Social Media on the Road

T0134636

Computer Supported Cooperative Work

Series Editor
Richard Harper, Socio-Digital Systems, Microsoft Research Cambridge, UK

Series Associate Editors
Dan Diaper, DDD Systems, Bournemouth, UK
Colston Sanger, London South Bank University, UK

Series Editorial Board
Liam Bannon, University of Limerick, Ireland
Prasun Dewan, University of North Carolina, Chapel Hill, USA
Jonathan Grudin, Microsoft Research, Redmond, Washington, USA
Carl Gutwin, University of Saskatchewan, Canada
Christine Halverson, Almaden Research Center, San Jose, USA
Leysia Palen, University of Colorado, Boulder, USA
David Randall, Manchester Metropolitan University, UK
Yvonne Rogers, Open University, Milton Keynes, UK
Kjeld Schmidt, IT University of Copenhagen, Denmark
Abigail Sellen, Microsoft Research, Cambridge, UK

For further volumes:
http://www.springer.com/series/2861

Oskar Juhlin

Social Media on the Road

The Future of Car Based Computing

 Springer

Prof. Oskar Juhlin
Interactive Institute
Mobility Studio
164 26 Kista
Sweden
oskarj@tii.se

Computer Supported Cooperative Work   ISSN 1431-1496
ISBN 978-1-4471-2588-4   ISBN 978-1-84996-332-9 (eBook)
DOI 10.1007/978-1-84996-332-9
Springer London Dordrecht Heidelberg New York

British Library Cataloguing in Publication Data
A catalogue record for this book is available from the British Library

© Springer-Verlag London Limited 2010
Softcover reprint of the hardcover 1st edition 2010
Apart from any fair dealing for the purposes of research or private study, or criticism or review, as
permitted under the Copyright, Designs and Patents Act 1988, this publication may only be reproduced,
stored or transmitted, in any form or by any means, with the prior permission in writing of the publishers,
or in the case of reprographic reproduction in accordance with the terms of licenses issued by the
Copyright Licensing Agency. Enquiries concerning reproduction outside those terms should be sent to
the publishers.
The use of registered names, trademarks, etc., in this publication does not imply, even in the absence of a
specific statement, that such names are exempt from the relevant laws and regulations and therefore free
for general use.
The publisher makes no representation, express or implied, with regard to the accuracy of the information
contained in this book and cannot accept any legal responsibility or liability for any errors or omissions
that may be made.

Printed on acid-free paper

Springer is part of Springer Science+Business Media (www.springer.com)

Preface

In the future, everyday life in traffic will be intricately meshed with city life. Today, motorways, city streets, toll roads, country roads, etc. are places where we spend a considerable amount of time, and where a large number of everyday encounters between people occur. Any road user's journey coincides with several, sometimes hundreds or even thousands of other people's journeys. But these encounters are brief and the interaction is slight. Mobile technologies and services provide us with new possibilities to support drivers and passengers beyond just helping them to reach their destination. We suggest that new technologies and applications could enhance social interaction in traffic and make life on the road more interesting and meaningful. We provide examples of some innovative applications such as car stereos that share music among drivers and digital games that interact with the landscape passing by outside the car windows.

Mobile applications could help people share their knowledge about what is going on in traffic, e.g. to warn of incidents or obstructions. In traffic encounters we already have to decide how to share the road surface so that everybody gets to where they are going in a reasonable amount time, without injuries or damage to vehicles. Much effort has also been put into making traffic encounters more efficient and safe. However, the role of social interaction as a resource in that effort has received only limited attention in traffic research, as well as from the car industry and transport authorities. To understand the potential of such new media, we must take a detailed look at the social interaction that occurs on the streets and highways in cities and in the countryside around the world.

Consider how people used the street before the car became a medium of mass transport. Human activities, which include everything from trade to gossiping, naturally took place where there were a lot of people and plenty of movement. Only a few decades ago streets would have been the places people headed for. People standing around here and there, shopping or walking by, did not impede the street's function—quite the opposite. In fact, they were a natural part of it. The arrival of mass automobility has in many ways changed what we do in the street. But it is also somewhat true that wherever people live and go to, there are still activities on the road which can only be understood as the "whole point of the journey." Rather than happening before or after the trip, these activities and experiences can only take place on the road. Car journeys are sometimes pleasant experiences, which are enjoyed for their own sake. Watching the motion of other drivers and vehicles provides for an interesting experience, as does looking at the passing scenery. But the experiential downside of traffic must also be recognized. Social interaction on the road is characterized by very brief encounters and by the participants being enclosed in the shell of a vehicle. This detachment occasionally makes what little interaction occurs monotonous, and in the end, driving becomes a lonely activity. Again, emerging technologies could be used to reintroduce some of the socialization that used to occur in the streets.

In our research at the Interactive Institute and the Mobile Life VinnExcellence Centre in Stockholm, we have studied social interaction on the roads and developed applications that support it in various ways. The increased availability of telecommunication and mobile computing technologies is a strong motivation for our interest in traffic. These technologies make it possible to think about designing new support for interaction between road users—support which may transcend the constraints upon social interaction that derive from the speed of the vehicles and the enclosed position of the driver when driving. Computers and telecommunications could make interaction possible in other ways than just brief visual interaction through the existing "car body-language." We could have a broader set of interfaces with other drivers, e.g. sound or graphics, and we could also prolong the time available for interaction. Technology could provide means of interaction before the physical encounter takes place, or it could sustain interaction when the brief meeting in person is over. We have developed, implemented, and evaluated a number of mobile services to investigate how increased interaction can provide improved coordination, better community life, and richer emotional experiences in traffic encounters. These services are prototypes that provide us with feedback on the experiences of road users and with an understanding of the technical constraints we are facing. But most importantly, these mobile services provide us with inspirational patterns (Löwgren 2005) that might inspire a discussion on how, in the future, we want to spend our time on the streets.

We envision that this book will primarily be used in higher education. It should be of interest to those studying human–computer interaction in mobile use contexts, as well as those interested in designing new forms of mobile applications and services. It may also be of interest to those whose object of study is traffic per se, for example people working within transport and urban planning. Finally, we hope that IT professionals and the general public will find it interesting to read about and reflect on the future of life in traffic. We examine a global phenomenon and our research is therefore of relevance in many countries. We draw on the experience of social life in traffic from both Europe and the US, and are inspired in the creation of new services by an international research community. Thus, although our own studies have mainly been conducted in Sweden, we believe that the results and the prototype applications we propose, are of a wider interest.

Kista, Sweden   Oskar Juhlin

Acknowledgments

The ideas in this book began taking form as early as 1991, when I was a young PhD student studying the social character of engineering knowledge. My thesis came to focus on technical practices such as testing and demonstrating various forms of information technology being developed to handle road traffic. The first publication (Juhlin, 1994) was a review and discussion of contemporary research projects in a field called Intelligent Transportation Systems. That study prefigured some of the basic arguments in this book, such as the importance of accounting for driving as a collaborative and social activity. The ideas emerged out of my initial misunderstanding of what the community of developers and researchers in this area were out to do. In my mind, they were digitally connecting the drivers and enabling them to communicate through various forms of data networks. But the mistake soon became obvious when I realized that they were rather linking cars and computers to each other. Still, after only an initial period of confusion, it became clear that the role of social interaction was an important, but missing topic in this gigantic research field. In the end, the misunderstood intentions of this particular community initiated a new research endeavor, which set out in a very different direction.

The various paths of this journey have been greatly enriched by Liselott Brunnberg, Mattias Esbjörnsson, Daniel Normark, and Mattias Östergren, all of whom have written their PhD theses on this topic. Their contribution to the research presented in this book cannot be underestimated. They have, since becoming PhDs, moved on to other areas of research and mobile industry, where I believe they will also have important roles to play. I would also like to mention two other colleagues. Lars Erik Sjöberg was a senior civil servant and sponsor at the Swedish National Road Administration when it all was getting started, and then became a research colleague and friend. Alexandra Weilenmann, my colleague and friend, has also been there for a long time to help me sharpen my arguments and improve the research. I would also like to thank a number of colleagues who in many ways have supported me in developing this research: Hans Glimell and Bo Dahlbom, who were both always around at the outset to support and guide; and my British friends Barry Brown, Eric Laurier, and Mark Perry, who really seem to have a similar "taste" in research topics as I have, and have constantly influenced this work. I would also like to thank Everett Thiele who has been around for several years to improve my English language, not least during the work with the this book.

My many colleagues at the constantly growing Mobile Life Centre, which emerged from a long-term collaboration with Lars Erik Holmquist and Kristina Höök, have been influencing the research in this book for a long time. The research has also allowed me to work with, and get inspiration from many previous members of our research group such as Mark Ollila and John Bichard. Here I would also like to mention my current colleagues Annika Waern, Arvid Engström, Ylva Fernaeus, and Maria Holm.

This research would not have been possible without a number of sponsors and research funders such as the Swedish Foundation for Strategic Research, the Swedish Governmental Agency for Innovation Systems (Vinnova), and The Knowledge Foundation (SITI). We have also received funding from Microsoft Research in Cambridge, Bergendahl's foundation, and the Swedish Road Administration. I would like to thank all of them for their support.

Last but not least, I would like to mention my dear family. It would, of course, have been possible to write this book without the love I get from my family, but it would have been a much more tedious job. Therefore, I would like to thank my family, that is, my partner Maria, my sons Benjamin and Leo, as well as my mum and dad, for being such a dear part of my life and for just being there.

July 17, 2010
Mobile Life Centre and Interactive Institute, Stockholm

Contents

Part III Sense and Social Interaction

Part I
An Empirical Program of Road Use

Chapter 1
Social Life in Traffic

This book provides a socio-technical foundation for thinking about our life on the road as social interaction. It focuses on how people coordinate and experience traffic as an ongoing practical achievement, and how that could be supported and expanded with new, emerging mobile media. It also concerns innovative design concepts and mobile technologies, which in various ways extend these particular forms of social interaction beyond the current practical restrictions on engaging with other people. Such restrictions include the driver being enclosed in the shell of a vehicle and the often very high speed, which limits the time available for interaction during each encounter.

Spending time in various kinds of vehicles is an important part of people's daily routine. If you can, take a look out of your window onto the street. If it is a crowded street you will probably see a bit of a drama every morning and afternoon, when many people in close proximity negotiate how to share the road space. Just the sheer view of this social activity is stunning. There are so many people traveling around in diverse vehicles, yet most of the time they manage to find their way without bumping into each other.

If we lift our view beyond the immediate road junction we find that road traffic is an immense and global activity. Statistics on how much time people spend traveling give us a better grasp of the importance of this social phenomenon. Many countries conduct travel surveys which detail how much time people spend on the roads. In the UK people on average made around a thousand trips per person per year, and the average time spent traveling was around 360 h between 1994 and 2003 (DFT 2005). Middle-aged men spent as much as 460 h traveling, whereas people older than 60 years spent approximately 300 h. Thus, each day of their lives people spend around an hour traveling somewhere. Thirty-seven minutes of that hour are spent in a car, around 9 min on a bus or train, and 11 min on foot. Long trips tended to be by public transport, whereas trips made by bicycle, car, and motorcycle took around 20 min. In the USA, people spent on average 24 min a day commuting in 2001, and those who used public transportation had to add another 16 min (Hu and Reuscher 2004). Busy middle-aged people spent more than 80 min per day in various vehicles. But it is not only people who travel to work that spend time on the roads. People over 65 years of age spent as much as an hour per day in their vehicles, and children younger than five spent three quarters of an hour a day in a vehicle.

O. Juhlin, *Social Media on the Road*, Computer Supported Cooperative Work 50, DOI 10.1007/978-1-84996-332-9_1, © Springer-Verlag London Limited 2010

The figures show that transportation is an enormously time consuming activity. If we stretch the statistics a bit, and smooth the figures out over a day, it is possible to say that at any given time an average of around 4% of the population is traveling. Thus, there might be as many as a bit over two million British citizens moving around somehow and somewhere. Similarly, there could be around 12 million US citizens, and alongside them also 350,000 Swedish people, who currently are on their way somewhere. Of course these are very crude estimates which do not take into account variations over the course of days, weeks, or months. But even so, they give an indication of the large amount of time we spend in traffic and underscore the importance of giving that part of social life special attention. Traveling adds up to a considerable part of most people's lives, and it is time spent in the company of others as a particular form of public life.

In the following we will unpack the details of this everyday social practice, i.e. how people interact with each other on the roads, and how new technologies can be designed to support these activities. We suggest that there are important things to learn about social life in cities.

Such studies might, for example, be of use in improving traffic safety. People aim for safety in maneuvering their vehicles. This book adds to the current state of the research through detailed accounts of how this is done as an everyday practice. When we account for the ongoing social interaction, we also get a new perspective on the relationship between mobile phone use and traffic safety. It seems like the connection between "distraction," which traffic research assumes to occur when making a phone call, and dangerous driving, is much weaker than previously thought. A focus on social interaction also reveals new possibilities to develop communication technologies which would help drivers to collectively increase their safety. Social life in traffic is also about more than just getting from one place to another as safely and quickly as possible. We have discovered aspects of community life where people enjoy brief encounters in traffic, very much like pedestrians in urban settings. It is, of course, obvious that people balance safety concerns with other needs and demands. The best way to avoid unsafe traffic is never to start the car, but we still do so. Safety questions, like all other aspects of using the roads, must be understood in specific social contexts.

Therefore, the study of on-going social interaction not only increases our understanding of the coordination of traffic, but also reveals something of a balancing game. In this book we investigate and discuss various dimensions of such an endeavor and suggest that when we undertake it we should look at street life as an integral part of urban life.

Finally, it is necessary to understand—already at this point—that we will not further consider whether the amount of transportation is increasing or decreasing, or the consequences of using private or public means of transportation. Discussions on the quantity of transportation and its fluctuations are important, and influence current public issues such as the impact on the environment and climate change (Kingsley and Urry 2009; Tengström 1991). Nevertheless, such questions are beyond the scope of this book. Here we instead invite the reader to think about how that time is spent.

1.1 Road Use and Traffic Encounters

We will here analyze a variety of ways in which social interaction occurs on the roads. In the following we will introduce some of these social practices and some of our key analytical concepts. Social life in traffic is not only about moving one's body from one place to another. Therefore, we would risk missing the point if we continued to refer to this activity as transportation or traffic. These concepts are closely linked to logistical connotations of changing the physical locations of bodies or goods. We will therefore apply the more inclusive term of *road use* to account for all activities that people engage in on the road. People use their time in traffic to make phone calls to their family. They also enjoy the journey as a means of escape from a stressful work life or problems at home. The concept of road use will keep us empirically focused on what people are actually doing on the road, and avoid a pre-conceived idea that misses out on these activities, since that form of road use might be outside the scope of, for example, traffic policy.

Traffic encounters are central to road use; i.e. there are frequent encounters between people as they pass each other in opposing lanes or travel in the same direction. Car drivers, and people who transport themselves in various other ways, encounter a lot of people regularly. A trip to work can involve passing thousands of other drivers going the other way and a number of people sitting by the windows of buildings near the road. In this sense, we are talking about people socializing en masse. However, it has to be recognized that the scant interaction which normally occurs between people on the roads is on the boundary of sociologist Anthony Giddens's definition of social interaction as ways of acting and reacting to those around one (Giddens et al. 2005). It is a somewhat odd form of social interaction as compared to, for example, the face-to-face interaction in an office meeting or a family dinner. In those situations people converse and interact in various ways for minutes or hours.

In traffic, there are seldom more than seconds available for social exchanges, and the means for interaction are restricted to gestures and using the clunky movement of the vehicles as a form of body-language. They are based on, or constrained by, the *speed* of the vehicles and the *enclosed* position of the driver. First, vehicles can move at anywhere between zero and well over a hundred kilometers per hour, which has consequences for the duration of the meetings. The encounters are often rather short, ranging from a couple of seconds if the cars meet in opposite lanes to minutes if they travel in the same direction. The speed of the vehicles also demands that the drivers pay attention to the handling of the vehicle itself. The consequences of a wrong move are serious and therefore the driver has always to ensure that the maneuvering is well handled. Second, the interaction is influenced by the drivers being inside vehicles made of steel and glass. This restricts the possibility to look at each other, but most importantly the possibility for verbal interaction. The means for interaction are restricted to gestures and using the clunky movement of the vehicles as a form of body-language.

This view on traffic, as constrained social interaction, is common among sociologists with an interest in car driving. In an overview of the perspectives on cars and society in French sociology, Inglis (2004) notes that it is shared by social critic André Gorz and historian Henri Lefebvre. The driver is caught in a paradox created by the car, according to Lefebvre:

> Motorized traffic enables people and objects to congregate and mix without meeting, thus constituting a striking example of simultaneity without exchange, each element enclosed in its own compartment, tucked away in its shell; such conditions contribute to the disintegration of city life. (Henri Lefebvre, quoted in Inglis 2004)

These meetings without exchanges are, according to him, examples of the ordered flow of commodities in an economy based on constant consumption, which in this case is supported by the marketing mechanisms of the auto manufacturers. Social relations in traffic reflect broader social structures, and are therefore not so unique. He also points to the downside of automobility: those cases where the smooth flow breaks down, which causes accidents and injuries. Similarly, Gorz describes traffic as individualistic and as a reflection of bourgeois ideology.

Freund and Martin (1993, p. 104) argue that car traffic allows people to mix without ever meeting, that the car becomes something between a private box and a public stage. In that sense, it serves as a filter against the abundant impressions of a modern city. The consequence of this peculiar form of engagement is an erosion of community life, especially in a society that generally values privacy, and fears contact with others. Fotel and Thomsen (2004), who studied children's mobility, argued that parents chauffeuring was part of a process of "insularization." The car is a "private space-bubble," that sustains families' social life, but negatively affects social interaction in public to the detriment of democracy and civil society. British sociologist John Urry has lately published extensively on the role of the car in society (2007). Central to his argumentation is that there is an "automobility system," consisting of vehicles and their manufacturing systems: the objects of private consumption; a complex network with other organizations and technologies such as petrol refining and distribution, road-construction and maintenance, and hotels; physical movements; a car culture; and finally, an environmental resources user. He describes traffic as individualistic and privatized, with the drivers locked into their vehicles:

> The car, one might suggest, is really Weber's "iron cage" of modernity, motorized, moving and privatized. People inhabit congestion, jams, temporal uncertainties and health threatening city-environments through being encapsulated in a domestic, cocooned, moving capsule, an iron bubble (Urry 2007, p. 120)

Again, traffic and transportation carry more than bodies and goods. In Urry's description they become a result of a more general modernization process. It follows that a driver is more inwardly oriented than social, and thus becomes attached to the technology, instead of engaging with people in the vicinity. The driver becomes a "car-driver hybrid." Thrift (2004) suggests that there will even be an increased hybridization between the driver and the car when new digital technologies, so called "non-humans," are introduced. He argues that individuals, who up to now have been "hidden" and anonymous in urban life, will be visible from a distance with new telecommunication and positioning technologies. Notably, Thrift does not foresee any intrusions in the local "iron-cage," but rather an urban life where the driver becomes connected to a non-local, or remote, society.

Sociologist Katz (1999) provides yet another account of traffic as constrained social interaction, based on a series of interviews to investigate so-called road rage, that is, various forms of expression of anger on the roads in California. He argued that strong emotions occur partly since the driver's possibility to interact with people in the vicinity is severely constrained. Drivers have little opportunity to take prolonged looks at the faces of other drivers. Thus, visual interaction, as occurs between pedestrians, is out of the question for drivers. The time available for such interaction is too short and the drivers are hard to see inside their vehicles. And there is no possibility to talk to people in the vicinity.

> Drivers are relatively free to look wherever and however they practically can just because their vision is itself relatively invisible to other drivers... For the same reasons that the vision of drivers is relatively unencumbered, the driver's ability to speak and, more generally, express his or her understanding and intentions to other drivers is severely impaired. (Katz 1999, p. 25)

This awkward situation leaves drivers with few ways of understanding the intentions of co-located drivers, which makes them struggle to figure out why other people do what they do. It is therefore, according to Katz, not only the behavior of other drivers that makes people angry, but also the frustration embedded in accounting for what people around them are doing with the limited means available for social interaction. It ends up as a "folk-sociology," where drivers make inferences from what they see and come up with explanations for traffic behavior drawing on concepts such as gender, class, and lately, mobile phone use. Furthermore, the driver's emotions are evoked since she is metamorphosed into a hybrid entity which includes her body and the vehicle. When, for example, another car cuts off the path in front of a driver, this is felt as an "amputation," which obviously makes people offended (Katz 1999).

Overall, the sociological literature above portrays social relations in traffic as severely constrained. The driver's possibilities to interact are bounded by the vehicle and the speed of the movement, in a similar manner as we previously argued. The observations are discussed as examples that support particular theoretical approaches, be they modernization (Urry 2007), bourgeois ideology, or consumption theory (Inglis 2004).

At the same time, it is evident that these statements can be seen as offhand or superficial comments since they are quick characterizations available to most of us through a glance at traffic, or just by thinking about our shared experiences of traveling in various vehicles. They are superficial also because there is no detailed analysis of the ways in which people do interact given the constraints. We argue that the way people orient themselves to each other in their brief and restricted encounters is important for both the flow of traffic and the experience of it. Although the interaction might be conceived of as meagre it is still worthy of investigation and analysis. Therefore, understanding traffic as constrained social interaction is just a starting point for detailed empirical investigation and analysis, and not the end-point where a general theory fits with social life.

Sociologist Mike Lynch, who pursues a so-called ethnomethodological approach, discusses social interaction on the roads in an appendix to his writings on scientific work (1993). He argues for a perspective that describes the orderliness of traffic from the participants', or the drivers', point of view. What from the point of view of traffic engineering, or a helicopter, looks like hydraulic streams bounded by the road network and halted at traffic lights or intersections is, from the participants' viewpoint, a "linear society." For example, at night drivers orient themselves in relation to lights ahead as a "visible presence of intentional actions within the line of traffic." During daytime, the surroundings are much more available as a graphic text in which she can read a line to follow. Lynch also points to the specifics of traffic and the way social interaction occurs in this situation. He claims that:

> Although the driver's body in the machine is still in play—as both an actual and presumed agent and source of significations—its actions in the field of traffic are circumscribed by the conventional modes of perception, gesture and communication within a speeding and nomadic assemblage of vehicular units. (Lynch 1993)

The speed of the vehicles and the drivers, and the extent to which the design of the car allows interaction, are factors that circumscribe or delimit the way social interaction can occur. Contrary to the other sociologists discussed, he argues that there is still room for various forms of interaction. There are plenty of variations in the flow of traffic, which supports a combination of ways in which "bodily expressions" can occur transmitting many different messages, such as complaints, to other drivers. Interaction in traffic might therefore not be as impoverished as one might first think. But again, Lynch's discussion of traffic is only a brief appendix which he invokes to juxtapose highly specialized scientific practices with commonly available and ordinary practices, such as driving, where there is no need for special tutorials to enable the readers to follow his general arguments. Therefore, we should not blame Lynch for his scant empirical references to the topic we are concerned with in this book. Instead we can see it as a source of inspiration for studying the detailed ways in which people go about interacting with each other on the roads, and then eventually intervening in it.

Basically, traffic encounters happen as a consequence of sharing a common section of a road. Drivers communicate with each other using blinkers, as well as making gestures with their heads or arms in order to negotiate how this resource should be shared in a safe and efficient manner. Even more importantly, drivers communicate by demonstratively positioning themselves in the road space, or deciding on a speed, both of which have a meaning to fellow drivers. The interaction is a kind of car-body-language about how to establish coordination given the intentions of drivers, formal rules, and their applicability in a particular situation. In addition to formal rules, their actions are also influenced by informal conventions, as we will discuss in Chapter 4. Maneuvering a vehicle in traffic is thus a cooperative activity. It follows that the drivers have to jointly decide who comes next. The availability of several rule sets, and the possibility to categorize a road context in various ways, make this less straightforward than might be expected. We argue that the way people agree on how to share the road space could be understood as a form of negotiation. We borrow the term *situated interaction* from sociologist Suchman (1987) to account for the way people negotiate right-of-way in actual situations given local variations and contingencies.

These constraints on social interaction negatively influence traffic safety. Consider all the encounters between different road users, which all depend on successful coordination, that take place just in one individual journey, and how this adds up when all road users are accounted for. This makes it seem easy to say that the social interaction that goes into coordinating traffic encounters works smoothly and well. But if we instead consider accidents occurring when vehicles collide, we get a very different picture. Far from all social interaction results in mutual agreement on how to use the road space, and the studies of everyday interaction can thus be used to inform and inspire new forms of technical means by which driver interaction can be altered.

At the same time, the previous list of various forms of social interaction might seem to require too much attention from the driver, given the effort she has to put into just safely maneuvering the vehicle. It is apparent that drivers must find safe ways of balancing their focus of attention between the vehicle and those they interact with. The particular ways in which road users reach agreements about what we in Chapter 5 refer to as *interactional adaptation*, are critical for social life in traffic. For example, the use of mobile phones when driving has been highly contested in many countries. We argue that drivers adapt to traffic in deciding when and how they use the phones. Conversations are adapted through the talk itself, e.g. when a driver notifies the person she is talking to about a troubling traffic situation that demands her attention. Another example is when drivers wait for specific situations in traffic to pick up the phone and make a call.

The interaction with other drivers and their vehicles in traffic also includes experiential qualities, making it boring or pleasant to be part of traffic. The constraints provide for an experiential downside. Brief contact, with the participants enclosed in the shells of their vehicles, characterizes the social interaction during encounters. This detachment occasionally makes interaction monotonous (Laurier 2002). Redshaw (2008) interviewed drivers who described their commutes as boring and often frustrating due to their repetitive nature and the necessity of such trips. They find traveling along trunk roads tedious when traffic is dense and they need to be somewhere at a particular time.

A lonely haulage driver (Nehls 2003, p. 40) is an obvious example of a person who does not always enjoy the isolation provided by this particular social setting. People who use their mobile phones to call friends and family while driving are other possible examples. Esbjörnsson and Weilenmann (2005) report a conversation between a bored salesman on the road and a shop owner who both treat the activity of driving as being "forced" upon them, and as something that could be made more pleasurable with some chatting. The way they make use of their mobile phones as they drive could be another indication of the road traffic being somewhat socially impoverished. They take the opportunity to socialize with family and friends instead of engaging with people around them.

But the restricted social interaction also has positive connotations for road users. Many drivers describe how satisfactory their highway experience is. They claim that they "like being alone," and that this is the experience they have when driving (Redshaw 2008). It is a pleasant feeling which is enjoyed for its own sake. In Chapter 9, we discuss how motorcyclists experience traffic encounters as central to their community life. The motion of the accompanying traffic provides for an interesting and sometimes appealing experience. Kevin Lynch and his colleagues argued in *The View from the Road* (Appleyard et al. 1964) that these encounters are essential to the driver's experience:

> Most impressive of all is the motion of the accompanying traffic, to which he is forced to be attentive, and which even passengers will watch with subconscious concern.

The experience of the visual appearance of traffic is aesthetically appealing per se. But the individual apprehension of traffic encounters possesses in many cases the same qualities as what allured the nineteenth century pedestrian strolling randomly along the Parisian boulevards fantasizing about what he saw. Mazlish (1994) quotes Charles Baudelaire, describing this figure, whom he called the flâneur, as a person who

> ...marvels at the eternal beauty and the amazing harmony of life in capital cities...He delights in fine carriages and proud horses, the dazzling smartness of the grooms...the sinuous gait of the women, the beauty of the children, happy to be alive and nicely dressed. (Mazlish 1994)

Similarly, we argue in Chapter 8 that the view of other cars and drivers in traffic queues, at traffic lights, and on the roads provides equivalent opportunities for day-dreaming. Driving along a freeway provides a fictional effect, or distraction, which consists of a partial release from the here and now, according to Margaret Morse (1990). It distracts people from understanding and engaging concretely with social activities along the road, but also with people they meet.

> It is also disengaged from the paramount orientation to reality—the here and now of face-to-face contact. Such encounter with the other is prevented by walls of steel, concrete and stucco in a life fragmented into enclosed, miniature worlds.

Although the driver is in close proximity to other drivers there are no occurrences of face-to-face contact, according to Morse. The practical constraints in traffic make social interaction impossible. In this situation, which she refers to as "mobile privatization," the driver can distract herself by combining a private world with an awareness of the outside environment.

The drivers' lack of experiences that are grounded in the outside world has been a concern in the study of the interaction between people in transit and people along the roadside who want to engage in interaction for various purposes and by various means. Several traffic planners argue that the modern way of designing streets, i.e. functional separation of people and activities into different spaces, deprives people of the possibility to meet and socialize (Hass-Klau 1990). Lynch and Southworth

(1974) discuss the topic with reference to what is called the Strip, that is, the main road through a US community. The Strip has been designed to take the growing automobility into account. But it has brought with it a new experience of being in a city. They claim that "strips bear no relation to their context," (p. 582) and that the direct contact with people and things has been lost (p. 584), which has consequences for the drivers' experiences.

> There is no coherent sequence of space and motion or view, such as might be displayed to someone in a moving vehicle. There is rarely any long view, or only a formless one. One is isolated within a metal shell, which dulls sight and hearing. (Lynch and Southworth 1974, p. 591)

Augé (1995) holds a similar position when he argues that modern roads are so-called "non-places," that is, places which lack identity and cannot be defined as relational or historical. On the other hand, Merriman's (2004) studies of stories of events on motor highways indicate that people seem to attach meaning to locations even along these roads, which may question the idea of motorways as non-places. Drivers make "momentary associations," for example to accounts of mysterious shadows beneath an overpass which were interpreted as a parked lorry and caused accidents.

The interaction between roadside communities and passing drivers, as mediated through various forms of road signs, was an important topic among the US architectural research community in the 1970s. Several studies note that road signs became larger and more attention-grabbing than before, in order to be readable to the swiftly passing driver. According to Lynch and Southworth (1974), the billboard first appeared in conjunction with the automobility era. In a similar vein, their architectural colleagues Robert Venturi and Denise Scott Brown saw bold signage as a way to reach out "in the vast and complex setting of a new landscape of big spaces, high speeds, and complex programs. Styles and signs make connections among many elements, far apart and seen fast" (Venturi et al. 1972, pp. 8–9). For example road signs could be of different magnitudes to communicate over various distances. A very large sign could be used to reach a driver at great distances. A medium-sized sign could be used for moderate distances and a small sign on a building could apply to close-up encounters (Lynch and Southworth 1974, p. 78). All the above architects recognized that this new media supported the possibility to vary the messages conveyed to passing drivers in relation to the surrounding architecture or the landscape in itself. But they differed widely in what they saw as appropriate content.

Lynch and Southworth's investigations of strips reveal an overwhelming use of private commercial road signs that present individual shops and products. The private road signs on the strips create first a clutter, and second a de-contextualization since the messages have little connection to the context.

> The pivot of motion on the highway today is all too likely a temporary shanty, and its goal a whiskey advertisement. On the other hand, a historic building, or the central stock exchange cannot be seen. (Lynch and Southworth 1974, p. 52)

Thus, the de-contextualized messages buy into the drivers' social situation of being "isolated within a metal shell, which dulls sight and hearing" (Lynch and

Southworth 1974). They call for some form of organization of the presentation of road signs, as well as messages that connect to the local context. Signs might be used for something more than giving directions or making a sale, and those advertisements that are most connected to the location should be favored.

Kevin Lynch and his colleagues wanted a modernist design of road signs that favored a strong connection between the sign and its context. Choosing between the social situation of the driver or the roadside inhabitant, they went for the latter. The signs should, in various ways, explicitly reflect local communities. Robert Venturi and Denise Scott Brown, on the other hand, saw the possibilities in retaining the weak connection between the driver and the roadside. In a classic book that came to be important for the emerging post-modernism, they analyzed the architecture surrounding Las Vegas's strip. The book evaluates the use of signs, symbols, orna-mentation, etc. as a way to meet the needs of automobility in particular, as well as current commercial and consumer demands. For them, the loose connection between driver and road context can be tedious, but it provides an opportunity to play around with new roles and heightened symbolism. The use of signs enables the creation of the imagery of the pleasure-zone based on "lightness, the quality of being an oasis in a perhaps hostile context, heightened symbolism, and the ability to engulf the vis-itor in a new role" (Venturi et al. 1972, p. 53). Thus, the signs along the roads enable more powerful forms of communication between roadside inhabitants and passing drivers. According to Venturi and his colleagues:

> The Strip shows the value of symbolism and allusion in an architecture of vast space and speed and proves that people, even architects, have fun with architecture that reminds them of something else, perhaps of harems or the Wild West in Las Vegas... (Venturi et al. 1972, p. 53)

In Chapter 10 we present a study of putting up signs as an everyday practice. Posters of signs communicate with the passing drivers for various purposes. Road authorities put up signs dictating the local application of the formal rules, etc. But there are many other people who want to convey messages to passing drivers. Most of these signs are commercially motivated—to market a local vendor or a locally available product. But there are also people who just want to say who they are, or keep alive the memory of a traffic victim, or just make fun of something. These private signs can vary between the cheapest paper poster to costly monuments in concrete and steel. This form of interaction between traditional neighborhood communities and passing drivers is something that we refer to as *intermediate inter-action* to denote how they straddle the gap between a tightly knit community and those passing in their vehicles. Sociologist Mark Granovetter (Granovetter 1973, 1983) has argued for the importance of such interaction when studying what he describes as weak ties. He claims that "groups making the greatest use of weak ties are those whose weak ties do connect to social circles different from one's own" (Granovetter 1983, p. 208).

To sum up, we have until now discussed how social interaction between drivers has been conceived in sociology, that is, as an interaction constrained by the speed of the vehicles and the enclosed situation of the drivers. We have also introduced a number of concepts to account for how that interaction is actually conducted as an ongoing practice. In the following we will expand on the analyses of the coordination and experience of traffic with reference to specific case studies. But keep in mind that our intention is to use this knowledge to influence the design of new forms of support for social interaction. The next step is therefore to present what such design concepts might look like and how they could be used. It is only when we have a dual focus on emerging technical possibilities as well as on available social interaction, that we are prepared to explore future life in traffic.

1.2 The Interactive Road

We will use the concept of an interactive road to describe life in traffic when future mobile technologies have become a more extended resource for people. The concept of interactivity has a double meaning. First, it refers to the ongoing social interaction on the roads, i.e. the way people act and react to each other. Second, it refers to the interaction between humans and mobile devices, sensors and networks. The concept of interaction is borrowed from computer science to denote the interplay between, on the one hand, different technical components such as keyboards or a mouse, and on the other hand, a user (Dourish 2004, p. 4). Its popularity comes from the need for an appropriate term to describe the fleeting relation between computers and users. It puts the focus not only on what happens between people and computers, but also on how it happens, dynamically and with reference to the specific situations. In the future we will see more interactive road settings. The roads are already crowded with people, and we envision an increase of computer use in this context. The ways in which this interaction will occur are, of course, still an open question, and how we conceive and design new technology will certainly influence the outcome.

In this section we provide a brief overview of how we propose that a future interactive road can be created. We will do this with examples taken both from academic research and industry, as well as examples from our own research. We argue that an interactive road might become more meaningful, aesthetic, fun, and safe. More specifically, there are opportunities to influence the interplay between drivers and others through the design of new mobile technologies, such as telecommunications and computers. The variation and constant development of such technologies, as well as their widespread adoption, inspire reflection about possibilities to alter the current constraints on social interaction. These new applications might make it possible to transcend current restrictions of time and place. First, new technologies can overcome current limitations that only allow interaction with road users who are nearby, with whom we have visual or audio contact, as is typical of face-to-face interaction. Second, new technologies can enable interaction between people who are in the same place, but at different times. Historically, a number of technologies for overcoming such restrictions have been used and discussed. Lorry drivers have used CB radio for a long time. It is sometimes used to organize get-togethers for coffee or lunch. More spectacular forms of its use are found in classic 1970s movies such as, for example, "Smokey and the Bandit," where lorry drivers and other car drivers converse over the radio to help each other elude pursuing police. Technologies have evolved since then. The police are now using automated speed traps, and drivers are using new mobile applications to help each other avoid them. Various systems are used to enable people to share information about where they are located. There are systems based on sending SMS-messages to a server which alerts subscribers to temporary speed traps (see Chapter 7). Thus, people collaborate to avoid complying with traffic laws. Although, this could provide for "deviant leisure" (Stebbins 1997), and also be of some practical use for the individual, it is questionable whether it can help to achieve smooth collaboration in traffic.

In Japan there have been several experiments, and also commercialized products, designed to augment the expressivity of drivers. Toyota and Sony investigated a new type of expressivity in a project that led to a concept car called the Pod (Masatsugu 2001). As one of its features it is said to express drivers' feelings, as well as its own emotions, by using an array of LED lamps on the front panel of the vehicle. This "face" can express ten different emotional states. For example, when the driver approaches, the car makes a cheerful expression by lighting up orange LEDs. When the driver brakes hard, the car gets annoyed which it expresses by using red LEDs.

Another Japanese company has developed a tail that can be attached to the back section of a car's roof. With this tail-antenna, called the "thanks tail," it is possible to express feelings and communicate (Akaike 2002). It wags and moves like the tail of a dog and can be used as an alternative to signal lights and horn. The engineers claims to being able to communicate the messages "thank you" and "sorry" by waving the rod on the car roof.

In our own research we have generated and designed a number of applications in the same area, which are informed by studies of social practices. In the following, we will briefly introduce some of them through practical scenarios.

We have previously discussed how the constraints within brief traffic encounters, and the enclosed situation of drivers, make it difficult to share knowledge about the state of the roads. Sandra, however, is using an application called Road Talk, which overcomes some of these constraints on social interaction.

The rain is pouring down as Sandra drives toward her country house. She sees a big nasty puddle of water further down the road and remembers how her uncle hydroplaned at the very same spot in October. She pushes a button and says: "Umm...big puddle here. Look out." The system saves her message and logs her position. Further up the road she meets opposing traffic. When they almost arrive at the same place, they suddenly hear Sandra saying "Umm...big..."

The system makes it possible for drivers to tell each other about their observations as they travel along the road network. They can share knowledge, which is collected as voice memos and recorded together with the geographical position. These messages are then spread from one car to another as they pass each other. They are played whenever a car approaches the location where a stored message was recorded.

Road Talk (Fig. 1.1) is intended to increase road safety by improving the means for social interaction. It draws on the fact that drivers often use the same section

Fig. 1.1 A road talk scenario where drivers communicate on the condition of a section of road

of the roads, that is, are at or near the same position, and it treats these co-visits as significant for interaction. Further, it trusts the drivers to handle traffic coordination in a similar manner to the way they collaborate today.

We have also discussed how the particular social setting in traffic provides for a specific experience. The driver is somewhat anonymous in a public sphere, and can glance at other people in the surroundings and reflect on who they are and how they look. It is an experience similar to what the flâneur feels when walking down a crowded sidewalk in the city center. In the following, we suggest that getting to know more about the people in the passing encounters would make the experience even better:

> Sandra attaches her mobile device, with built-in Wi-Fi card, to the dashboard and starts the Sound Pryer application. As she hits the road, it plays her favorite music on the car stereo. After a while, the icon of a red lorry appears on the screen of the device. She says to herself: "It must be that one over there," as the latest Cardigans song fills her loudspeakers. It returns to playing her own music after she passes the lorry and sees it fall behind in the rear-view mirror.

The metaphor used to guide the design of Sound Pryer (Fig. 1.2) is that of a "collaborative" MP3 player. A user can play her own music, but also tune into other players and hear what they are playing as long as she is within close proximity. The Sound Pryer application draws on the idea that people take an experiential and aesthetic interest in the surrounding traffic, and that they are willing to share music, since people are effectively anonymous to each other in that situation. The visual, and now audio, contact provides for a special and titillating shared experience, that of prying into other cars. It is a form of a shallow sociality, which sociologist Erving Goffman refers to as unfocused interaction, which "occurs when one gleans information about another person present by glancing at him" (Goffman 1963, p. 24).

Fig. 1.2 Sound Pryer allows joint music sharing in traffic

In social life, interaction obviously extends to more sustained forms of engagement with each other. We argue that even such activities can occur and be explored in road traffic, such as when motorcyclists head out on the road to enjoy themselves. Then new mobile technologies can improve the possibilities to socialize even in such unlikely places.

It is Sunday afternoon and the sun is shining. Eric thinks it is a great day for a ride together with some motorcycling friends. He picks up his Hocman-device and browses through the log of bikers he encountered yesterday while spending a couple of hours on the curvy roads south of Stockholm. He decides to contact "Mini-potato" and "Madhonda" whom he has met a number of times before, that is, met for a couple of seconds on the highway and a bit longer on the internet. They decide to meet at Bulky Burger on Main Street for a ride.

Motorcycling is a strikingly social activity. Bikers like to meet other bikers, especially along the roads. Naturally, such meetings tend to be rather brief and geographically dispersed. Hocman (Fig. 1.3) is a prototype service designed to spark and further social interaction by building on these traffic encounters. It is based on handheld computers capable of establishing computer networks with other devices in the vicinity, without the need for any additional telecommunication systems. When the bikers head out on the road the software continuously senses similar devices nearby. If another device is in the vicinity it makes a sound to alert the biker that a meeting is taking place, and an automatic exchange of web pages takes place between the devices. The sound alert has already proven to be highly appreciated by bikers. The personal web pages may contain contact information, for-sale ads, pictures, etc. When the biker gets off his bike he can examine the log and read the pages captured. The pages can be helpful when planning future encounters, or when referring to rides in discussions in other prevalent media such as the internet.

Finally, we will present a type of application which draws upon the interaction between people passing on the road and the roadside residents. Lynch (1976, p. 35) argues that the most interesting roadside objects to look at from a car are various forms of human activity or traces of it. A mobile application could draw on people's curiosity about the roadside to heighten their experience.

Traveling in a car can be very tedious for children. But any trip can become an exciting adventure with a "Journey Game" (see Figure 1.4). The game turns churches, bridges, and other roadside objects into a fantasy land filled with virtual creatures, treasures, and adventures. By pointing the gaming device towards objects as they pass by, players can, e.g., defend themselves against attacking creatures or criminal gangs.

Fig. 1.3 Hocman provides digitally enhanced community life among motorcyclists

Fig. 1.4 Journey games make the passing environment more real and unreal

Dave is sitting the back seat of his parents' car on the way to visit relatives in a nearby city. The car is moving along a country road. He looks at a field, a barn, and a power line visible in the distance. His peaceful observation of the surroundings is suddenly interrupted by a crackling sound. He turns his attention from the scenery outside to the walkie-talkie in his hand. A man's voice is heard over the radio: "Agent Bravo to agent Alpha. I just saw your car passing by. We are here on the other side of the *golf course* searching for the robbers. Over!" He looks up and indeed sees a golf course in the field just behind the barn. He decides to pull out his directional surveillance microphone and starts sweeping the surrounding landscape for suspicious activities. From the forest on the other side of the golf course a couple of birds can be heard among the trees. Everything else seems to be dead quiet. The sun is disappearing behind the tree line and the landscape is beginning to fill with long, dark shadows. Then, suddenly, the deafening sound of a gunshot pierces the quiet. He quickly reaches for the walkie-talkie in order to contact the nearby team of agents over the radio.

As the agents engage in a search to find out the location of the shooting, David continues to use his surveillance microphone. From one of the buildings to his right some suspicious voices can be heard. He keeps the device pointed at the building in hope of catching some of the conversation going on. Finally he picks out a few words, something about ammunition. He decides to call in the team. He contacts the agent and tells them to be careful since the suspects seem to be armed. Moments later he gets a report back over the phone. The agents were unfortunately a little bit too careful and by the time the building was stormed whoever was in there had escaped. A gruesome discovery was made, however. Left in the building on the floor was the dead body of a man.

A journey in a car provides a specific experience, fuelled by the ever-changing scenery and lots of brief encounters. It might be used to design a new form of mobile games that include the vivid and dynamic mobile context, e.g. the experience of traveling along a road. Here the children interact, not only through experiencing a landscape and, for example, looking at human activities, but also through interacting with imaginary people and real roadside objects.

To sum up, we suggest that mobile technologies provide a means for re-thinking the ways in which social interaction occurs. This includes supporting various needs of the road users, as well as different approaches for achieving these goals. Thus the quality of the time spent in traffic could become rather different in the future.

References

Akaike M (2002) A car that can wag its tail. Japan for sustainability-disseminating environmental information from Japan volume. http://www.japanfs.org/en_/column/a02.html. Accessed 9 November 2009

Appleyard D, Lynch K et al (1964) The view from the road. MIT Press, Boston

Augé M (1995) Non-places: introduction to an anthropology of supermodernity. Verso, London
DFT DfT (2005) Focus on personal travel: 2005. DFT, Department for Transport, London
Dourish P (2004) Where the action is. MIT Press, Boston
Esbjörnsson M, Weilenmann A (2005) Mobile phone talk in context. In: Proceedings of the fifth
    international and interdisciplinary conference modeling and using context. Springer, Berlin
Fotel T, Thomsen TU (2004) The surveillance of children's mobility. Surveill Soc 1(4):535–554
Freund P, Martin G (1993) The ecology of the automobile. Black Rose Books, New York
Giddens A, Duneier M et al (2005) Introduction to sociology. W.W. Norton & Company, College
    Books, New York
Goffman E (1963) Behaviour in public places:—notes on social organization of gatherings. Free
    Press, New York
Granovetter MS (1973) The strength of weak ties. AmJ Sociol 78:1360–1380
Granovetter MS (1983) The strength of weak ties: a network theory revisited. Sociol Theory 1:
    201–233
Hass-Klau C (1990) The pedestrian and city traffic. Wiley, London
Hu PS, Reuscher TR (2004) Summary of travel trends: 2001. National household travel survey. U.
    D. FHWA.
Inglis D (2004) Auto couture: thinking the car in post-war France. Theory Cult Soc 21(4/5):
    197–219
Juhlin O (1994) Information technology hits the automobile? Rethinking road traffic as social
    interaction. In Summerton J (ed) Changing large technical systems. Westview Press, Boulder
Katz J (1999) How emotions work. University of Chicago Press, Chicago
Kingsley D, Urry J (2009) After the car. Polity Press, Cambridge
Laurier E (2002) Notes on dividing the attention of a car driver. Team Ethno Online
Löwgren J (2005) Inspirational patterns for embodied interaction. In: Proceedings of Nordic design
    research conference, Copenhagen, Denmark
Lynch M (1993) Scientific practice and ordinary action:— ethnomethodology and social studies of
    science. Ambridge University Press, New York
Lynch K, Southworth M (1974) Designing and managing the strip. In: Banerjee T, Southworth M
    (eds) City sense and city design: —writings and projects of Kevin Lynch. The MIT, Cambridge,
    pp 579–616
Masatsugu A (2001) Toyota's expressive POD concept for Tokyo Motor Show. CarDesign-News.
    http://archive.cardesignnews.com/autoshows/2001/tokyo/preview/toyota-pod/. Accessed 9
    November 2009
Mazlish B (1994) The flâneur: from spectator to representation. In: Tester K (ed) The flâneur.
    Routledge, London
Merriman P (2004) Driving places: Marc Augé, non-places, and the geographies of England's M1
    motorway. Theory Cult Soc 21(4/5):145–167
Morse M (1990) An ontology of everyday distraction—the freeway, the mall and television. In:
    Mellencamp P (ed) Logics of television—essays in cultural criticism. Indiana University Press,
    Bloomington
Nehls E (2003) Vägval. Etnologiska föreningen i Västsverige. Göteborg, Sweden
Redshaw S (2008) In the company of cars—driving as social and cultural practice. Ashgate
    Publishing, Aldershot
Stebbins R (1997) Casual leisure: a conceptual statement. Leis Stud 16:17–25
Suchman L (1987) Plans and situated actions: the problem of human-machine communication.
    Cambridge University Press, Cambridge
Tengström E (1991) Bilismen—i kris? En bok om bilen, människan, samhället och miljön. Rabén
    and Sjögren, Stockholm
Thrift N (2004) Driving in the city. Theory Cult Soc 21(4/5):41–59
Urry J (2007) Mobilities. Polity Press, Malden
Venturi R, Brown DS et al (1972) Learning from Las Vegas: the forgotten symbolism of
    architectural forms. MIT Press, Boston

Chapter 2
Juxtaposing Traffic Research and Social Computing

Our research in mobile applications that support social interaction in traffic, as well as our sociological investigations, are grounded in and inspired by research conducted in two different areas. The juxtaposition of these areas plays an important role in framing our research in its current form. Each of these research orientations will be presented, to illustrate how they form a foundation for the work presented in the remainder of the book.

We have been influenced by research which has traffic as its topic, e.g., traffic planning and intelligent transportation systems. These mature fields have a long history and include various traditions with different views on social interaction and how it should be organized. We will also discuss marginal traditions that understand social interaction as crucial in designing the cityscape and the roads, but regard such interaction as contingent and complex. An ambitious normative theory of design for public life in cities, which derives from research on the design of public roads, is of particular importance, as well as specific design approaches which have made very interesting efforts to promote and support complexity and diversity on the roads. We will also present dominant traditions which understand social interaction more as a problem that has to be diminished and limited by various means. We review how the use of information technology has been conceived within traffic research and transportation planning, basically to control and delimit social interaction.

We also draw on the results of research in the area that can broadly be referred to as human–computer interaction. Here computer support for social interaction is explored, both for work and leisure. We will account for the turn from computers being a tool for control and surveillance in work-related practices, to perspectives where technologies are important means for supporting social interaction, collaboration, and community experiences of various kind.

2.1 A Design Theory on Traffic and City Life

Kevin Lynch, who was professor of architecture at MIT, summarized many years of research on possibilities and requirements of public technology in the book *A Theory of Good City Form* (1981). It brings together experiences of the involvement of architects in the construction and design of the urban highway system at the peak of this historic era. There are important parallels between that research and the focus in this book on designing mobile services for social interaction on the roads. Traffic and transport are already important to Lynch as he outlines his theory, and we will specifically refer to these studies in his work. Furthermore, Lynch's book is very much a reflection based on his innovative research spanning more than 30 years. His interest in the lived social life of traffic is still challenging and inspiring when we engage in the design of mobile services. Lynch's theory is about establishing the critical dimensions for architecture to support good urban quality of life through design guided by criteria such as *vitality, sense, fit, access,* and *control.*

He argues that it is important to secure a healthy environment, or what he refers to as *vitality.* This includes our need for a good supply of clean air and our concern to avoid bodily accidents. Furthermore, it is about ensuring that the city should be in consonance with the basic biological structure of the body. Vitality, in all these senses, is at the core of the concerns of research and planning of road use. It is the topic of the environmental research on traffic; and the quest for increased safety on the road generates a large body of research and design. Finally, consonance with our basic biology is the subject of human factors research, which is an important field in the area, not least for the car industry.

Lynch argues further that it is necessary to account for what he calls the *fit,* which means the match between the form of the design and its purpose. The design has to deliver what it is supposed to do in a satisfactory and comfortable way. According to Lynch, traffic congestion is an obvious example of a poor fit between what the users want to do and what the system can provide. The benefit of getting *access* to all kinds of activities, through transportation and communication, is the most basic argument for life in cities. The ideal city should provide access to an enormous variety of people, goods, and services. Access to activities such as work, residence, and education is of importance in designing the physical settlement. Easy access was once the privilege of a few. But with the advent of private cars and other modern means of transport and communication, it is now available to many more.

Furthermore, the use of space must be *controlled.* This is traditionally done through ownership, rights of presence, or rights of use. The way space is controlled can either be explicit and codified, or implicit in informal social rules. Again, such regulations are highly relevant for the topic of social interaction on the road, where the code of law strongly influences how we behave.

The establishment of fit, access, and control is a central part of transportation planning and traffic research. However, Lynch cautions against focusing too strongly on these requirements when designing the road infrastructure, since that would underestimate other qualities in road use. Traveling is not just a necessary evil for getting access to what is really interesting. Lynch writes: "Driving for pleasure is the most common form of outdoor recreation in the United States. A pleasant trip in good company through a fine landscape is a positive experience. . .It is possible to provide fine roadscapes, pleasant vehicles, and opportunities for work, entertainment, or companionship en route" (Lynch 1981, p. 194). Currently, the separation of activity and road use, which is at the bottom of the traditional access concept, is being increasingly challenged by road users applying new mobile technologies. As we have discussed earlier, activities such as work and family life, which are thought to lie "outside" the area of road usage and take place only before or after the journey, are increasingly becoming part of the road use itself as the drivers chat away their time on the roads.

By *sense*, Lynch (1981) means the "clarity with which it [*the settlement*] can be perceived and identified, and the ease with which its elements can be linked with other events and places." This quality of public life is rarely addressed when discussing transportation and traffic, and we will therefore outline it more carefully. It lies at the root of personal feelings and is based on identity, transparency, and legibility. *Identity* is the extent to which a person can recognize a place as distinct from other places. A place with an identity can occasionally provide sheer delight through the play of light, sounds, colors, forms, etc. This is particularly true when traveling on roads, as Lynch discussed in other books such as *The view from the road* (Appleyard et al. 1964). *Transparency* denotes the possibility to directly perceive operations of various functions, e.g. social functions. The concept of transparency conveys a sense of life. The demand of transparency is balanced against motives such as privacy, modesty, and control. *Legibility* is that important part of sensibility that is about the degree to which inhabitants are able to "communicate accurately" with each other via symbolic physical features in the landscape. Signs are posted about ownership, status, group affiliation, etc.

Finally, we add design for *delight* and *play*. Kevin Lynch's design ideal is clearly that of a modernist. He wants the roadscape to be designed as a language, able to fully convey the meanings and intentions of the people who live in the cities and along the roads. The requirement of *sense* is then different from Venturi and Brown's semiotics, which allows the roadside architecture to both play with intended meanings and convey fictitious narratives. They wanted it to provide a sense of lightness, heightened symbolism, and role playing. It could be argued that qualities such as delight, play, and narration relate to Lynch's concept of sense, since these qualities are so influential in social life that the fiction of city life has to be conveyed as clearly as possible. However, we do not believe that requirements of a clear and distinct "language" are enough to bring out the role of delight and play in social life. These characteristics must be made explicit in their own right.

Summing up, researchers in architecture of the roadscape such as Kevin Lynch, Robert Venturi, and Denise Scott Brown, and the experiences of this period of urban design, inspire us to address the role of traffic in urban social life beyond obvious goals of traffic research such as safety, pollution, and efficiency of flow. It underscores the variations in social use of the road spaces, and the broad range of requirements which could be of relevance in design.

2.2   Traffic Design for Vitality and Sense

The design theories of Kevin Lynch are ambitious and broad. To address such a range of issues in a particular design case could be an overwhelming task. At the same time, there are instances of road design principles that make an effort to encompass aspects such as vitality and sense. The existence of such approaches is important to recognize when considering the scope of the design of the next generation of mobile technologies.

We will therefore, in the following, specifically discuss traffic planning principles that have been intended to generate road traffic which is vital, fitting, and sensible. We will be presenting a way of designing residential streets known by the Dutch term *woonerven* [living yards]. This points partly to why social interaction is a relevant concern and partly to the specific problems of designing for increased interaction using traditional construction materials such as concrete, stone, and asphalt.

In 1963, Niek De Boer presented a design concept to bridge the disparity between children's play and car traffic on an urban street (Hass-Klau 1990). This concept was based on the idea that the car driver should feel that he or she was driving in a farm-yard environment. De Boer named the new street "*woonerf*." His idea was adopted by Delft municipality in conjunction with a major street renovation in 1969. Four planners adopted De Boer's concept, and also invited the residents of the streets to be renovated to contribute their own ideas. It was agreed to avoid the typical separation between pavement and roadway, and instead to integrate them as a road surface which would give the visual impression of a yard. This effect would be reinforced with trees, benches and other design elements. The first *woonerf* was created in a low-income area—which was in great need of playing areas for children—and which was also home to a large number of students. The students came to play an important role, primarily through their enthusiasm and their ability to involve other people living in the area. The use of the *woonerf* principles was an instant success, and many Dutch towns began street renovations of this kind. They also attracted international interest, on Germany's part to such an extent that Delft became the "magical" place to which German planners made pilgrimages (Hass-Klau 1990).

The road-users' individual wishes, and the planners' positive attitude towards them, gave rise to versatility and variation in the designs. These designs were characterized by a balancing of the various interests, where e.g. some children's idea of a football pitch had to be weighed against a number of car-owners' interpretation of the same design as a "steeplechase course." Nor was it the planners' intention to arrive at a universal design for a *woonerf*. On the contrary, the variation was viewed as an important message to its users that the design, as well as its use, was open to negotiation and local input (Hallqvist 1994).

A *woonerf* should primarily be located in a residential area, and for this reason the volume of traffic should normally be low. There must also be sufficient parking space for residents and visitors, and the lighting should be good. The playgrounds should be distinguishable from the areas intended for traffic, but they must not give the impression that the children cannot play in other areas as well (Trafiksäkerhetsverket 1991). Despite the variations in design, certain general characteristics have come to the fore, including the fact that a *woonerf* tends to have very narrow driving lanes, even when there is two-way traffic. The lanes are often demarcated by a change in the material used to make the road surface, e.g. from asphalt to stone. The lanes are laid out so that cars cannot drive forwards in a straight line, but have to zigzag. There might be raised sections in the roadway made of a light-colored material so that they are clearly visible to the road-users. A *woonerf* is often lined with trees, playgrounds, benches, walls, etc., as well as bollards of various materials and designs.

Evaluations of *woonerven* indicate that the residents' attitudes are primarily determined by their satisfaction with design features not directly related to traffic (Ben-Joseph 1995). Space is a scarce resource in the Netherlands and must to a significant extent be shared between different activities, which is why the design of an area will be characterized by the way in which various activities' need for space are mutually adjusted (Vahl and Giskes 1990). Researcher Anne Moudon (1987) sees the underlying concept behind the *woonerf* as re-establishing the social character of the street in order to achieve better neighborhood relations. Others, such as Jonquiere (quoted in Hallquist 1994) point to a desire to break the dominance of traffic and instead to try to integrate the street's traffic function and its function as a meeting place and a living space for the residents.

The *woonerf* concept was formally established in 1976 through special legislation. The legislation presupposes that there is cooperation regarding its use. The legislation can rightly be perceived as a codification of the mutual adaptation between road-users which the street environment itself should generate (Hallqvist 1994). There are also special instructions regarding how to mobilize local involvement in the design and management of a *woonerf* (ANWB 1979). The legislation envisions a *woonerf* as serving as a meeting place for residents and visitors, as well as offering opportunities for children, adults, and the elderly, as well as mopedists, bicyclists, and car drivers to use the street for their own particular requirements (Directorate 1980). This encompasses a number of minimum standards as regards physical design, which are supplemented with special traffic legislation. One renowned standard maintains that "the entire shared yard street in a *woonerf* is a pedestrian domain, and it is therefore essential to avoid kerbs which separate pedestrians and motor vehicles." Article 88 of the traffic legislation for *woonerven,* from which the following quote is taken, is equally renowned:

> Pedestrians may use the entire street within an area defined as a "*woonerf*"; playing in the street is also allowed...Within a "*woonerf*," motorists may not drive faster than walking pace. They must take into consideration the possible presence of pedestrians, including children at play, unmarked objects and raised sections in the road surface, as well as an irregular road line. (Directorate 1980)

During the 10 years immediately following the first trials in Delft, more than 800 individual streets became *woonerven* in the Netherlands. But practical and economic constraints on the (strict) application of the *woonerf* idea gradually emerged.

Nevertheless, the basic concept of shared road usage has proven to be a robust idea. There are plenty of references to *woonerven* in planning literature. You also come across modifications of the basic concept in various guises and under various names. One example, from the beginning of the 1980s, relates to an entire road network in a newly-built area in the Waterwijk neighborhood in the Dutch town of Lelystad, which was planned in order that "open areas should be used and shared between users in a better way" (Vahl and Giskes 1990). Another early application came about in Munich at the end of the 1970s, when two town planners and a traffic engineer were awarded a contract to redesign the street network in a small suburb of the *city*. They wanted to apply Delft-inspired ideas under the name *Wohnstrassen* (living streets). The federal transport research institute was initially hesitant about their ideas, but finally provided a research grant to study how the streets were used before and after the redesign. Their *wohnstrassen* are reminiscent of *woonerven*, but the codification of road usage, which the legislation in the Netherlands had been striving for, is missing. The results of the "before and after" studies surprised the previously skeptical traffic engineers (Hass-Klau 1990). Significantly more pedestrians now used the streets. They stayed there for longer and there was more communication. They felt safer and their behavior changed inasmuch as they took more notice of each other. There were fewer accidents even though the number of "conflicts" remained the same, and no dangerous behavior by motorists was reported.

Another example, also from Germany, is the "soft separation" design principle, which is used as a "transitional form" between the principles of separating and mixing road-users (Schweig 1993). It is influenced by *woonerven* to the extent that soft separation is characterized by the roadway and the pavement not being separated by curbs, but rather being indicated by different surfaces, shallow water drainage channels, or bollards. In a number of applications, considerable improvements in the interaction between road-users are being noted, despite the high traffic intensity and the fact that there have been no reductions in speed limits.

A final example is Ben-Joseph's (1995) discussion about "shared road usage" with particular reference to the USA. He proposes a road concept called a "shared road," which after local development work can be adapted to local regulations and requirements. He believes that shared road usage is possible even in the case of a traditional road design in the form of a grid of roads. Ben-Joseph emphasizes the strength of local activities, which can operate independently of a central authority's yardstick, as a key factor for achieving change.

Despite the fact that these ideas have attracted a great deal of interest, they have never gained a firm foothold in the world governed by the traffic planners, and as a result have only had a marginal influence on the design of residential streets. The ideas about user-participation and support of local interaction have also been diluted as a consequence of the fact that traffic planning has gradually come to focus on road traffic safety in a comprehensive and large-scale perspective, and also has favored other methods to achieve these goals. One reason is that it is very expensive to rebuild streets in the way needed to establish the rich form of interaction that is sought after.

To sum up, the specific design principles discussed above have all acknowledged social interaction among road users as a critical topic. The idea has been to introduce strict speed limits in order to provide more time for people to come to agreements on how to share the road space. They aimed to generate vitality and a good fit by supporting people's own negotiations. Equally important, they also designed for longer traffic encounters, to generate more sense in the city; i.e. to increase socialization.

However, planners and traffic researchers in favor of *woonerf* principles and similar ideas do not seem to have been as interested in information technology as their other colleagues in traffic research. Still, the way information technology has been conceived in this area is important when deciding on how well it maps onto available social interaction.

2.3 Intelligent Transportation Systems and Telematics

Traffic planners and engineers have had high hopes for the use of various IT-based solutions to improve transportation (Emberger 1993). Instead of the blunt tools which have previously been used to handle traffic, new information technology is thought to offer significantly better opportunities for control and surveillance of traffic (Chen and Miles 1999). The term Intelligent Transportation Systems (ITS) was coined in 1994 (Walker 1998) and defined as:

> The application of information and communications technology to the planning and operation of transportation systems. (McQueen and McQueen 1999, p. 20)

In general, transportation and traffic are regarded as a large system of roads and vehicles that must be controlled to achieve a smooth and safe traffic flow. The traditional means for maintaining a functioning transportation system (i.e. vehicles, roads, road markings, signs, and traffic lights) should be complemented with more technologically advanced solutions, consisting of information and communication technologies. One of the most ambitious goals of the introduction of new high-tech solutions is to improve the operation, control, and surveillance of the transport networks (Chen and Miles 1999) to achieve greater efficiency in the form of lower travel times and costs. It is also important to note that the concept covers all aspects of transportation, ranging from people driving their own vehicles to the use of public transportation.

The development of ITS is based on the assumption that the demands of future daily life, sustained by an increase in mobility, will be secured through increasing use of private cars. As a consequence, the burdens on the transport infrastructure, which is already thinly stretched, particularly in urban areas, are multiplying. The very freedom of movement that cars have provided is now being degraded into traffic congestion. To solve these problems, a combination of new policies and information technology (Camus and Fortin 1995; Chen and Miles 1999) are capable of opening up new ways of achieving a sustainable mobility. The overall idea is that traffic problems are linked to incomplete information provision, which can now be remedied through the compilation and communication of "real-time data." This can best be explained as a collection of services that aim to reduce the number of accidents; help relieve congestion; support environmental monitoring and protection; increase productivity and operational efficiency; and, finally, provide comfort factors (Chen and Miles 1999). There are a number of different stakeholders whose concerns the field of ITS must address; these range from city planners to managers of the transport network, vehicle manufacturers, fleet operators, authorities, travelers, and drivers.

The applications are normally categorized into a list of service categories including systems for traveler information, traffic management, vehicle systems, public transport management, emergency management, electronic payment, and safety (Catling 1994; Libbrech and Ryd 1992; Walker 1998; Whelan 1995).

As an example, these services provide real-time information to the road users, but also means for collecting data on the traffic situation and the condition of infrastructure. According to overviews of the services proposed by ITS, the new technologies offer a number of centralized solutions for control and surveillance. They will support traffic management by monitoring the road conditions from traffic management centers, using data from sensors (video, pressure, speed, temperature, number of vehicles) built into the road, or placed along the roadside. Furthermore, the centers can handle emergency calls from motorists and collect various fees from the road users. Consequently, they can be used as an automatic traffic police, identifying vehicles which are breaking the law. With the help of automated data collection and processing from its computerized systems, sensors, and video, ITS can provide feedback to the road users and thereby influence and manage the demand for road usage in terms of time and space. It is possible that the technology will be able to influence the potential to park and/or to access a road. Fees can also be charged for road usage, so that the price is in direct relation to the level of congestion. The centers can also offer services to drivers such as updated travel information to help them avoid queues and accidents.

The field of transport telematics is similar to ITS, but here it is the car industry that is the key player, rather than the road authorities. Telematics is defined as "two-way communication between a vehicle and a service centre (i.e. to and from the vehicle) by means of wireless technology" (Gabinus 2003, p. 6). Within this field, there are services to enhance safety such as collision avoidance, pre-crash restraint deployment, and vision enhancement to warn of hazards ahead. In some 2003 Volvo models the dashboard includes an automatic collision mayday system that determines the severity of a crash and automatically calls for help. General Motors provides a similar service. Their "Air Bag Deployment Notification" is activated in the event that the front air bag is set off. The vehicle sends a signal to a control center, where an advisor will attempt to contact the driver and inquire whether or not assistance is needed. Emergency help will be notified and the location will be provided if the driver cannot answer. Telematics is also used to track stolen cars and to perform remote diagnostics, where sensors detect problems in the vehicle and send this data directly to a service center for analysis and to book a time for repair.

There is also a great deal of interest in bolder functionalities which depend on gathering and processing data from sensors on the vehicles. These applications are autonomous and do not utilize any centralized features or control rooms. The idea is rather to build expert systems in the form of artificial drivers (Catling 1994; Whelan 1995). These would be able to detect and communicate with each other, as well as communicate with nearby vehicles, traffic signals, and road signs.

To sum up, both the concentration on vitality in designing ITS and telematics, and the specific design approaches, resemble dominant traffic planning principles.

Thus, in this sector the introduction of information technology is new, but the way they intend to apply it is not. Therefore, we believe that the discussion on the role of social interaction in traffic stands to gain from making ITS's relationship to that tradition explicit.

2.4   The Foundation of ITS in Traditional Traffic Planning

We argue that the way information technology has been designed is founded on the dominant tradition within transportation planning and traffic research. It is rooted in a perspective where the problem of coordination is understood and handled through analytic models and sets of rules for road usage which are intended to be universal, i.e. which apply in general situations over large geographical areas, and under idealized categorizations of road use.

To make those principles visible we will discuss ITS with reference to classic transport planning studies which emerged almost half a century ago. Colin Buchanan, who led a major British traffic study at the end of the 1950s and beginning of the 1960s, was an influential transport planner who advocated perspectives which have lived on into the design approaches in the ITS community. Traffic planning was an established activity in the 1950s, but Buchanan wanted to raise the level of ambition to encompass the design of urban road networks in their entirety (Banister 1994, p. 26). The first edition of the final report *Traffic in Towns* was published in 1963, and a paperback edition was issued soon afterwards by Penguin Books (Buchanan 1964). Few traffic studies have had such a public impact as this report. It was also extremely important elsewhere in Europe, and is therefore well suited for a discussion about the principles of the handling of road usage coordination by traffic planners.

The Buchanan report focused on the growth of mass motoring, and pointed to the fact that the steadily increasing volume of traffic was creating serious social problems in the form of road accidents and pollution. Buchanan's solution to the problem was "a matter of rationalizing the arrangements of buildings and access ways" (1964). The design of towns and roads should be carried out by a new type of expert with the support of a town planning policy. He proposed a hierarchical structuring of road types into "primary," "district," and "local distributors." These roads should reach "environmental areas" where the actual activities took place. The report refers to the modern major hospital as a metaphor for the design of a town which should be able to house mass motoring: "In principle it would be like a gigantic building with corridors serving a multitude of rooms" (1964).

Traffic planning should be carried out by special experts. These should carry out analyses of road usage and then "organize" the combined road activity in such a way that the number of "conflicts" is reduced. Junctions are regulated with traffic signals. Roads are divided into lanes, pavements, and cycle paths. The lanes are used for vehicular transport. The pavements are used by pedestrians and the cycle paths for bicycle transport. Children should be kept away from roads and their immediate vicinity. Buchanan's analysis of the essence of road usage has become something of a self-fulfilling prophecy, although a great deal remains to be done before it could be said to control and regulate road usage completely.

The study had a major impact on traffic planning far beyond the UK's borders. It has also characterized Swedish traffic planning, as can be seen in the comprehensive models for traffic planning which were developed in the 1960s and 1970s (Gunnarsson and Lindström 1970; Lenntorp and Wiklund 1980, p. 47). Principles similar to the perspective in *Traffic in Towns* were specified:

> Separation of different types of traffic, so that conflicts are eliminated between traffic with differing properties;
> Differentiation, so that traffic flows are homogenized;
> Simplification and standardization, so that surprises are avoided and decisions and actions made easier.

The above guidelines are now almost half a century old, but similar arguments can be seen much later. The Netherlands is often seen as a pioneer as regards traffic planning and road traffic safety. In a report by the National Institute for Road Traffic Safety Research, their proposal for a new national policy is set out with clear reference to the described perspective:

> Roads are built with one major function in mind: to enable people and goods to travel, the so-called traffic function... The concept of sustainably safe road transport comes down to the removal of all function combinations by making the road mono-functional. Multi-functionality leads to contradictory design requirements and also to higher risks. (SWOV 1997)

Consequently, there has been no lack of ambition among traffic planners to push their design approach. The principle of introducing hierarchical systems and control mechanisms, as well as the efforts to focus on Katz's concept of vitality, runs throughout the way information technology has been conceived under the ITS umbrella. The ability of people to coordinate movements and other forms of road use by themselves is not trusted and must be restricted in various ways. There is also a fundamental disregard of social aspects related to "sense" qualities (Lynch 1981), e.g. the possibility to display identities and interact as a community. Again, this lack of interest is visible in traditional traffic planning and how it excludes such topics already in the definition of road usage, which is first defined as transport and second as a *non-activity*. Buchanan defines it by asking about the function of road use, and more precisely what function does movement have. He sees the movements as results of activities in which drivers are involved. These activities take place in other situations outside of the road network, and often inside buildings.

> Traffic is a function of activities, and traffic is concentrated in towns because activities are concentrated there. It is characteristic of activities in towns that they mainly take place in buildings, or in places such as markets, depots, docks and stations... In towns, therefore, traffic can be said to be a function of buildings. (Buchanan 1964, p. 48)

To sum up, the way IT support for traffic (ITS) has been conceived is influenced by traditional transport planning. This explains why so little attention has been given to support for social interaction. This neglect has consequences for people on the roads and the design of urban quality of life, but it might also be of importance for those struggling to implement ITS in practice. Despite their efforts, ITS has not yet resulted in a shift regarding how traffic is organized. As early as 1998, an overview of the state of the art of Intelligent Transport Systems (ITS) claimed that

> In contrast to cellular radio... ITS has stubbornly defied predictions and refused to take off commercially, even though it has a long technical history. (Walker 1998, p. 407)

And the industry is still not taking off. General Motors' commercialization of ITS services, called On Star, is one of few, albeit weak, commercial successes. Ford's rival system, called Wingcast, flopped altogether in 2002. The struggles of the car industry and government authorities to put mobile technology to use motivate a closer look at other areas of IT-research for inspiration and expertise.

2.5 Social Interaction in Computer Science

We now turn to computer science, and more specifically, the recent interest in technologies which support collaboration in various ways. By doing so we hope to learn more about how spontaneous, non-hierarchical social interaction can be supported by IT. There are two reasons for providing this background to the research presented in this book. First, it underscores the importance of applying a user-centric perspective, which takes detailed studies of humans and their computer interaction seriously when designing collaborative applications. An interest in social and interactional practice, as well as in the appropriate methodological tools, is fundamental to research areas such as Computer–Human Interaction (CHI), and especially, Computer-Supported Cooperative Work (CSCW). Second, by accounting for how it emerged as a central topic in these areas, we can grasp the underlying reasons for shifting from a perspective that views organizational work only in terms of large systems that can easily be managed, to one that looks at the contingent and situated collaborative aspects of, for example, distributed groups.

Computers were initially used for complex and manually demanding calculation tasks, such as modeling ballistic trajectories and controlling technical systems. Computer technology was first applied commercially in the 1950s to automate offices (Esbjörnsson 2005; Johansson 1997), including procedures to automate accounting (Nurminen 1988). When computerization took off in the 1960s (Grudin 1994), the technology become useful as information systems for business management (Borghoff and Schlichter 2000), together with associated research fields such as the area of management information systems (often referred to as MIS) (Brown 1998). An MIS is comprised of all the components that collect, manipulate, and distribute data or information (Esbjörnsson 2005). In all, computerization became a successful tool for handling large data sets and complex technical systems in factories but it proved to be less effective in rationalizing and controlling offices' activities (Nurminen 1988). In order to compensate for its deficiencies the companies collected more and more information at an increasing cost (Attewell 1996). The systems approach that had been so useful for controlling complex technical systems, did not apply equally well for administration, which contains contingent and situated collaboration (Dahlbom and Mathiassen 1993). It was in this situation that the research area of workplace studies (Brown 1998; Luff et al. 2000) took as its starting point an organization's dependence on local collaboration (Orr 1996) and investigated the possibility to improve it with digital technology. Those ambitions developed into the area of Computer Supported Collaborative Work (CSCW) (Crabtree 2003; Greif 1988), which was defined as research concerned with understanding and developing technological support for the activities and relationships that hold between people working together in groups. The focus on group work has since then decreased, and CSCW is currently more conceived as a broader field which investigates cooperative work and digital technology support in general (Bannon and Schmidt 1991). Recently, research has focused on the relation between the mobility of the personnel and organizational work. Historically, a popular research area has been controllers' collaborative work in traffic control rooms of various kinds (Heath and Luff 1992; Juhlin and Weilenmann 2001; Pettersson et al. 2002). For example, Hughes et al. (1992) and Mackay (2000) show how control managers make use of available resources to make their own work visible to their colleagues, and how their peripheral awareness, is an important way to, e.g., repair mistakes. Watts et al. (1996) have considered audio communication support for airspace management.

The area has also been concerned with collaboration in mobile work. A majority of the research focuses on the ways in which white collar work is conducted in specific "office" settings, and the ways in which office workers access information irrespective of time and place (Bellotti and Bly 1996; Luff and Heath 1998). Bellotti and Bly (1996) discussed how workers' physical mobility in office spaces, and their lack of desktop tools, prevented them from doing such organizational work, e.g., long distance collaboration. Similarly, Heath and Luff (1992) study the local mobility of underground station managers. They found that the managers had much less awareness of the workplace activities when they left the control room to move around the station.

Research in these fields includes not only sociological analysis, but also the design of new technology. Recently the term embodied interaction has been used to describe design that is informed by studies of social interaction, as well as research on support for tangible or physical interaction with computers, to provide computing which "moves beyond the traditional confines of the desk and attempts to incorporate itself more richly into our daily experience of the physical and social world" (Dourish 2004). The idea emerges from our bodily and socially based knowledge of how to act in the world when there is no apparent "problem" to be solved. According to Paul Dourish, humans focus on the way in which we experience the world "as embodied actors interacting in the world, participating in it and acting through it, in the absorbed and unreflective manner of normal experience" (2004).

In his theory of embodied interaction he states that computing occurs in specific settings, which are organized and dependent on collaboration between many people and physical objects. Thus, embodied computing "exploits our familiarity and facility with that everyday world, whether it is a world of social interaction or physical artifacts" (Dourish 2004). It is integrated with physical artifacts as a way to augment everyday objects in the world and provide for interaction through such objects. Finally, it recognizes that computers are design objects with an aesthetic.

In general, the way in which we interact with environments has been a key topic within the area of Computer–Human Interaction. The oft-cited paper "Re-placeing space" (Harrison and Dourish 1996) has been influential in the discussion on how to design support for interaction in virtual environments. It establishes a distinction between the concepts of space and place. *Space* describes geographical arrangements that might "structure, constrain and enable certain forms of movement and interaction" (Dourish 2006). Thus, they recognize movement as contingent on geography. In collaboration, geographical arrangements constrain such things as relational orientation, possible actions which require proximity, or presence (Harrison and Dourish 1996). *Place* refers to the social meanings of an environment, which it acquires through conventions, roles, and use. In this book we bring the physical *movement* to the forefront, arguing that being a road user brings with it a specific way of orienting oneself in the dimensions of both place and space.

2.6 Towards a New Research Agenda

Kevin Lynch argued for a broad set of requirements when designing public technology, which included recognition of the role of social interaction (1981). We have also presented some attempts within transport planning to account for the role of local social interaction, both to achieve coordination of movements and other more experiential qualities. On the other hand, the design approach vis-à-vis information and communication technology has been narrow and focused on aspects of the vitality of the city, e.g. on safety and congestion. Furthermore, the approach has been influenced by a perspective aiming to reduce local social interaction through the introduction of hierarchical control solutions. A comparison with other areas of computing, where traffic is not the topic, reveals many similarities. Computerization of office work has traditionally built on a preference for hierarchical structures, which also favor task separation. The interest in more general research on human–computer interaction has turned to the details of local collaborative work, partly in order to account for the high cost of building such systems, and partly due to the interest in new technologies that support communication between peers. Furthermore, there is a growing interest in what Lynch would refer to as the sense qualities of the interaction, i.e., the role of local communities, experiences, and aesthetics. A recent approach is to design an "embodied" relation between computers and humans (Dourish 2004).

In this chapter, we have juxtaposed research areas which currently overlap only minimally. Putting these areas side by side—transportation planning in a broad sense and research in the area of human–computer interaction—creates new opportunities which inspire inquiry into the role of social interaction on the roads and how it could be supported by mobile technologies. The next step is to decide on where and how to start such an undertaking.

References

ANWB (1979) Woonerf. ANWB, Haag

Appleyard D, Lynch K et al (1964) The view from the road. MIT Press, Boston

Attewell P (1996) Information technology and the productivity. In: Kling R (ed) Challenge. Computerization and controversy. Academic Press, San Diego, pp 227–238

Banister D (1994) Transport planning. Taylor & Francis, Oxon

Bannon L, Schmidt K (1991) CSCW: four characters in search of a context. In: Benford SD, Bowers JM (eds) Studies in computer supported cooperative work. North-Holland Publishing, Amsterdam, pp 3–16

Bellotti V, Bly S (1996) Walking away from the desktop computer: distributed collaboration and mobility in a product design team. In: The proceedings of the conference on computer supported cooperative work. ACM Press, Boston

Ben-Joseph E (1995) Changing the residential street. APA J 61(4): 504–515

Borghoff UM, Schlichter JM (2000) Computer-supported cooperative work—introduction to distributed applications. Springer, Berlin

Brown B (1998) Working notes: how groupware is used in organizations. PhD thesis, Department of Sociology, University of Surrey

Buchanan C (1964) Traffic in towns—the specially shortened edition of the Buchanan report. Penguin Books, Hammondsworth

Camus J-P, Fortin M (1995) Road transport informatics—institutional and legal issues. European Conference of Ministers of Transport, Paris

Catling I (1994) Advanced technology for road transport: IVHS and ATT. Artech House Books, London

Chen K, Miles JC (eds) (1999) ITS handbook 2000—recommendations from the World Road Association (PIARC). Artech House Publishers, London

Crabtree A (2003) Designing collaborative systems—a practical guide to ethnography. Springer, Berlin

Dahlbom B, Mathiassen L (1993) Computers in context—the philosophy and practice of system design. Blackwell Publishers Ltd., Oxford

Directorate ARS (1980) Woonerf. Haag, ANWB & Road Safety Directorate

Dourish P (2004) Where the action is. MIT Press, Boston

Emberger MP (1993) The contribution of Prometheus to European traffic safety. In: Parkes AM, Franzén S (eds) Driving future vehicles. Taylor and Francis, London

Esbjörnsson M (2005) Enhanced social interaction in traffic. PhD thesis, Department of Applied Information Technology, IT University of Göteborg, Gothenburg

Gabinus T (2003) A prospectus for growth in telematics. The Telematics Valley, Gothenburg

Greif I (ed) (1988) Computer supported cooperative work: a book of readings. Morgan Kaufmann, San Mateo

Grudin J (1994) Groupware and social dynamics: eight challenges for developers. Commun ACM NY 37: 92–105

Gunnarsson OS, Lindström S (1970) Vägen till trafiksäkerhet. Rabén och Sjögren, Stockholm

Hallqvist B (1994) Woonerfgator och Nordiska Tillämpningar av den Holländska Planeringsfilosofin. Tekniska Högskolan i Lund, Institutionen för trafikteknik, Lund

Harrison, S, Dourish P (1996) Re-place-ing space: the roles of place and space in collaborative systems. In: Proceedings of the international CSCW conference. ACM Press, Boston

Hass-Klau, C (1990) The pedestrian and city traffic. Wiley, London

Heath C, Luff P (1992) Collaboration and control: crisis management and multimedia technology in London underground line control rooms. Comput Support Coop Work 1:69–94

Hughes JA, Randall D et al (1992) Faltering from ethnography to design. In Proceedings of the 1992 ACM conference on computer-supported cooperative work, Toronto, Canada, pp 115–122

Johansson M (1997) Smart, fast and beautiful—on rhetoric of technology and computing discourse in Sweden 1955–1995. PhD thesis, Department of Tema, Linköping Studies in Arts and Science No 164, Linköping

Juhlin O, Weilenmann A (2001). Decentralizing the control room: mobile work and institutional order. In: Proceedings of the seventh European conference on computer supported cooperative work. Kluwer, Bonn, pp 379–397

Lenntorp B, Wiklund T (1980) Grepp på bilismen—Om prognoser och framtidsplanering inom transportsektorn. Liber, Stockholm

Libbrech R, Ryd PO (1992) Subfunctions, functions and application areas of advanced transport telematics—CORD project. ERTICO, Brussels

Luff P, Heath C (1998) Mobility in collaboration. In: Proceedings of the 1998 ACM conference on computer supported cooperative work. ACM Press, Seattle, pp 305–314

Luff P, Hindmarsh J et al (2000) Workplace studies—recovering work practice and informing system design. Cambridge University Press, Cambridge

Lynch K (1981) A theory of good city form. MIT Press, Cambridge

Mackay WE (2000) Is paper safer? The role of paper flight strips in air traffic control. ACM Trans Comput Hum Interact 6(4):311–340

McQueen B, McQueen J (eds) (1999) Intelligent transportation systems architecture. Artech House, London

Moudon AV (ed) (1987) Public street for public use. Van Nostrand Reinhold Company, New York

Nurminen M (1988) People or computers: three ways of looking at information systems. Studentlitteratur, Lund

Orr J (1996) Talking about machines—an ethnography of a modern job. ILR Press/Cornell University Press, Ithaca

Pettersson M, Randall D et al (2002) Ambiguities, awareness and economy: a study of emergency service work. In: Proceedings of the 2002 ACM conference on computer supported cooperative work, New Orleans

Schweig KH (1993) Soft separation—a design principle to a better streetscape and to more security in main thoroughfares. In: PTRC 21st summer annual meeting, University of Manchester, Manchester

SWOV (1997) Sustainable solutions to improve road safety. Research activities, vol 8. SWOV Institute for Road Safety Research, Leidschendam

Trafiksäkerhetsverket (1991) Gårdsgata. Trafiksäkerhetsverket, Sweden

Walker J (1998) Advances in mobile information systems. Artech House, London

Watts JC, Woods DD et al (1996) Voice loops as cooperative aids in space shuttle mission control. In: Proceedings of the 1996 ACM conference on computer supported cooperative work, Boston, pp 48–56

Whelan R (1995) Smart highways smart cars. Artech House, London

Chapter 3
Investigating and Designing for Social Interaction

The purpose of this book is not to provide optimal solutions to a well-defined problem. Instead, our topic is a "wicked problem" (Rittel and Webber 1973). Rittel and Webber argue in their classic text that some planning problems are particularly hard to handle. These require that decisions be made in situations where, on the one hand, people have different normative opinions on the quality of a solution, and on the other hand, the solutions are generated in a complex and dynamic setting. Wicked research problems are vexed by the complications of deciding on the goal of the work before determining what is possible to achieve. Furthermore, such problems are hard to delimit, which makes it difficult to decide when to stop analyzing or when a solution is optimal. There are many things that could possibly influence a specific problem and any number of alternative solutions. Evaluations of a suggested solution are equally difficult to conduct. According to Rittel and Webber, planning or design should not be understood as a straightforward process starting with a problem definition, and then proceeding through investigations and the identification of solutions.

Since our interest in designing for social life in traffic easily qualifies as a wicked problem, we must have an open and explorative approach that identifies problems and solutions in parallel. To account for the uncertainties involved in deciding on the most interesting questions and then determining if they have been answered, Redström (2001) suggests that we instead account for the research as an investigation of a design space. In this case, it concerns road users and social activities on the road, as well as the affordances of mobile technologies. Our investigation will provide a number of brush-strokes within this area, but unfortunately never give us the full picture.

First, we choose social scientific methods, which make visible some of the wickedness of life in traffic. We associate these studies with technical research, to generate new designs, though acknowledging that design does not need to be determined by these studies. Second, the choice of cases studied is an important part of the research itself. What part of social life in traffic we look into strongly influences what part of it we see, and what kinds of applications that will be generated.

In the following we will present the method of ethnographic field observation, and more specifically our interest in detailed studies of ongoing practical interaction. We discuss how that knowledge is associated with technical competence in mobile

O. Juhlin, *Social Media on the Road*, Computer Supported Cooperative Work 50,
DOI 10.1007/978-1-84996-332-9_3, © Springer-Verlag London Limited 2010

technology as a way to invent new applications. Finally, we argue for the selection of the specific cases studies which in various ways contribute to our research topic.

3.1 Analyzing Social Interaction

In this book we are concerned with the role of social interaction on highways and streets. We are interested in understanding how and why road users act and react to each other. In this sense, the studies share their topic with sociology and especially so-called ethnographic research. The ethnographic tradition, with its roots in anthropology, has been useful (Crabtree 2003). Basically, the term refers to a collection of techniques to gather and organize field material to uncover not only how people interact, but also their motivations for doing so. It is often conducted with the guidance of three important principles: participant observation, inclusion of members' viewpoints, and holism (Prus 1996, p. 109). First, the method is based on the assumption that the researcher must share the day-to-day activities of those studied to be able to describe them thoroughly. Second, the researcher must not only represent what is visible, but also the underlying intentions, norms, etc. that make the activities rational from the members' perspectives. Thus, the method depends on familiarity with the members to understand their motivations. Third, human conduct must be understood with reference to the naturalistic setting in which it occurs.

The sociologist Gusfield (1981) is a champion of ethnographies of traffic events. He has argued for close analysis of everyday activities to understand traffic behavior.

> My intent in raising the question of purpose and the meaning of the driving event was to focus attention on the immediate context in which the event occurs... It concentrates on how the event emerges in interaction with others... To look at traffic safety at its microlevel is to understand how the actual situations of using traffic are enacted. (Gusfield 1990, p. 7)

Recently, sociologists like Katz (1999) and the geographer Laurier (2002) have conducted ethnographic research on traffic. The importance of a detailed understanding of how users' practices fundamentally influence the requirements of new technology has also been recognized in specific areas of computer science such as Human–Computer Interaction and Computer-Supported Cooperative Work (Randall et al. 2007). As such, ethnographic fieldwork is increasingly being used in conjunction with technical research. When used in the area of systems development, it could be seen as a way of gaining insight and understanding into everyday practices (Hughes et al. 1992). The fast-growing body of ethnographic research and its popularity in CSCW is explained by the need to account for problems with the use of information systems, as well as new demands to understand social interaction when designing information technology (Heath and Luff 2000). It is central to ethnography to see users' activities as taking place within a socially organized sphere (Hughes et al. 1994). Due to the familiarity of their everyday situations, many important activities are taken for granted by those who perform them. Consequently it is not sufficient to simply ask people about their practices. Furthermore, people generally find it difficult to articulate their knowledge, to describe their way of performing tasks (Hughes et al. 1992). Therefore, in addition to interviews, ethnography relies on observation.

Most importantly, the methodology above is intended to make the researcher knowledgeable about intentions and norms, i.e., things that have to be interpreted from behavior. However, native people, i.e., those whom the sociologist studies, find themselves in a similar situation. They do not a priori understand the motivations and the intentions of the people they meet. Instead they need to work out such rules in the situation at hand. Thus, to understand social interaction we should also study the methods people themselves use to inquire into the motivations of others and thereby achieve social agreements. The study of such ethnomethods derives from the work of Garfinkel (1967/1996). According to Martin and Rouncefield this approach

> places methodological emphasis on the rigorous description of the situated practices through which a setting's activities are produced and accomplished. (Martin and Rouncefield 2003)

The goal is to study the details of how the interaction is done. It is pursued by means of thorough analysis of the ways in which people act and react to what is observable and/or audible in the empirical material. It might concern what is said by the participants, as well as their movements, and how they use different artifacts. Accordingly, the emphasis is more on how they organize activities than their motivations.

> Ethnomethodology turns away from the structures and theorizing of traditional sociology, concentrating instead on the details of the practices through which actions and interaction are accomplished. (Button and Dourish 1996, p. 19)

The focus of attention is usually activities that are mundane, normal, or unremarkable in nature. In line with the increased interest in field observations, designers have found ethnomethodology a rich resource for insights about the organization of social interaction, and especially work, as compared to more theoretically oriented sociological positions.

We suggest that the topic of concern in this book, interaction between road users, brings with it some methodological ramifications. We learn from ethnomethodology that we should focus on the ethnographic methods of people in traffic. This implies studying the details of the interaction by which people orient themselves in relation to each other, e.g., when people initiate mobile phone conversations while driving; when a road inspectors prepare to stop in the vicinity of an identified defect during their daily rounds; or when motorcyclists use an Internet message board to organize a joint trip. For that purpose we have utilized a number of different data collection methods ranging from taking field notes to copying documents, taking photos, recording interviews, printing conversations on message boards, and video recordings. In each specific project, the methods have been chosen depending on our questions and the level of detail needed, as well as the practical possibilities of collecting data. At the same time, we also recognize that we want to reveal people's motivations for being involved in these activities, as a way to inspire design, and that the brief and meager interaction, e.g. in a traffic encounter, does not always lend itself to such an analysis. Therefore, we recommend that detailed analysis be complemented by traditional interpretative ethnographic approaches.

3.2 Designing for Social Interaction

This book is as much about inventing new applications to support social interaction on the roads, as it is about studying such interaction. We think it is apparent that the design principles underlying the area of ITS, which, e.g., treat road use as a non-activity per se, constrain the everyday life of road users. We accept that contradictory design requirements with respect to multi-functional road use are true challenges. However, these challenges should be confronted, as a wicked problem, by multi-faceted experimental design, and studies of social interaction. This could be done in a similar way as the Dutch *woonerf* design approaches, rather than with traditional reductionistic and controlled expert-management approaches.

An important issue is how to move on from the accounts of people's practices, as previously discussed, to the invention of new and interesting technologies. Although ethnographic accounts are often claimed to be relevant to the design of computer systems, especially within the research field of computer-supported collaborative work (CSCW), there have also been complaints and concerns about its usefulness in design. The fleeting and superficial nature of the social interaction that occurs in traffic also limits its value as a source of inspiration. Therefore, our statement that fieldwork and analysis of fieldwork have been of use for the research presented in the book needs further clarification.

The challenges faced by using ethnographic fieldwork to inform design are three-fold. First, road use, like many other mobile activities, is basically not a work activity, and the theories and experiences of the field of CSCW may therefore be less suitable. However, theories emerging from ethnographic fieldwork within CSCW have been extended to include studies on social interaction and leisure activities (Brown and Chalmers 2003; Grinter and Palen 2002). This shift illustrates the possibility of applying traditional CSCW research methods to these non-work contexts, but also the relevance of findings from these contexts to core CSCW issues (Brown and Chalmers 2003). Second, road use is a "truly mobile" (Sherry and Salvador 2002) activity that may occur almost anytime and anywhere, which makes it difficult to limit the study and, e.g., choose when and from whom to collect data. Furthermore, it is hard to select the community to be addressed, since boundaries between insiders and outsiders are blurred. Abundant meaningful interaction occurs between unacquainted, as well as acquainted, participants. It differs from traditional CSCW ethnographies on social interaction in geographically bounded settings such as underground, air-traffic, and emergency rescue control-rooms. Third, it is not always the case that detailed empirical investigations contribute to design. In the CSCW community, ethnographers criticize designers for lacking knowledge about the subtleties of the activities addressed, whereas designers criticize the ethnographers for not coming up with anything but vague and obvious design implications

(Plowman et al. 1995). The problem could be due to the understanding of ethnography as, at best, determining design. Such an approach has been suggested in the form of an "iterative" process where findings from the fieldwork are used to deduce services (Ljungberg et al. 1998). However, such an approach implies first that there is a "problem" to be solved, and second that the description of it can be comprehensive and accurate (Fällman 2003). We suggest that these methodological issues can be handled through a design approach that *associates* the ethnography with design and evaluation, as will be discussed in the following.

We follow a course in which research and design are better understood as a form of associative work (Latour 1986), in which materials and people are combined and recombined (Latour 1988) as a local activity to generate innovative mobile services. Associative design emerges when participants in design establish a sustained collaboration involving dialogue and shared handling of material objects. The participants in the design process engage in such collaboration because they acknowledge its necessity for generating innovation. They further recognize disparate interests in their individual professional identities, making it easier to engage in mutual work.

The first step towards associative design is to treat the generation of ethnographic field-data as a topic in a dialogue between the project workers, rather than documents in lectures on ethnographic findings. Dourish (2001) argues that ethnographers and designers could engage in modest dialogues while preserving their theoretical orientation and interest in sharing their knowledge. Ethnographic field data can inform design without forcing the ethnographers to become designers.

> Design implications of such studies should arise through an explicit dialogue between researchers from different disciplines (rather than require social scientists to be able to engage in design, or vice versa). (2001, p. 156)

We argue for an even more committed involvement, in which the activity of the ethnographers overlaps the work of other participants during the different phases of the project. The willingness for mutual engagement is sustained first and foremost by an understanding of design as necessarily undetermined by ethnography. Thus, the ethnographer does not believe that his role is just to deliver an ethnographic account and then leave. Moreover, the participants focus on the diversity and openness of their individual orientations and interests instead of seeking specialization, which should open up for collaboration.

We also suggest moving beyond the dialogue to account for material aspects of design work, both in terms of the tangibility and physicality of the materials brought back to the lab by ethnographers, as well as the materiality of the prototypes. First, ethnographic data is brought to the place where the fieldworker and the designer work together—the laboratory. This data is in the form of images, videos, notes, etc. In accordance with Latour (1986), we argue that the power of research labs can be explained as their being sites where huge numbers of inscriptions are brought together. Labs are sites where:

> Domains which are far apart become literally inches apart; domains which are convoluted and hidden become flat; thousands of occurrences can be looked at synoptically...

In our cultures "paper shuffling" is the source of an essential power, that constantly escapes attention since its materiality is ignored. (Latour 1986, pp. 54–55)

He draws attention to the representation of other objects and how these are arranged and rearranged at a local site, such as the lab, to create innovation with an impact on the world outside. Thus, we must not only look upon the interaction between ethnographers and designers as a conversation, but also look at the necessity of gathering data at a specific place and collaboratively shuffling them around. The sustained relation between the researchers and the designers, as well as the opportunity to juxtapose technology and inscriptions, was essential to enable interesting associations. Thus, the design is linked with the empirical findings, but also with available technology, and with findings from other closely related areas.

To this end we combine and associate knowledge of road use collected in the fieldwork with various computer-science issues. Ideas are abandoned if they are deemed unsuitable, or not likely to add value to the situation. Furthermore, if a particular design is deemed technically difficult to achieve it may eventually be discarded. We finally settle for preliminary versions of a concept that would add value to the specific situation. These are developed into prototypes which are fully functional, are focused on making the conceptual idea visible for the users, and whose functionality should be possible to evaluate.

Finally, we suggest that the implemented applications are partly seen as inspirational patterns (Löwgren 2005). A prototype can be observed and used in itself. It carries a value beyond those that are documented in evaluations. The implemented example plays an important part in design-oriented research such as architecture, and lately also in computer science. We suggest that the resulting applications presented in this volume should be seen as such inspirational patterns, which contribute to an emerging understanding of our design domain, and not as tools which solve clearly defined problems.

3.3 Evaluating New Applications

Evaluating new applications is important. First, we learn how well the implementation fits the design requirements, which is useful for an eventual re-design of the application. Second, we get a better understanding of the phenomenon initially studied, since the underlying ethnographic analysis, which influenced the design, is also evaluated to a certain extent. Third, the use of the applications can lead to new forms of social interaction, or make us identify forms of social interaction previously not accounted for.

We have chosen to conduct field experiments (Borovoy et al. 1998) in natural settings, since we have been interested in evaluating our conceptual ideas in as realistic a setting as possible. Field experiments provide us with initial data for understanding how the concepts work, although the technology is often unstable and only of limited availability. We have interviewed the test persons, and occasionally also invited them to answer questionnaires.

Video recordings have been the most important tool for collecting data both during field experiments and ethnographic field work. Video recorders are increasingly used to collect data during HCI evaluations (Hindmarsh et al. 2002). As of yet there is no common standard for transcribing video recordings similar to the coding schemes in conversation analysis (Heath and Hindmarsh 2002). Consequently, we have developed coding schemes that account for the details of the drivers' activities of relevance for the particular evaluation being conducted. It is important to note that the video captures only some of the visual details that demand the drivers' attention in any situation, and only some of what she does. Thus, the video camera was not a way of assembling a comprehensive collection of visual data. Rather it was a tool which provided more data than field notes and audio recordings alone. The recordings have been transcribed and categorized into a set of themes which emerged when analyzing the data, in line with the tradition of interaction analysis (Jordan and Henderson 1995).

As we have previously argued, the prototype applications provide us with inspirational patterns. The design concepts should not be seen as our final statement on the services that we argue will flood the streets and be essential for the future of everyday life in traffic "beyond just getting there." Instead, these services are both an invitation to think about how to understand road traffic and an opening for inventing new ways of supporting that interaction.

3.4 Selecting Case Studies

As argued, we are interested in social interaction on the roads both as a way to achieve agreements on how share the road space, and as a way to socialize in a broad sense. The next step involves presenting the cases selected, and making explicit the underlying reasons for our choices. Since we presume studying social aspects of road use to be an intrinsically "wicked" problem, where means and ends are hard to delimit, we do not expect our research to capture the fundamentals of this form of public life. Still we can be somewhat strategic in what we choose to focus upon. In general we have selected cases which are salient regarding vitality, i.e., social interaction to ensure healthy environments and bodily safety, as well as significant regarding social interaction for sense experiences. Thus, the selected cases must involve users within the design space, and the investigation is facilitated by their spending a lot of time on the road. Second, they should cover diverse groups of road users who spend time on the roads for different purposes. Third, to ensure that we get empirical data on social interaction in traffic, it is convenient if they are in some way explicit in the way they use the roads. Fourth, since the research includes designing new services, it is favorable if the users already use mobile technology.

Based on the criteria above, the following studies have been selected. We selected four cases where vitality was a critical topic. First, we chose to study students at a driving school. Here we addressed the ways in which social interaction helps students safely maneuver through crowded streets. This instructional setting was chosen because the students were both driving and discussing their driving at the same time. Students and instructors not only drive, but articulate what they are doing as well.

The second case focuses on lorry drivers and their mobile phone use practices. Mobile phone use in cars is a huge social phenomenon, and is thus important to our social interaction in traffic. The topic of the study is the way in which social interaction through and with the phone is performed in conjunction with other driving activities. We argue that adapting mobile phone use to driving is a practical concern for ensuring safe driving, and depends on specific forms of collaboration. Drivers adjust their phone handling to the collaboration in traffic, and likewise they adjust the conversation to the traffic situation by making non-present conversational partners aware of problematic traffic situations. Lorry drivers were chosen since they spend a considerable amount of time in traffic, which would make the topic more empirically available. The third case continues to investigate mobile technology in traffic, but also commences the intervention into the design realm. It focuses on road inspection, that is, maintenance of large trunk roads, where the road inspectors travel long distances to identify defects and disturbances, either to take care of the problems or to delegate the tasks. Road inspectors were selected because they use an advanced, mobile, position-based reporting system, which has been up and running for a number of years. However, the study illustrates that the system fails to assist the individual inspectors on the roads. It is instead a beneficial tool for administrative tasks performed at the office. Based on the findings of the empirical study, we introduce a prototype application supporting mobile reporting, which will handle reminders, the delegation of tasks, and reporting. We also present how the new applications were received by the inspectors. One of their work tasks is providing road information. Thus, we have taken a first step towards developing new systems that will increase information sharing to improve the coordination of traffic.

In the fourth case study, which concerns the vitality of life in traffic, we will bring this design issue even further. The topic is in part existing mobile services, and in part the design of a new tool for sharing traffic information between drivers. Drivers use the current system to avoid police speed traps, and thus get to where they are going faster. However, we use this study in combination with our findings from the driving school to influence the design of a system to increase the vitality of road use.

We selected six cases which in various ways investigate and design for both *sense* and *delight*. They are about social interaction as a way to create or generate identities or visibility for social practices, as well as interaction concerning aesthetic and emotional experiences. First, motorcyclists belong to a group of road users who spend a lot of time on the roads for the simple reason that they enjoy it. They are also explicit about their interest in others, since they normally greet other bikers they meet along the road. By following this group we can learn more about the social aspects of road use. They also put a lot of effort into making an impression through their choice of bike, modifications, personal equipment, and style of driving. This study inspired a new design concept called the Hocman. Second, inspired by sociological theory, we singled out everyday commuters and drivers in the Sound

Pryer study. The third case considers posters of non-official road signs, or what we refer to as public road signs. Here the focus is on the practical ways in which they struggle to give a location transparency and identity.

The final three case studies (Backseat Game, Backseat Playground, and the Road Rager) all consider passengers in vehicles, and especially children sitting in the backseats of cars. We are interested in how they experience the passing roadside, and their use of mobile computer games, as well as how these experiences could be combined. These three case studies variously explore what part of the landscape should be given more of an identity and greater transparency, in the context of delightful and exciting location-dependent games as well as multiplayer games.

References

Borovy R, Martin F et al (1998) GroupWear: nametags that tell about relationships. In: Proceedings of CHI'98. ACM Press, New York

Brown B, Chalmers M (2003) Tourism and mobile technology. In: Proceedings of ECSCW'03. Kluwer, New York, pp 335–354

Button G, Dourish P (1996) Technomethodology: paradoxes and possibilities. In: Proceedings of SIGCHI conference on human factors in systems design. ACM Press, New York, pp 19–26

Crabtree A (2003) Designing collaborative systems—a practical guide to ethnography. Springer, Berlin

Dourish P (2001) Where the action is—the foundations of embodied interaction. MIT Press, Cambridge

Fällman D (2003) Design-oriented human–computer interaction. In: Proceedings of the SIGCHI conference on human factors in computing systems (Ft. Lauderdale, Florida, USA, April 05–10, 2003). CHI '03, ACM, New York, NY, pp 225–232

Garfinkel H (1967/1996) Studies in ethnomethodology. Polity Press, Cambridge

Grinter RE, Palen L (2002) Instant messaging in teen life. In: Proceedings of CSCW;02. ACM Press, Ft. Lauterdale, pp 21–30

Gusfield JR (1981) The culture of public problems: drinking-driving and the symbolic order. University of Chicago Press, Chicago

Gusfield JR (1990) Concept, context and community: sociological perspectives on traffic safety. In: Rothe JP (ed) Challenging the old order—towards new directions in traffic safety theory. Transaction Publishers, London

Heath C, Hindmarsh J (2002) Analysing interaction: video, ethnography and situated conduct. In: May T (ed) Qualitative research in practice. Sage, London

Heath C, Luff P (2000) Technology in action. Cambridge University Press, Cambridge

Hindmarsh J, Heath C et al (2002) Creating assemblies: aboard the ghost ship. In: Proceedings of CSCW 2002, Nov. 16–20, New Orleans, USA

Hughes JA, Randall D et al (1992) Faltering from ethnography to design. In: ACM conference on computer supported cooperative work. ACM Press, Ft. Lauterdale

Hughes J, King V, Rodden T et al (1994) Moving out from the control room: ethnography in systems design. In: ACM conference on computer supported cooperative work. ACM Press, Ft. Lauterdale, pp 429–439

Jordan B, Henderson A (1995) Interaction analysis: foundations and practice. J Learn Sci 4(1): 39–103

Katz J (1999) How emotions work. University of Chicago Press, Chicago

Laurier E (2002) Notes on dividing the attention of a car driver. Team Ethno Online

Latour B (1986) The powers of associations. In: Law J, (ed) Power, action and belief—a new sociology of knowledge. Routledge and Kegan Paul, London

Latour B (1988) Drawing things together. In: Lynch M, Woolgar S (eds) Representations in scientific practice. MIT Press, Cambridge

Ljungberg F et al (1998) Innovation of new IT use—combining approaches and perspectives in R&D projects. In: Proceedings of PDC'98, Seattle, Washington, USA

Löwgren J (2005) Inspirational patterns for embodied interaction. In: Proceedings of Nordic design research conference, Copenhagen

Martin D, Rouncefield M (2003) Making the organisation come alive: talking through and about the technology in remote banking. Hum Comput Interact 18(1 and 2):111–148

Plowman L, Rogers Y, Ramage M (1995) What are workplace studies for? Proceedings of ECSCW'95 – the 4th European conference on computer supported cooperative work, Kluwer, New York, NY, pp 309–324

Prus R (1996) Symbolic interaction and ethnographic research—intersubjectivity and the study of human lived experience. Suny Press, Albany

Randall D, Harper R, Rouncefield M (2007) Fieldwork for design—theory and practice. Springer, London

Redström J (2001) Designing everyday computational things. Gothenburg Studies in Informatics, Göteborg University, Sweden

Rittel HWJ, Webber MM (1973) Dilemmas in a general theory of planning. Policy Sci 4:155–169

Sherry J, Salvador T (2002) Running and grimacing: the struggle for balance in mobile work. In: Brown B et al (eds) Wireless world—social and interactional aspects of the mobile age. Springer, London

Part II
Vitality and Social Interaction
on the Roads

Chapter 4
Traffic as Situated Interaction

Roads are often crowded places which many people would like to use at the same time. In this chapter we focus on the ways in which drivers coordinate their vehicles' movements and how they come to agreement on the sharing of the road space. The drivers have to sort this out even though, as we have previously discussed, they are confined within the shells of their vehicles, and often meet other drivers for only a short span of time. Obviously the availability of a set of formal traffic rules makes interaction easier. Furthermore, there are a number of informal rules discussed by sociologists (Dannefer 1977) which in some sense prescribe how to behave given the shape of the roads and the relations between vehicles (hereafter referred to as *setting-specific* conditions), and rules which draw on the identities of the drivers. According to sociologist Redshaw (2008), people's driving behavior is directed by cultural norms and habits. For example, young men are confident about their driving skill, but do not necessarily conform to formal rules or the needs of others. Edensor (2004) sees national belonging as contributing to how drivers behave on the roads.

We argue that the availability of several rule sets and the possibility to interpret the context of a road setting in various ways make misunderstanding of other drivers' activities possible. We are here interested in how rules are actually used in naturally occurring interaction out on the streets. We introduce the notion of *situated interaction* to account for how agreements are negotiated as a local activity. Such negotiations must, of course, be finalized in seconds, since there is little room for more sustained forms of interaction. If situated interaction plays an important role in traffic it will have implications for how the information technology for coordination should be designed.

4.1 Mutual Understanding Through Plans or Situated Actions

Road use is understood as a cooperative activity, since a number of actors share a common resource (the road) and through its use change the conditions and possibilities for other users (Schmidt and Simone 1996). They are forced to show consideration, or at least adapt their activities to each other, i.e., coordinate them, in order to avoid accidents and disturbances.

O. Juhlin, *Social Media on the Road*, Computer Supported Cooperative Work 50, DOI 10.1007/978-1-84996-332-9_4, © Springer-Verlag London Limited 2010

Understanding how people interact and achieve common understanding is a central issue in social science. For example, sociological and anthropological methods have been applied to the study of artificial expertise and how it fits with social contexts (Collins 1995). In a groundbreaking study within computer science, presented in Lucy Suchman's book *Plans and Situated Action* (1991), two different ways of understanding social interaction were discussed: the planning model, which has been influential in the efforts to construct so-called expert systems; and the situated-action model. In the planning model, mutual understanding is achieved between individuals because they have the ability to represent a situation, e.g., a traffic situation, similarly. Furthermore, they have a similar set of plans available as means to achieve a specific goal. If an individual performs a particular behavior in a particular situation, the other individuals can reconstruct what he/she is up to by interpreting the relationship between the behavior and the situation as belonging to a specific category of events.

In the case of traffic, it could seem reasonable to view the formal traffic rules as the plans by which road users achieve coordination in a specific and commonly understood situation. A formalized set of rules has been developed, mostly by government authorities, to solve the problems of coordination. The individual driver is required to drive on the right-hand side of the road and to follow the speed limit, otherwise she will be punished. However communication between drivers is still essential in traffic. Traffic researchers Swan and Owens (1988) focus on this interaction as important in understanding the coordination of traffic and the cause of accidents:

> Fitting lines of action together or establishing joint-action in the driving environment requires taking note of the action of others as indications are made. This assumes that the meaning of the indications are shared by the actors in the environment. (Swan and Owens 1988, p. 59)

> Thus, for drivers to fit their actions together smoothly and reduce accidents, they must understand the intended meaning of one another's gestures and must interpret the actions similarly. The whole process of driving interaction depends upon the ability of the driver to take another's role, and thereby to understand what other drivers are thinking and planning to do. (Swan and Owens 1988, p. 62)

Their understanding of social interaction is close to what Suchman labeled the planning model. According to Suchman, this perspective begs the question of how the individuals come to understand the situation similarly. Many ethnomethodologically informed studies show the openness of the representation of situations. The representation of a situation seems to depend on a choice of priorities. In addition, a specific behavior can always be interpreted as a sign of many different intentions. In the latter perspective, situated actions create and sustain shared understanding on specific occasions of interaction. Social constraints on appropriate action are always identified in relation to some unique set of circumstances.

Therefore, Suchman recommends a perspective where the actors struggle back and forth to work out a common understanding and to establish cooperative actions.

With reference to the sociologist Harold Garfinkel, she understands the users' activities as following "the documentary method of interpretation" (Suchman 1991, p. 66). Garfinkel writes:

> The method consists of treating actual appearance as "the document of," as "pointing to," as "standing on behalf of," a presupposed underlying pattern. Not only is the underlying pattern derived from its individual documentary evidences, but the individual documentary evidences, in their turn, are interpreted on the basis of "what is known" about the underlying pattern. Each is used to elaborate the other. (Garfinkel 1967/1996)

Each event confronting the actors who share a resource is unique. Thus the cooperating individuals must also work to make sense of it, and identification becomes more than just a simple recognition and categorization procedure. Despite the difficulties, actors often succeed in establishing agreement on how to achieve coordination. But this work should be taken into account, rather than taken for granted, in a theory of social interaction. Suchman writes:

> The stability of the social world, from this standpoint, is not due to an eternal structure, but to situated actions that create and sustain shared understanding on specific occasions of interaction. Social constraints on appropriate action are always identified relative to some unique and unreproducible set of circumstances. (Suchman 1991, p. 66)

To better understand coordination Suchman proposes an empirical focus on the occurrence of mutual understanding, instead of an a priori attribution and identification of plans as the basis of establishing mutual understanding and coordination. In this case the focus should be on road users as they solve coordination problems with other road users understood by the actors both as following the formal set of rules, or doing something else. The unit of analysis is road users' work of achieving coordination, and specifically activities whereby road users try to influence each other.

Here, a useful distinction is drawn by the sociologist Goffman (1990). He distinguishes between coordination achieved between individuals without anyone having the purpose of communicating with others, and coordination involving such activities. A clear case of the first kind is when two drivers just pass each other in two separate lanes on a major road without trying to communicate. However, in other cases the opposite is applicable. Goffman refers to instances of this form of interaction as performances: "A performance may be defined as all the activity of a given participant on a given occasion which serves to influence in any way any of the other participants" (Goffman 1990, p. 26).

4.2 Analysis

The study was conducted at a driving school in Stockholm during the summer of 1998. The training of drivers was observed as they practiced in and around the city center. We participated in twenty sessions, and recorded the conversations. The driving school used camcorders in one of their cars as part of the training. When this equipment is used, the teacher and the student meet directly afterwards to view the videotape and discuss the lesson. In these cases too, we copied the tape and recorded their conversations. We have specifically chosen to focus on the cooperation with other road users, that is, the sequences in the conversation where they refer to, e.g., other drivers or pedestrians. Since the subject is often raised, it seems to be an important issue in the training (Groeger 1993). This main category has been further analyzed and interpreted, which has resulted in a number of subcategories, some of which are presented in this chapter.

In most cases, a driver treats his compatriots in the vicinity as inaccessible for collaboration. They are more or less viewed as physical projectiles on a steady course. Thus, there is only coordination without performance. Coordination is settled without road users intending to communicate with each other. In other situations, a driver chooses to constitute the presence of road users as a possibility to perform. The interaction could be brief, e.g., making an "appeal" and receiving an answer. The means for interaction include blinkers, hand or other bodily gestures, and demonstratively positioning oneself in the road.

She can use the blinkers to send a message to fellow road users that she wants to change lanes or make a turn. During the lessons, it is primarily the proper use of this signal that is discussed. But she can also use eye contact to send the same message. If the car that constitutes the audience is close behind, a distinct turn of the driver's head could be enough to make a plea. Speed and its variations also give opportunities to influence other road users. In the following case, it is used to say, "go ahead":

> Instructor: Good! You clearly show her that you will wait, then you can start to move directly. So, you don't really need to stop the car. You can aim at passing behind her as soon as she has started to walk.

A single pedestrian stands at the edge of a zebra crossing looking towards our vehicle. We are a bit away and the student brakes with a distinct jerk. The teacher interprets this tiny, but marked, adjustment of the speed as the driver sending the message "I have seen you, and will give you right-of-way." The pedestrian seems to understand it similarly and starts to cross the street. Thus, the way we maneuver the car is not only a means for moving our body from one place to another, it is also a means to account for our intentions in our interaction with other road users. The maneuvering of the car is a sign in the "body" language of vehicles.

4.2.1 Rules as Resources to Interpret Behavior

In the discussion between student and teacher many different forms of rules or goals are used as resources to interpret road users' intentions. In the study we identified three main categories of rules. They include both formal and informal rules, which apply to various setting in traffic. In an article on the coordination of traffic, sociologist Dale Dannefer discusses rules governing recurrent setting-specific interaction:

> Such interaction patterns are governed by universalistic norms, applicable to all drivers regardless of their characteristics or the characteristics of their vehicles. These norms are purely situational — generated by the problems of co-ordination to which they apply. (Dannefer 1977)

We regard the law and its concern for general safety requirements as the *formal* rule set. But there are also a number of *informal* norms, which refer to general categories of traffic situations. Finally, we identified informal rule sets which refer to the *identities* of the drivers.

The code of law: Traffic regulations were, not surprisingly, the most commonly referenced rule set in the conversations between driver and instructor. This does not mean that the interpretation of such rules is easy. Although the traffic regulations are mostly to the point, parts of them are vague and very general. For example, in Sweden, the overarching rule in the traffic code is that you should drive "safely." In many cases the general discourse on safety equates to following more specific rules such as driving on the right-hand side of the road. In practice, however, those ambitions could be at odds with safe driving. The student can, e.g., be requested to drive faster than the regulations stipulate in order to be "safe." In the next case, the student is heading north, entering a major road into the center of Stockholm. There is heavy traffic on this trunk road.

> Instructor: Good preparation! Good speed to enter!
> Student: There was rather heavy traffic.
> Instructor: Yeah, you have to find a gap. Did you think about the speed on the ramp?
> Student: 70 a bit ahead.
> Instructor: Yeah, 70. But what was it on the ramp?
> Student: Didn't see. But I was driving 50.
> Instructor: Yes. It was 50 so to speak. But if you think about the speed necessary to enter the road, then it is idiotic beyond belief that you're supposed to drive at a certain speed on the ramp, and then enter a road where the other cars are driving at least at the speed limit. No one can dispute that if you're entering a road with a speed limit of 70 you may drive at that speed. For safety reasons. Not just because you are enjoying driving fast, but also that if you see a gap you must be able to match the speed of the other drivers.

Excerpt 4.1 Driving school conversation on the conflict between driving safely and following formal rules

The speed limit on the ramp is 50 km/h, while it is 70 km/h on the road itself. She can indeed disturb the coordination if she enters the traffic stream on the highway driving much more slowly than the other drivers. Therefore the teacher gives two rather different recommendations, that both seem to contradict the formal traffic laws. First, she says that the student should drive on the ramp at the speed prescribed on the road signs on the main road. Second, she says that she should match the speed of the traffic. The principal justification is to avoid danger for all of the road users.

Hence, following the concrete formal rules and driving safely are not always conceived to be the same thing. To put it in another way, the formal rule set can occasionally be self-contradictory.

Setting-specific rules which give priority to traffic flow: Both sociologist Dannefer (1977) and the instructor discuss a setting-specific, informal rule called the principle of "flow priority." The concept of flow was frequently used during the lessons to invoke special forms of priority. But its application referred to such heterogeneous characteristics as speed, quantity, road structure, and the identity of other drivers. In the following, we will give an example of prioritizing speed:

> Instructor: He chose to reverse. Think about that here...did you see the blue
> sign? In any case you should go first...slow down there. It could be that he
> can't see that well in the beginning.
> Student: No.
> Instructor: Slow down. If someone would be in the middle, then you could let
> him pass first. To get better flow in the traffic.

Excerpt 4.2 Helping achieve flow in traffic

In this case, the student is told to give a car priority although it is coming from the left. The difference between them was that we were driving slowly, and the other car had a much higher speed. "Flow" is here defined as a single car with a higher speed. The flow-priority principle can be understood as a general concern that drivers not only think about their own rights, but also respect other people and what they do on the streets. Being a competent driver is therefore not only about correctly executing the rule set, but being a considerate fellow-citizen as well.

Identity rules: Coordination is also achieved with reference to the characteristics of the people involved. The instructor and the student discuss the behavior of other drivers in terms of "oldies," "poor creatures," "lunatics," and "men." With reference to Dannefer (1977), we refer to these as identity-based rules. In the following example, the behaviors of other drivers are explained by the student-driver sign on the back of our car. Thus other drivers treat the driver of our car as a beginner, which influences the way they act and negotiate the sharing of the road space. Another car is overtaking us on our left in the following example. The driver signals with his horn as he passes us. The teacher comments on the situation by saying that he only used his horn because the sign on our bumper said "student driver":

He wouldn't have honked if it had said "Your Neighborhood Plumber," and we had been driving a van.

Various actions in traffic are interpreted differently given the meaning that is read into the vehicle's appearance. A "Plumber's van," presumably driven by a middle-aged man, is allowed to do things which other drivers are not. Another teacher interpreted the frequent overtakings, and drunk pedestrians waving their fists, as hostility towards our driver's student identity: "people get allergic when we come."

But the student identity could also be favorable in the coordination of road use. According to one of the teachers, the other road users become more helpful when they face a beginner in traffic. Furthermore, at the test to get the driver's license, the magnetic sticker on the back of the car is removed precisely in order to avoid other drivers helping the novice. Summing up, there are several rule sets available when interpreting other people's activities and deciding what to do. Some of them depend on the road setting and some on whom you meet.

4.2.2 Coordination as a Local Situated Activity

The discussion between student and instructor indicates that many different rules are of relevance in traffic collaborations. Most of these norms refer to the context of the meeting between road users, rather than to their identities. These rules can be both formal, such as the regulations prescribed by the authorities, or informal, such as, e.g., the flow-priority rules. According to Dannefer (1977), both informal and formal rules are setting specific because they refer to the characteristics of the infrastructure or the vehicles, rather than to the behavior of other road users. At the same time, these characteristics are recurrent, making the situations repeat themselves. Thus situations could be classified as belonging to a more aggregated series of events, given a stable set of backgrounds provided by the road infrastructure. However, the empirical material seems to speak against such an interpretation of the concept of situations. Instead the road infrastructure seems to also be constructed or interpreted as a result of the cooperation per se.

Most of the rules discussed by the teachers, with the exception of the identity rules, interpret the situation with reference to generalized representations of the road setting, e.g., the rule prescribing the use of the right-hand lane. Rule following of that type depends on the interpretation of the situation according to specific classes of roads. However, the empirical material reveals that the classification of the infrastructure is ambiguous and is based on a specific interpretation of the situation, where many alternatives seem to be possible. The following conversation between the student and instructor reveals uncertainties about the classification of the infrastructure:

> Instructor: Now you are coming in at the speed limit, which he wasn't. He is getting upset and wants to overtake you. In this phase, the ramp is widening, making room for two cars beside each other. No markings indicating two lanes. And you thought: "what a wide and nice lane. I'll put myself in the middle." That lane! But according to the law it's two lanes if there's enough room for two four-wheeled vehicles, even though there's no center marking. So, you can't see it clearly from this camera angle, but you can see it anyway (Student: yeah) that there is very little space left on that side. And I bet he's not that comfortable in this situation. Because he doesn't know if you will continue gliding over as he overtakes you, and he hasn't got much to choose

from. Because he just has a pole over there. So, there is nowhere to go. And
here I felt that you really scared him. Really!

Student: I felt it myself. It wasn't that good. Clearly!

Excerpt 4.3   Interpreting the context

The student seems to be uncertain about what kind of infrastructure she is moving
in. Should she act like the road consists of one or two lanes? The teacher, on the
one hand, is certain that the situation was caused by erroneous interpretation and
disturbances from the infrastructure, but, on the other hand, she admits that the road
was gradually widening. The issue in this situation is a problem of boundaries. At
what particular point should a specific part of the infrastructure be classified in one
rather than another category? The driver has to make his or her actions function in
that fluid setting.

Similarly, road signs are interpreted in specific situations. A student is driving
through a tunnel headed towards downtown in the following example:

Student: I am staying in the right lane.

Instructor: On what do you base the decision?

Student: Signs with two arrows

Instructor: What does that mean?

Student: Two lanes. Here, the sign has only one arrow, and then I became a bit
uncertain. Then, I saw...

Instructor: Did you see that it was a bit sooty? Someone has bumped into it
there. Actually, there used to be an arrow there too. I can understand that you
started to wonder. But it's better that you start to look ahead, and try to get
new information from the next sign.

Excerpt 4.4   Interpreting road signs

The student is uncertain about how to interpret the road sign. Is it a dirty two-
lane marking, or is it a dirty one-lane marking? The sign itself cannot tell her how to
interpret it correctly. Thus, the details of the situation influence the driver's action.
Furthermore, the infrastructure (the road) is not a stable backdrop for the road user's
activity of coordination.

4.2.3 Constructing the "Background" through Social Interaction

From the previous examples it is evident that cooperation between road users is
filled with uncertainty. It is not even conducted on the basis of a road structure as
a given background. This does not mean that it is necessarily dangerous or requires
remedying. Rather, it is necessary to look for those practices that sustain cooperation

despite the presence of uncertainty. Here, "the documentary method of interpretation" could be of interest (Garfinkel 1967/1996). In the cooperation between road users, an individual user switches between interpreting the behavior of other users, the contexts, and the responses to her own behavior, to establish a working behavior in a situation.

In the following example, road users' activities are used as "documents" when interpreting the characteristics of the infrastructure. The student sees parked cars ahead of her and uses them to interpret the formal rules applicable to that section of road. The student and the instructor discuss the situation as they watch a videotape of the driving lesson:

> Instructor: What does it look like on the ground? (Student: Yeah) Do you see any arrows pointing to the right there?
> Student: No!
> Instructor: It is a bit hard since the truck is standing there.
> Student: Yeah. I didn't get it. Then I became too occupied to see the road sign.
> Instructor: Was it okay to drive straight ahead?
> Student: Yeah [*hesitating*]
> Instructor: Of course, it was allowed. You can drive straight ahead here. The reason you got a bit thrown off was because you can see a row of parked cars over there. (Student: Exactly) So, there was only enough room in that single lane to drive straight ahead. Then you have to change lanes. Still, you can drive straight ahead.
> Student: Exactly.

Excerpt 4.5 Discussing the fit between the traffic code and the setting

The student chooses to turn right at the junction since she is uncertain about the formal rules applicable to the lane she is using. She is not sure if it continues straight ahead. Maybe it requires its users to turn right? The activities of other road users influenced her decision to turn. First, parked cars in the continuation of her lane after the junction can indicate that the lane is not supposed to be used for through-traffic. Second, the truck in her lane could have blocked a traffic sign. The student asks the teacher to rewind the tape. She wants to read the road sign at the side of the road to see if she was mistaken:

> Student: I believe there's a road sign somewhere around here, or farther ahead. It says something about "Bantorget." Here! I don't know where it will come. No, farther ahead. Just before the truck. So that you don't see all of it. Somewhere around there! There! Or is it a road sign? Is there some kind of tree [*teacher laughs*] in the way? All you can see is half of the sign. And then I think that there's an arrow pointing towards Bantorget.
> Instructor: So, there was some kind of impulse from a sign?
> Student: Exactly. As well. . .

The activities of other road users are interpreted as indicators of the markings on the street and the presence of road signs. But it is not enough for her to only organize her own activities as a response to the other drivers' activities and the infrastructure. Her own presence is interpreted similarly by them, according to the teacher:

> Instructor: You're a bit indistinct to them, as you're driving slowly. They want to stop. And then you start to drive really slowly, and then they start to wonder "Ooooh, did I miss any road sign? What's up? Are they about to run out of gas?" (Student: Yeah) Often you think that it is not possible to drive too slowly. It can't go wrong. You can never be too careful. But sometimes in traffic, it could imply that you give very indistinct signals to the other road users. Like in this case, you had the right-of-way, and they had started to slow down. There wasn't really any problem. And yet, you started to slow down and drive much more slowly, and looked really carefully at them. They were standing still and weren't a danger.

Like in the previous example, the road users' activities are interpreted as signs of the infrastructure's characteristics and the formal rules applicable in that situation. The issue is not what speed to choose, but who has right-of-way. Generally, it is difficult for a road user to know if she really has seen all the signs applicable in a situation. One possibility, such as in these cases, is to interpret what the other road users are doing as documents of the existence of specific signs. The drivers see the other road users' activities as "documents of," or as "pointing at" the formal rules, in line with the documentary method of interpretation. But they also interpret the other road users' activities in line with "what is known" of the underlying pattern, e.g., the formal rules in that situation.

The following sequence provides yet another example of how they construct an understanding of the setting through their cooperation, rather than simply interacting to communicate information. The student makes use of other road users' application of the documentary method of interpretation:

> Instructor: That thing about communication with your fellow road users, you'll see that it is rather pleasant. It is better for you to have complete control of what you are doing, and what all the others are doing. You also get better treated if you, so to speak, dare to meet the gaze from another car or pedestrian. You radiate more confidence yourself.

The teacher's advice is ambivalent. She promises full control through communication. Uncertainty can be cured by more information about other road users' activities. But their activities cannot be isolated from the student's own activities. So uncertainty can also be reduced if the student acts as though she already had the information. If you perform "as if" you are certain, the situation will become certain; i.e., you "get treated better." The advice could also be formulated as "fake it till you make it." If that advice is taken as a general feature of road use coordination, the individual is caught in an interpretative process concerning the documents as information on what the other road users want and documents as a comment on her own activities. Other road users' activities are interpreted as documents of what they want, what they will do, or documents of other road users' actions as affirmations that everything is all right: "you are doing okay."

4.3 Social Interaction for Safety and Access

The study shows how social interaction among drivers is strongly linked to the vitality and accessibility of street life. Drivers need to find ways to agree on how to share specific sections of road, both to avoid physical accidents as well as to ensure that they will access destination points. The successful interpretation of other road users' activity is an essential component of driving as early as driver training, and it is not as straightforward as just learning the formal rule set. Our research supports the presence of many different types of rules in the interpretation of other road users' behavior. But these seem to figure as weak resources in contingent situated activity. The learning process by which the students become aware of the meaning of other peoples' behavior is hardly explained by the formal application of rules to an easily given and structured context. The road users achieve coordination despite three theoretical problems. First, the identification of the situation, or the background for the coordination, is not simple or given. The fieldwork makes visible the interpretative flexibility of "the background." Second, it seems that many rule sets are applicable to a particular background such as various formal and informal rules. The informal rules are either applicable to the context, or to the individual road users involved in the coordination. Third, the drivers understand what the other road users want to do by interpreting their activities as documents of an underlying plan. But a single action can be interpreted as an expression of many different plans, according to sociologist Collins (1995). Acceleration by a nearby car could be a document of him following the flow-priority rule, that he is following a formal rule of which the other driver is not aware, or just a message telling the other driver that he is incompetent or has acted wrongly. These "inconsistencies" are mostly solved in local situations. Mutual understandings of how to achieve coordination seem to be reached anew in each situation. Thus, driving is more a matter of "muddling through" despite uncertain background knowledge.

4.4 Designing for Movement Coordination

There are at least two consequences of such an understanding for the design of information technology to support road use. First, acknowledging that driving is both a collaborative and situated activity might influence our expectations concerning automatic driving systems. Since the start of the Prometheus program in 1986, which was a joint research program among the European car manufacturers, a considerable amount of work has been carried out by engineers to develop the idea of the artificial driver (Catling 1994; Whelan 1995). In the spring of 1998, a demonstration was held in the Netherlands by European and American researchers of "Automated Vehicle Guidance" (AVG 1998). Automated vehicle driving is understood as being implemented in three steps: "beginning with. . .automated highway systems providing 'information' to the driver for collision avoidance and other safety-related issues, moving on to AVG for control-systems that assist the driver and take over some of the driving tasks, and ultimately leading to. . .fully automatic systems for inter-city transportation." The description of the demonstrations included fully automated steering systems that detect the curve of the road and keep the car in its lane. It also included cruise-control systems that adapt to the speed of cars in front, or "platooning," where the manned first truck in a column controls the following unmanned trucks. The number of demonstrations, and the discussions by the designers, show that confidence in the possibility of artificial driving was strong in the research community of ITS.

However, in the pursuit of the automatic driver it is essential to recognize that the model on which the computer algorithms are based should not be that of the individual driver's brain and its interaction with the car, but rather that of a driver situated within a driving context. In a broader discussion on expert systems, sociologist Harry Collins argues for taking into consideration how such systems work in a social context:

> When we build an expert system it is meant to fit into a social organism where a human fitted before. An ideal expert system would replace an expert, possibly making him or her redundant. It would fit where a real expert once fitted without anyone noticing much difference in the way the corresponding social group functions. (Collins 1990, p. 15)

The social context of an artificial driver is, of course, traffic where drivers (artificial or real) interact with other people to work their way through the road net. Finding out what the other road users are doing and what they are up to is the most important thing for avoiding accidents (Swan and Owens 1988, p. 59). As in social interaction in general, a driver has to interpret other people's intentions by interpreting their behavior.

In designing this new technology, irrespective of whether the computers are to serve as drivers, co-drivers, or teachers, it is essential to understand how drivers themselves achieve coordination. The research should not aim at mimicking an individual driver's mental structure, but at imitating his or her activities in traffic. Computers, running by rules or algorithms, must function together with other road users. They must adapt to them, or the drivers will have to adapt to the new machines. If the artificial drivers are socially incompetent, this could put serious strains on other road users. The designers of ITS have acknowledged the importance of modeling even this aspect of driving (Groeger 1993). However, the subject is rarely treated in behavioral research in the area (Parkes and Franzén 1993).

The ITS research community should be expected to have a thorough understanding of traffic, as the artificial driver will be introduced in a setting where inappropriate design could have fatal consequences. An interpretation of traffic as a situated social activity, where rules only figure as weak resources in establishing mutual understanding, increases our sensitivity to the consequences of this type of technology. Our study calls for extended evaluation before such systems are introduced in traffic. Here, the issue is not only to present a cognitive model of a general driver but also to understand how people coordinate their shared road use, that is, the social aspects of traffic.

Second, our empirical findings could also inform another design approach with more modest design principles for road use. In the field of CSCW, empirical studies of collaborative work employing computers have raised a call for less interfering tools. Instead of developing expert systems, they suggest the use of technologies to support human experts in their work, such as message and communication systems. In traffic, a similar perspective could, e.g., stress technologies to support road user interaction such as enhanced communication systems beyond blinkers and horns. However, before leaping into such a design approach, it is important to focus on the way current communication systems and mobile devices are used by drivers of various kinds.

References

AVG (1998) 3AVG demo project Rijnwoude

Catling I (1994) Advanced technology for road transport: IVHS and ATT. Artech House Books, London

Collins H (1990) Artificial experts: social knowledge and intelligent machines. MIT Press, Boston

Collins H (1995) Science studies and machine intelligence. In: Jasanoff S (ed) Handbook of science and technology studies. Sage, London

Dannefer D (1977) Driving and symbolic interaction. Sociol Inq 47(1):33–38

Edensor T (2004) Automobility and national identity representation, geography and driving practice. Theory Cult Soc 21(4/5):101–120

Garfinkel H (1967/1996) Studies in ethnomethodology. Polity Press, Cambridge

Goffman E (1990) The representation of self in everyday life. Penguin Press, London

Groeger J (1993) Degrees of freedom and the limits of learning: support needs of inexperienced drivers. In: Parkes AM, Franzén S (eds) Driving future vehicles. Taylor and Francis, London

Parkes, AM, Franzén S (eds) (1993) Driving future vehicles. Taylor and Francis, London

Redshaw S (2008) In the company of cars—driving as social and cultural practice. Ashgate Publishing, Aldershot

Schmidt K, Simone C (1996) Coordination mechanisms: towards a conceptual foundation of CSCW systems design. Comput Support Coop Work 5:155–200

Suchman L (1991) Plans and situated actions: the problem with human machine interaction. Cambridge University Press, Cambridge

Swan AL, Owens BM (1988) The social-psychology of driving behaviour: communicative aspects of joint-action. Mid-Am Rev Sociol 13(1):59–67

Whelan R (1995) Smart highways, smart cars. Artech House, London

Chapter 5
Interactional Adaptation for Achieving Safe Mobile Phone Handling in Traffic

Mobile phone use is a recent and important part of the social life in traffic, and a salient example of how mobile technology is appropriated in traffic. People make and receive calls when going to and from work as well as during their free time (Goodman et al. 1999; NTHSA 1997). A recent study in the USA shows an increase in mobile phone use. During 2004, 5% of the drivers on the road were holding mobile phones to their ears, compared to 4% in 2002, and 3% in 2000 (Glassbrenner 2005). When including the use of hands-free systems, the figure reached approximately 8% during 2004 (Ibid). The safety of this activity has become a central topic in the public debate and among legislators. It has been subject to legislation in most of the countries in the European Union, Australia, a couple of provinces of Canada, and a number of states in the United States (McEvoy et al. 2005). Despite the legislation, observational studies reveal that close to 2% still use mobile phones while driving in Australia (McD Taylor et al. 2003) and in the UK (Johal et al. 2005).

The concerns surrounding the safety of mobile phone conversations in cars as well as the specific design of the driver support systems are informed by extensive research in the field of traffic psychology (Alm and Nilsson 1995; Brookhuis et al. 1991; Fairclough et al. 1991; McKnight and McKnight 1993; Manalavan et al. 2002; Reed and Green 1999). A number of studies have addressed the impact of mobile phone use on driving, through controlled experiments where the driver takes part in staged conversations. The studies support arguments that mobile phone use dramatically increases the cognitive load on the driver, which multiplies the risk of an accident. The increased demand on the driver's attention is explained either by the need to handle the phone device per se, or to handle the conversation.

We argue that these conclusions are based on theoretical and methodological assumptions that are questionable from a sociological approach. First, traffic safety and mobile phone use is approached from a cognitive perspective. We argue that safe driving is not only the responsibility of the individual driver. As we have discussed in previous chapters, traffic is a social activity where risks are handled in

---

This chapter has previously been published as Esbjörnsson et al. (2007). Reprinted from the publication with permission from Taylor and Francis.

collaboration. Mobile phone talk is equally a social activity taking place in this context. Second, safety is not only a concept which draws upon traffic theory and research. It is of practical and everyday concern for drivers, and as such has to be investigated in real-use situations. Third, the emphasis to control the data collection in earlier research has raised concerns about the validity of these experiments (Goodman et al. 1999). "The relationship between the intelligence test Q&A dialogues and the content of normal cellular communication is unknown. [. . .] A better understanding of the nature of actual cellular telephone communications in business and private calls is sorely needed." (ibid.)

Based on a study of naturally occurring mobile phone use in cars, we present findings on how mobile phone use is fitted with road use to accomplish safe driving. Similar to the topic in the experimental studies, we focus particularly on the use of the phone alongside the maneuvering of the car. Further, we focus on the unfolding moment-by-moment activities of driving in complex traffic situations, where the demand on drivers to maneuver and coordinate their movement with others is high. The empirical material includes many situations of that kind, primarily from the study of a lorry driver delivering food in downtown Stockholm. We focus on only one person, but our results have larger implications in that we analyze the details of this practice rather than quantifying how mobile phone use is combined with driving. The detailed level of the analysis provides insights into how this work is concurrently and collaboratively organized.

Our findings show how the driver relies on a number of resources to fit talk to driving. First, we show that the traffic situation is made visible in the phone conversation. This is done when the traffic situation becomes more complex, and the driver puts increased focus on the maneuvering of the car. Second, drivers adjust their phone handling to collaboration in traffic. We call strategies by which drivers fit their engagement with the phone with their driving and vice versa, *interactional adaptation*. Interactional adaptation includes both interaction with people in the immediate surrounding and with the remote people on the phone, as well as interaction with the technologies at hand such as the car and the phone. We add to the research by showing how the work of maneuvering the car is handled alongside the conversation to achieve safe driving.

5.1 Background

In the previous chapter we discussed how driving a vehicle in traffic is a collaborative and social activity, since drivers have to share the road space with others. Collaboration is essential when two drivers compete for the same part of the road. Disagreements may lead to crashes and accidents, whereas successful coordination provides a specific order in which the drivers can move forward. In order to establish a functioning collaboration, routines and rules are used as resources. Formal rules are provided and sanctioned primarily through the work of the authorities. Coordination also depends on informal rules (Dannefer 1977), which are on-goingly interpreted by road users depending on the setting, and in negotiation with other drivers. The social character of traffic is also visible in the way in which drivers are held morally accountable for specific decisions on the use of the road space. Some decisions by a driver are visibly supported by other drivers, whereas other decisions are equally visibly disliked.

Previous studies of driver support systems in general, and mobile phone use in particular, fail to address the situated and social character of driving, as they are based on experimental setups. In the following, we give an overview of a number of such studies, and finish off by summarizing why this is a problematic approach.

Driving and mobile phone use have been extensively studied in traffic psychology, and the policy discussion is influenced by the results in this field. An overwhelming majority of the studies on safety issues connected with mobile phone use while driving are performed as controlled experiments, either in driving simulators (Alm and Nilsson 1994, 1995; McKnight and McKnight 1993; Manalavan et al. 2002), or in more realistic settings, i.e., "on-the-road" studies (Brookhuis, et al. 1991; Fairclough et al. 1991; Reed and Green 1999). The drivers are exposed to traffic situations as they use the mobile phone. A controlled secondary task is introduced, to produce measurable differences depending on variations in phone use or traffic situations. Some studies concern the effects of making a call, i.e., dialing while driving (Reed and Green 1999), whereas others concern the impact of the conversation per se.

Conversations are staged in two different forms. First, the majority of conversations concern mathematical tests, where the driver has to solve various mathematical problems. For example Alm and Nilsson have the driver interact with a tape-recorder, which provides problems to be solved (Alm and Nilsson 1994, 1995). Brookhuis et al. (1991) provide the driver with mathematical problems, as do Kircher et al. (2003). In Serafin et al. (1993), the driver converses with a computer. There are also studies which include drivers engaged in casual conversations, e.g., on what to do next time they are off-duty, or about TV shows (Svenson and Patten 2003). Both types of conversations have an impact on the drivers' traffic behavior, though casual conversation does so to a lesser extent.

A number of "compensatory behaviors" whereby drivers adapt their phone use to make it safer have also been identified. Drivers attempt to compensate for the attention deficit during a mobile phone conversation, e.g., by slowing down (Alm and Nilsson 1994; Fairclough et al. 1991; Goodman et al. 1999; NTHSA 1997). Similarly, Kircher et al. (2003) report that drivers place their phones on the wheel when dialing, which makes it easier to watch the road and look at the phone at almost the same time. Further, the studies recognize that people make calls before starting, or stop the car for outgoing calls. Still, the researchers claim that, "compensation cannot be expected to be sufficiently strong to outweigh the decrease in driving performance accompanying a mobile phone conversation—in particular in sudden critical traffic situations" (Svenson and Patten 2003). But their interpretation of the risks at stake is made even more uncertain when recognizing available crash data, which in some sense should reflect actual accidents where mobile phone use has been the cause. Crash data analysis suggests that the number of crashes that may be attributed to mobile phone use is much smaller than would be predicted in a statistical model based upon driver inattention factors (NHTSA 1997). The second major crash data study made in the UK came to a similar conclusion. Here, mobile phone use is only one of several " distractions" which in general are present in 2–6% of the reported accidents (Svenson and Patten 2003). Two epidemiological studies from 1997 and 2005 present figures comparable to the top range of the results from the crash data analysis (McEvoy et al. 2005; Redelmeier et al. 1997). Both studies were conducted through analysis of phone billing records from drivers involved in car crashes. The rate of phone use in a specified time span in proximity to the crash was compared to the use rate at control intervals of 24, 72 h, and 7 days before the crash. Both studies came to the conclusion that there was a fourfold increase in the relative risk of an accident if the person was using the phone. McEvoy et al. report that 9% of drivers used the phone during the hazard interval, whereas only 3% used it in the control period.

Traffic researchers such as Svenson and Patten (2003) interpret the figures from the crash data analysis as a major difference vis-à-vis the controlled experiments, which point to higher figures than reported from actual crashes. This could be explained as a result of either insufficient crash data or inadequately designed experiments. Svenson and Patten (2003) blame crash data analysis saying that "epidemiological post hoc data are always difficult to interpret," and that the UK "numbers quite likely underestimate the true figures" (ibid., p. 7).

Another possible explanation is that the experiments are insufficiently valid. First, the type of staged conversations, interacting with a tape-recorder providing queries or mathematical problems to be solved, must be quite rare in traffic. Second, the driving situation is far from realistic when performed in a driving simulator. The collaboration with other road users is restricted, and the drivers do not need to consider potential risks of their driving behavior. Third, irrespective of whether the experiment is done in traffic or in a driving simulator, the driver is forced to use the mobile phone. Accordingly, the test-subject cannot fully adapt his behavior, regarding the timing of mobile phone use in relation to the traffic situation.

Drawing upon the work of social science methods such as ethnography, ethnomethodology, and conversation analysis, we advocate the need to consider interactional adaptation in its proper context. In a commentary on mobile phone research, Schegloff, one of the founders of conversation analysis, emphasizes the importance of studying new technology in its context of use.

> For the many who appeal to other sorts of data to ground their inquiries, let me just suggest again the long-term pay offs of setting new technological inventions in the proper context, an analytically conceived context. For they are like naturalistic versions of experimental stimuli: given precise analytic characterizations of the field into which they are introduced, their effect can be revelatory. Examined as objects in their own right, they may yield only noise. (Schegloff 2002, p. 298)

Hence, in line with Schegloff's arguments this chapter concerns the study of mobile phone use while in traffic. We advocate the benefits of studying driving and mobile phone use with observational ethnographic methods, where these activities are everyday concerns of a driver. This is in line with ethnomethodologically inspired ethnography. Ethnomethodology has been taken up in the design-related disciplines (e.g., Computer Supported Cooperative Work and Human Computer Interaction) for its strength in showing the ways in which the social organization of work is an ongoing practical accomplishment by the members of the setting. This is a useful approach when trying to grasp interactional adaptation, since it will reveal the moment-by-moment organization of adaptation including the temporal aspects thereof. Thick descriptions of a number of cases where interactional adaptation is taking place can be useful resources when thinking about the design and deployment of new technologies.

However, the ethnographic studies are criticized. The main criticism concerns how an "ethnographic study of a single, small-scale setting (or of a small number of such settings), at a particular point in time can have relevance for a wide audience" (Hammersley 1992, p. 5). Nevertheless, in order to better understand mobile phone use and driving, we need to focus on the unfolding moment-by-moment activities of maneuvering the car while using the mobile phone.

One example, if not the only previous example, of such an approach to driving and phone use, is Laurier and Philo's investigation of the adaptive behavior of drivers (Laurier and Philo 1998). In their studies of the office work taking place in cars, they argue that when people engage in doing other things than driving, this is integrated into the driving task in the same manner as the maneuvering depends on moment-by-moment coordination in a contingent situation. Combining driving and office work is not so new and obscure as we initially imagine (ibid.). They are combined in the same manner as we, for instance, coordinate looking through the windscreen and in the rear-view mirror:

> There are legitimate involvements of driving that could cause an accident but are dealt with as part of the commonsense grounds of driving: looking for too long at the speedo, fuel gauge or rear view mirror. Learner drivers have to learn how to divide their attention appropriately between monitoring the road ahead, the rear view mirror and the instrument panel. (Laurier and Philo 1998)

Further, they argue that the attention put to office work, such as reading documents, is always secondary to driving, and takes place when the car is moving slowly as traffic is queuing up on motorways. In these situations, some of the mobile workers bring forth their paper documents and even their laptops. According to Laurier and Philo, fast-moving traffic and traffic in smaller cities preclude this type of work. From studies such as this, we can gain an increased understanding of the role of the conversation and the resources available to fit talk to traffic.

5.2 Method and Data Collection

We have studied drivers by sitting in the front passenger seat, observing and video recording their activities. The data collection took place during 2002. Motivated by the increasing proportion of commercial drivers on the roads, which currently amounts to approximately 25% in the Stockholm region (SOU 2003), we chose to follow seven drivers working with sales and deliveries. The decision was further motivated by the lack of detailed ethnographic studies on how either private or commercial drivers handle mobile phones in traffic. Hence, in line with Sacks's arguments on choosing a topic for exploration, that "one gets started where you can maybe get somewhere" (Sacks, in Silverman 1998, p. 72), the group of professional drivers provides an advantageous case for an exploratory study. Further, professional drivers were chosen since availability is an important aspect of their everyday work. They spend a considerable amount of time in their vehicles, and handle their mobile phone conversations while in traffic. In average, mobile phone use while driving reaches approximately 8% (Glassbrenner 2005), and the frequency of interactional adaptation should be seen in light of this number. However, the choice of professional drivers increased the likelihood that we could observe and video-record conversations and driving in a natural setting. The participants agreed to being recorded, and we promised to present the results in a way that maintained their anonymity. They were also requested to inform us if they wanted a recorded conversation to be deleted.

In the following we present data from one single participant, here called Anders. He works as a lorry driver, delivering food to supermarkets in the downtown Stockholm area. Anders was observed during the course of 3 days. He used two hand-held phones: one for work calls and one for private calls. During the time he was studied he made 11 calls and received five. In total, the study generated a substantial body of recordings. We collected a corpus of 95 phone calls, all of them performed while seated in the vehicle. However, numerous other mobile phone conversations were observed during the fieldwork, unfortunately several of these were not recorded due to technical reasons. The analysis presented in this chapter relies on the whole corpus, although we have chosen to present empirical data on Anders. The various strategies of interactional adaptation he frequently applied were perceptible in view of the fact that he regularly used the mobile phone while driving in the dense inner-city traffic. Hence, these situations provided more obvious moments of interactional adaptation than what is accessible from the data on phoning and driving on the highways.

5.3 Analysis

The video data reveals a number of ways in which people adapt driving and phone use to each other. During the fieldwork, we were able to observe what drivers did to situate calls within the driving, how they preferred specific traffic situations for handling the device, and how they provided awareness of the traffic situation to the non-present conversational partner to adapt the talk to the complexity of driving.

The participants in the study noticeably consider the car as an appropriate place for mobile phone conversations, irrespective of whether they are driving at 110 km/h on a highway or are in dense city traffic. In a majority of the recorded conversations, the mobile phone use takes place while driving. The choice of the driving situation, and consequently the car, as a suitable place for conversation is evident both in how they are using the phone, and in the conversations. The transcription notations are adapted from Jefferson (1985), as related in Atkinson and Heritage (1985, pp. ix–xvi).

5.3.1 Making the Traffic Situation Visible in the Phone Conversation

Anders made the traffic situation visible to his conversation partner several times in the phone conversation, especially when it became more complex and he needed to focus more on the maneuvering of the car in order to ensure safe driving. Accordingly, when more attention on the traffic is required, conversational strategies are used to keep the conversations going with minimal contributions from the driver.

In the following two excerpts from the same phone conversation, presented in the sequence they occur, problematic traffic situations are made visible in the talk. In the first part, Anders is about to make a left turn, but is hindered by construction work. In the second part he comments on the narrow street which, as he states, forces him to focus on driving.

Table 5.1 Anders provides the remote conversationalist with awareness of the traffic situation

Time	Conversation	Car	Traffic situation	Pictures
01:26	And then (..)Yeah I was probably home around eight and then Ulla came over (2.3)		The car in front overtakes a cyclist, by driving on the "wrong" side of the street.	
01:31		Hits the turn signal, to indicate a left turn at the intersection/ traffic light.		
01:32	He he he. (.) hehe (2.7)		The white car in front of him turns left at the intersection. A number of orange road signs indicate a construction work, and a backhoe loader is partly blocking the street.	

Table 5.1 (continued)

01:35		Slows down to make the left turn.	Several orange signs on the left side of the street.
01:37	Yes yes yes it's sad there I couldn't drive (3.6)		
01:38		Turns off the turn signal indicating left turn.	The traffic light turns yellow. The distance to the cars in front increases, as they accelerate.
01:43	Exactly	Shifts gear with his right hand.	The street is still narrow, with cars parked along the right side.

As Anders prepares to turn left, he discovers construction work on the street making it impossible for his large truck to pass. The complicated situation is introduced in the conversation as he says: "there I couldn't drive" (01:37). This is delivered in the same tone of voice and tempo as the talk preceding it. There is no pause after the previous statement ("it's sad"). Although we cannot see the consequence of this utterance, since we do not have access to the other end of the conversation, it is noteworthy how smoothly he comments on the traffic. It is as if he is conveying that there are some concerns, but it is not a big deal that needs to take more space in the conversation. Still, he could change his focus of attention a bit by making the tricky situation available to his conversational partner. Making the problematic situation visible in the conversation allows him to continue the conversation but without continuing on the previous topic, by switching to talking about traffic.

Also, it is noteworthy that this is the first time in this particular phone call that it becomes evident from *the talk* that Anders is driving while having this conversation. There has been no explicit mention of the fact that Anders is in the car. However, it might be that the person on the other end can assume this because of traffic noise in the background. We can assume that having missed the left turn he needs to figure out how to approach the destination at the same time as he is talking. The reference to the traffic situation is accordingly a resource that prepares the remote conversational partner for oncoming difficulties.

Anders and his co-conversationalist then get to the reason for the call. This part of the conversation is left out of the transcript below. Anders has helped a friend to sell sweaters, and now there has been a mistake. A woman has received a blue sweater instead of a black one. When we come back into the conversation, they have just agreed that there is no black sweater in XL.

Table 5.2 Anders keeps the conversation running while handling the complex traffic situation

Time	Conversation	Car	Traffic situation	Pictures
02:43	What was I going to say:: eh::: (2.7)	Turns left. Using his left hand, in which he also holds his phone book.		
02:43	Yes yes yes:: (4.4)			
02:51		As soon as he drives straight on the street, he lets go of his phone book. Throws it on the seat to the right. He lets go of the steering wheel, and takes the phone in his left hand.		
02:54	Yes (2.7)	Changes gear with his right hand. Takes the phone book with his right hand.		
02:57	Yes yes, yes (4.1)	Hits the turn signal with his right hand, through the steering wheel, while holding the phone book.		
03:00	What was I going to say:::: (5.5)	Puts the phone book back on the seat. Takes the steering wheel with his right hand. Looks to the left in the intersection before turning right.	Decreases the speed. There is a car to the left, who lets him pass.	
03:06	°I have to keep my tongue in the middle of my mouth° (idiomatic expression: I have to be careful) (3.8)	Looks to the right while making a right turn onto a bigger street.		

Table 5.2 (continued)

03:11	I'm at Väster-malm where it's so damn narrow (2.8)		
03:16	What was I (1.2)	Lets go of the steering wheel with his right hand, scratches his right ear.	
03:18	No but a medium blue	Moves his right hand back to the steering wheel, but immediately moves it to the gear stick. Changes gear. Looks to the left in the intersection.	Slows down before passing the intersection. Continues straight ahead

Here Anders is busy handling his phone, his phone book, the steering wheel, and the turn signal. During these activities, his contribution to the conversation is reduced. Two times he says "What I was going to say. . ." (02:43, 03:00), but without getting to what he was going to say. This sentence, along with the repeated use of "yes," is a way to fulfill his obligation in the conversation, i.e., to provide some material for each turn, though without providing any new information. These strategies give him more time to focus on the traffic situation, and less on the conversation. Still, he does not have to engage in explaining to the conversational partner what is happening.

He also has the opportunity to make the problematic traffic situation a topic of the conversation. When traffic forces him to leave the current topic, he explains why: "I have to be careful" (03:06). This displays a current problem. He then explains what sort of problem it is, i.e., that he is driving in a particular part of the city where the streets are narrow: "I'm at Västermalm where it's so damn narrow" (03:11).

Perhaps this explicit reference to the fact that he is in a complex traffic situation is a way to account for why he has not been more active in the conversation. Another "what I was going to say" would not be appropriate. This time he has to come up with an explanation. By explicitly referring to the traffic situation he explains his rather passive contribution to the conversation, at the same time as he again makes the remote conversationalist aware of his need to focus on traffic.

Summing up, there are various ways in which the conversation per se could be used to provide the non-present conversationalist with an understanding of the traffic situation, or just allow the driver to focus on traffic. The shift of attention between driving and talking is interactionally adapted using different conversational resources. This aspect of mobile phone talk has hitherto not been studied in traffic research. It is apparent from the conversation that he is not just doing talking on the mobile phone; rather he is doing talking on the phone while driving.

5.3.2 Adapting Phone Handling to Collaboration in Traffic

The driver has different opportunities to fit the phone handling with his pressing concern for maneuvering the vehicle and coordinating with surrounding drivers to increase safety. The intensity of the traffic situation, and the complexity of the maneuvering, vary during a journey. Our findings support the hypothesis in previous research that drivers actively make use of these variations when engaging in other tasks than driving. Laurier (2002) has shown that slow-moving traffic, and especially car queues on motorways, were chosen as suitable situations for office work. Further, Svenson and Patten (2003) suggest that drivers choose suitable traffic situations when they make calls. Such activities frequently occurred in our study.

In the following we will examine a situation where Anders makes a call when driving in the city center. The excerpt shows the way in which he adapts the maneuvering of the vehicle, with attention to the traffic, to the making of a call. When we enter the conversation, Anders is driving his lorry towards a roundabout and decreases the speed. As the vehicle comes to a stop, he brings out his phone and starts to make a call.

Table 5.3 Anders chooses a situation of slow movement to dial

Time	Conversation	Car	Traffic situation	Pictures
00:04	Anders: Normally he calls	Slowing down to full stop. Holds the phone in his left hand, and moves his right hand from the gear lever to the phone. Looks down on the device.	Approaching a roundabout.	
00:05	Observer: hehehe (2.5)			
00:07	Anders: You ( ) (10.6)	Looks up, and puts his right hand back on the gear level.		
00:08			A cycling postman appears on the pavement on the left i.e. the other side of the street going towards the roundabout.	
00:10		Looks at the phone again, and presses some buttons with his left hand.	Heavy traffic in the roundabout	

Table 5.3 (continued)

00:11			Two pedestrians cross the road leading into the roundabout
00:12			A red car in front of him, probably waiting for the pedestrians to cross, accelerates towards the roundabout.
00:16		Looks down at his mobile. Continues to dial. Accelerates very slowly.	A gap occurs between his lorry and the roundabout.
00:18		Looks up. Lifts the phone to his left ear with the left hand.	The cycling postman passes on the zebra crossing in front of the lorry.
00:19		Lifts his right hand, from the gear level, and waves to the postman.	
00:20	Anders: °You're welcome° (1.1)	Grabs the steering wheel with his right hand.	
00:21	Anders: It wasn't my intention to let you go first (6.4)	Brakes to full stop again at the edge of roundabout. Looks at the cars. Moves his right hand from the steering wheel, to the gear level.	
00:26		Waits for the traffic in the roundabout to decrease. Puts his right hand back to the steering wheel.	A gap occurs in the traffic in roundabout.

Table 5.3 (continued)

00:28	Anders: (turn around) (6.7)		
00:33		Moves his right hand to the gear level, and back to the steering wheel.	
00:35	Anders: Hi man!	Accelerates, and starts a conversa- tion in his mobile.	

Anders has stopped behind a red car which is standing still in front of a zebra crossing. The red car has yielded for two pedestrians who are about to cross (00:11). Anders makes a call (00:04). The situation is convenient for phoning because the coordination work with the surrounding people is settled for the moment, giving first the pedestrians, and then the red car right of way. That makes it possible to do something else. Further, the halt frees him from the practical work of maneuvering the vehicle. When the pedestrians have crossed, the red car accelerates towards the roundabout (00:12). But it accelerates only very slowly (00:16). This creates a gap between the red car and the zebra crossing.

The gap between the red car and the lorry could in this situation be filled either by Anders and his lorry or by the cycling postman (00:08), who has been advancing in parallel. Anders engages in dialing, and meanwhile the postman uses the gap to cross the street. Anders raises his arm and waves towards him saying rather silently "you're welcome" (00:20). The postman apparently had gestured to thank him for allowing him to use the empty space first. We interpret Anders's wave as an answer to the postman's gesture. However, the postman could not hear him talk. Thus, "you're welcome" is more likely said to himself or to the observer, i.e., the researcher present in the car. Then he says in a much louder way that "it wasn't my intention to let you go first." Although explicitly addressing the postman ("you"), this could also be addressed to the observer to account for why he was allowing the postman to use this particular gap. His comment displays that the gap did not occur because he gave the "turn" to the postman; it occurred as a consequence of him standing still and attending to his phone. Put another way, he opts out of his turn in traffic and instead chooses to prolong his standing still, with the intention to dial. This situation make visible the ways in which he engages in the traffic situation in such a way that the phone use is convenient, and is interactionally adapted to other participants in traffic.

Further, we learn that he has to account for the way he uses and creates gaps in traffic. In this case, he was explicitly praised by the postman for generating a gap and then allowing him to use it. The opposite is, of course, also an alternative where drivers scorn each other for hindering each other in traffic (Katz 1999). The humorous comment (00:21) probably also draws on the paradox of being thanked for standing still in traffic to dial, something which could provoke anger. If drivers just stopped their vehicles on a busy street they would usually be held accountable for this behavior. Needless to say perhaps, none of the drivers in our study simply stopped their vehicles in traffic to make a call. However, in the previous case, Anders can allow himself to prolong the halt and affect the traffic without being accountable for the obstruction, since another person benefits from the gap he causes.

Further, we argue that the choice of the entry to the roundabout as a place to make the call was chosen for the low speed. The conversation itself provides no clue as to why he chose that particular occasion to make a call. However, during our study, Anders makes 11 calls as he drives, and looking at them in general helps us to better understand the situation. The great majority of his call initiations occur either when decreasing the speed of his vehicle or when standing still for a while. The dialing takes place either when he brakes as he is coming up to a red light, or in conjunction with braking before making a turn in a junction. The number of such occasions of co-occurring dialing and slow movement indicates that this situation was chosen by Anders to make a call because the vehicle was moving slowly and coming to a full stop.

To sum up, the interactional adaptation of phone handling to the collaboration with other road users, allowing for the most convenient interaction with the phone, is an important and empirically available activity. Such adaptation to the situation positively affects traffic safety, and must be accounted for when discussing the impact of phone use on traffic safety in general.

5.4 Discussion

The aim of this chapter is to influence the design of new technologies supporting mobile phone use while driving. We discuss our experiences along two lines. First, we provide a discussion of the findings of relevance for safety concerns of this practice in general. Second, we discuss how our findings can influence the design of technologies to be used in cars.

5.4.1 Safety as an Achievement in Mobile Work

Previous studies clearly show that there is an increased risk associated with the use of mobile phones when driving a car. However, the level of that specific risk, as well as which particular activities of mobile phone use that generate the problems, is still debated. We add to this discussion by arguing that the two activities of driving safely and handling mobile phones should be considered in parallel. The act of dividing one's attention between the phone and the maneuvering is an everyday thing, as is the dividing of attention between all the other small tasks that take place while driving. The study reveals previously unrecognized *interactional adaptation*. The driver fits the conversation to driving, which includes collaboration with the remote conversational partner, and the driver fits the mobile phone handling to the interaction with surrounding drivers, cyclists, and pedestrians.

Our study reveals a practice where the drivers adapt their driving and their mobile phone conversations to each other to achieve safe driving. First, the field study illustrates how the drivers make the traffic situation visible in the phone conversation. This is done when the traffic situation becomes complex, and the driver puts increased focus on the maneuvering of the car. The balancing of attention between driving and talking is coordinated by different conversational resources such as shift of tempo, turn taking, and choice of topic. The use of these resources, as well as the way in which traffic is more explicitly accounted for, makes the non-present conversational partner aware of the traffic situation. Thus, they can collaboratively converse in a way that is adapted to the traffic situation. Second, it is found that drivers adjust their phone handling to the collaboration with other road users, to allow for the most convenient and safe interaction with the phone. When there is a pause in the traffic flow, e.g., a stop at a red light or at a roundabout, this can be used to initiate a phone conversation. These situations are sometimes prolonged more than the traffic situation calls for, to make an opportunity to engage in phone use. The fact that one is standing still is observable to other road users, and these places are the type of places where cars can be expected to stand still, thereby not resulting in unsafe traffic situations.

These findings have consequences for our understanding of the previous research in traffic psychology, which has been influential on the lively policy discussion and legislation on phone use in cars. Goodman et al. (1999) suggest that the difference in the number of crashes predicted by the experimental studies and the figures derived from crash data analysis could be explained by a compensatory behavior of the drivers.

Our study, which reveals interactional adaptation, underscores the concern about the validity of previous studies. The drivers do not just pursue their mobile conversation unaffected by the traffic situation. Rather, they actively make the situation as smooth as possible. Thus, the residual between theoretical predictions from experiments and the crash data, as discussed by Svenson and Patten (2003) could be explained by the efforts made by the driver to make the talk as safe as possible. We suggest that the drivers' own work to reduce risks could be an explanation of the difference between the number of actual crashes due to mobile phone use, as identified in crash data analysis, and the risks as suggested based on controlled experiments.

The consequences of our findings could be that the concerns about the danger of using phones, which are based on experimental studies, are overvalued. It seems that the activity of driving and handling phones is less dangerous than these studies suggest. It follows that policies to limit the use of phones in cars are less important than what the experimental studies suggest.

At the same time, the ethnographic method itself has its limitations when it comes to the generalizability of the results. However, we argue that the methodological approach taken in this study, to focus on the details which concern the drivers in a naturalistic setting, is of further importance. Our study is only a first step towards understanding phone handling and driving in an uncontrolled but realistic environment. Fieldwork methodology has much to offer when understanding how drivers engage with their phones.

5.4.2 Technologies to Support Interactional Adaptation

Various existing technologies are supposed to make mobile phoning in cars more safe and convenient by freeing both hands for maneuvering the car, and some countries make the legality of phone use dependent on such systems (McCartt and Geary 2004). As argued earlier, there is a growing understanding that the decreased safety is not due to the need to occupy a hand with the phone. However, the identification of interactional adaptation as important when combining driving and phone use, points in another direction for design. The results of our study provide empirical support for the possibilities to design collaborative technologies which could increase the convenience and safety of phone handling in cars, thereby benefiting drivers. Such technologies could either improve safety through providing increased awareness of the traffic situation to a remote conversationalist, or provide increased awareness of phone handling to surrounding drivers.

In the first case, increased awareness could be technically mediated, e.g., visually or aurally, to the remote conversationalist without the involvement of the driver. It could provide the remote conversationalist more means to interpret the current traffic situation than through available oral cues. Further, it is possible to imagine services where the driver is actively involved by getting extended support to negotiate the conversation to make it fit with the traffic situation. The current systems could be improved by introducing simple interaction techniques like pressing a single button or uttering specific sounds which are automatically recognized. The interaction would then trigger the phone to put the line on hold and inform the remote conversationalist of the upcoming situation. This would be similar to the "signaling method" suggested by Manalavan et al. (2002) for mitigating the risks involved. In their experiments the remote conversationalist was provided with signals such as beeping, squealing brakes, a police siren, or a synthesized voice message, during critical traffic situations (ibid.).

In the second case, technologies could make the adaptation easier for other drivers in the surroundings by increasing the visibility of phone handling, e.g., by providing other visual cues. Thus, it would be easier for people in the surroundings to see that the driver is engaged in a conversation, and adapt to this situation.

These two directions for design share the assumption that the technologies should be a support for drivers and conversationalists in better performing interactional adaptation. We argue against Manalavan et al.'s idea, where they imagine "a cell phone capable of receiving real-time localized traffic data," interpreting the data, and then signaling to the remote conversationalist when the driver can no longer attend to the conversation. We do not believe that interactional adaptation through and by the system would be as useful as the skillful interactional adaptation we have identified. For example, we have seen a number of examples where the drivers make calls in specific situations such as when approaching traffic signals. Drawing on Manalavan et al.'s idea, we could suggest a context-aware system which only allows the driver to engage in button pressing where the conditions resemble those that the driver looks for, e.g., a red light. Although traffic lights were favored places for making calls, they were a resource rather than a determinate precondition for this activity. Anders sometimes favored calling at places where the car might come to a stop, rather than choosing a place where this is less likely. Thus, the traffic situation does not decide what the driver can do. A context-aware system, which takes decisions, could be disturbing for the driver who does not act and think of particular situations as determined for phone calls, or in the latter case, unsuitable for calling.

5.5 Achieving Safe Driving in Mobile Phone Use

We have shown how drivers actively work to avoid physical accidents while speaking on the phone in a vehicle, and the ways in which this is an intrinsically social activity. Thus, the vitality of street life is based on situated and collaborative activities also when it comes to the use of new mobile communication technologies.

Safety is an underlying concern for all mobile phone use taking place in cars, and has to be considered as such. It is particularly an issue with the increasing amount of in-car applications and mobile technologies aimed to be used in the car. Future drivers will likely have access to several applications that can potentially distract them from driving. We have taken a closer look at the everyday practice of using mobile phones in cars, and how this is managed to achieve safe driving.

Our study reveals a number of strategies of interactional adaptation used by the drivers to make their phone use fit with driving, which are not previously accounted for in the numerous controlled experiments dealing with phone use in cars. The analysis of the empirical data shows how the drivers seek to accomplish safe driving by adapting their handling of the phone, as well as the conversations, to fit with the traffic situation. They use suitable situations in traffic to retrieve phone-numbers, or to dial. They provide remote conversationalists with awareness of any eventual problems in the traffic situation which may require more focus on driving. Further, they adapt their driving to fit with the mobile phone use, and with nearby road users.

The empirical findings have relevance for our understanding of the validity of previous studies and indirectly for policy and legislation concerning mobile technology use in cars. In contrast with previous studies in more experimental settings, we have found that drivers do not just pursue their mobile conversation unaffected by the traffic situation. Instead they make the situation as smooth as possible, in collaboration with other drivers and with remote conversationalists. Thus, the residual between predictions from experiments and crash data could be a result of the efforts made by the driver to make the talk as safe as possible. Based on our findings, we suggest that the drivers' own work to reduce risks could be an explanation of the difference between the number of actual crashes due to mobile phone use, as identified in crash data analysis, and the prognosis based on the risks as suggested by controlled experiments.

The results have bearing on the design of technologies to be used in cars. In order to ensure safe mobile phone handling, there are two possible ways to design such technologies: either to provide awareness of the traffic situation to a remote conversationalist, or to increase the awareness of phone handling to the surrounding road users.

References

Alm H, Nilsson L (1994) Changes in driver behaviour as a function of handsfree mobile phones—a simulator study. Accid Anal Prev 264:441–451

Alm H, Nilsson L (1995) The effects of a mobile telephone task on driver behaviour in a car following situation. Accid Anal Prev 27:707–715

Atkinson JM, Heritage J (1985) Structures of social action: studies in conversation analysis. Cambridge University Press, Cambridge

Brookhuis KA, de Vries G, de Waard D (1991) The effects of mobile telephoning on driving performance. Accid Anal Prev 23(4):309–316

Dannefer D (1977) Driving and symbolic interaction. Sociol Inq 47(1):33–38

Esbjörnsson M, Juhlin O, Weilenmann A (2007) Drivers using mobile phones in traffic: an ethnographic study of interactional adaptation. Int J Hum Comput Interact 22(1):39–60

Fairclough SH, Ashby MC, Ross T et al (1991) Effects of handsfree telephone use on driving behaviour. In: Proceedings of the 24th ISATA international symposium on automotive technology and automation

Glassbrenner D (2005) Driver cell phone use in 2004—overall results. Traffic safety facts—research note, February, DOT HS 809 847

Goodman MJ, Tijerina L, Bents, FD et al (1999) Using cellular telephones in vehicles: safe or unsafe? Transp Hum Factors, 11:3–42

Hammersley M (1992) What's wrong with ethnography? Routledge, London

Johal S, Napier F, Britt-Compton J et al (2005) Mobile phones and driving. J Public Health 271:112–113

Katz J (1999) How emotions work. University of Chicago Press, Chicago

Kircher A, Törnros J, Vogel K et al (2003) Mobile telephone simulator study. Vetenskaplig rapportsamling—Vägverkets utredning om användning av mobiltelefoner och andra IT-system under körning. Publ: 92, Swedish National Road Administration, Borlänge

Laurier E (2002) Notes on dividing the attention of a car driver. Team Ethno Online, No. 1

Laurier E, Philo C (1998) Meet you at junction 17: a socio-technical and spatial study of the mobile office, Glasgow. Dept. of Geography, University of Glasgow and ESRC, Swindong. http://web2.ges.gla.ac.uk/~elaurier/texts/proposal.htm. Accessed 17 January 2010

Manalavan P, Samar A, Schneider M et al (2002) In-car cell phone use: mitigating risk by signaling remote callers. In: Proceedings of CHI—extended abstracts on human factors in computing systems. ACM Press, New York, pp 790–791

McCartt AT, Geary LL (2004) Longer term effects of New York State's law on drivers' handheld cell phone use. Br Med J 10:11–15

McD Taylor D, Bennet DM, Carter M et al (2003) Mobile telephone use among Melbourne drivers: a preventable exposure to injury risk. Med JAust 179(3):140–142

McEvoy SP, Stevenson MR, McCartt AT et al (2005) Role of mobile phones in motor vehicle crashes resulting in hospital attendance: a case-crossover study. Br Med J. doi:10.1136/bmj.38537.397512.55

McKnight AJ, McKnight AS (1993) The effect of cellular phone use upon driver attention. AccidAnal Prev 25(3):259–265

National Highway Traffic Safety Administration (NTHSA) (1997) An investigation of the safety implications of wireless communications in vehicles. Department of Transportation. http://www.nhtsa.dot.gov/people/injury/research/wireless. Accessed 17 January 2010

Reed PM, Green PA (1999) Comparison of driving performance on-road and in a low-cost simulator using a concurrent telephone dialing task. Ergonomics 428:1015–1037

Redelmeier D, Tibshirani RJ (1997) Association between cellular telephone calls and motor vehicle collisions. New Engl J Med 336(7):453–458

Schegloff E (2002) Beginnings in the telephone. In: Katz J, Aakhus M (eds) Perpetual contact: mobile communication, private talk, public performance. Cambridge University Press, Cambridge

Serafin C, Wen C, Paelke G et al (1993) Car phone usability: a human factors laboratory test. In: Proceedings of the human factors and ergonomics society 37th annual meeting

Silverman D (1998) Harvey sacks—social science & conversation analysis. Oxford University Press, New York

SOU (2003) Trängselavgifter. Statens Offentliga Utredningar. 2003:61. http://www.regeringen.se/sb/d/263/a/1912. Accessed 17 January 2010

Svenson O, Patten C (2003) Information technology in the car: mobile phones and traffic safety—a review of contemporary research. In Vetenskaplig rapportsamling—Vägverkets utredning om användning av mobiltelefoner och andra IT-system under körning. Publ 2003:92, Swedish National Road Administration, Borlänge

Chapter 6
Driving and Articulating the Road Context with the PlaceMemo Application

Road inspectors, the subject of this study, are a form of advanced users of mobile technologies. For a number of years they have utilized a mobile system, which they could bring with them from the office into the vehicles, which attaches a geographical position to the information they report into the organization's databases. As in the previous chapter, proper coordination of their driving and handling of mobile devices is critical and has to be accounted for in the design.

The purpose of this case study is to increase the knowledge of social interaction and mobile work on the roads, which includes driving and interpreting the road context, as well as to evaluate current technical support. Furthermore, we wish to identify services and applications that could be used to develop the inspection work. We are particularly interested in systems containing information on geographical position, hereafter called position-based information. We saw the road inspectors as a form of advanced users in our general design space, who scan the road context for obstructions similarly to regular drivers, but are part of an organization that also shares such information and takes care of the obstructions.

Road inspection includes the identification of defects in the road infrastructure and the handling of these problems.[1] It is a collaborative activity drawing on the skills of the inspectors to make interpretations of roadside objects. The primary concern is to detect objects that could obstruct drivers' free passage. However, collaboration and sharing of information is hampered by the relatively isolated position of the road inspectors in their vehicles. First, their ability to collaborate is reduced by the distance to other colleagues. Second, they are restricted by the mobile work situation, as they are almost constantly on the move. In this situation, infrastructure maintenance could be supported by mobile technology, which would provide the organization with new forms of collaboration and sharing of information. The ability to localize objects would be facilitated. The information associated with these objects would be easier to recall, and the sharing of information would be viable.

Co-authored with Mattias Esbjörnsson
VINNOVA The Swedish Governmental Agency for Innovation Systems, Stockholm, Sweden

[1]This chapter draws upon the paper Esbjörnsson and Juhlin (2002). It also draws on the paper Esbjörnsson (2006). Reprinted from the publication with permission from Springer Verlag.

6.1 Articulating Collaboration in Infrastructure Management

Our understanding of road inspection draws on previous experiences from research in the field of Computer Supported Cooperative Work (CSCW). Here, a distinction is made between two approaches to designing information technology for organizational work. The first approach focuses on automation. This is considered suitable in those cases where an activity is carried out by routine, or as if according to a stable plan, and the context of the work is highly stable and predictable. The second strategy focuses on support of *articulation* work. It is founded on the argument that automation will be less successful if the task is complex and characterized by constant deviations from what is to be expected, and if you constantly have to take new situations into consideration (Schmidt and Simone 1996). Here, work is understood as a local and contingent activity. This implies that all activities performed by humans include a level of *articulation*. The particular way in which an organizational rule should be followed in that situation has to be expressed there and then (Mantovani 1996; Schmidt and Simone 1996; Suchman 1987). It is a way to account for the difficulty of simply following routine paths. Participants often have their own ways of working and solving problems, and the decisions are connected to a particular situation that makes it hard to reuse knowledge in new contexts. There can also be reluctance to share personal skills with other people since one's individual advantages will be lost (Grudin 1994). Since contingency and complexities are more the rule than the exception, they must also be accounted for when designing support for collaborative work (Grudin 1994; Schmidt and Simone 1996). This includes support for articulation work, and support for sharing information. Finally, it has also been recognized that successful systems need to support both group work, and individual tasks.

6.1.1 Infrastructure Management in Vast Areas

Recent studies of occupational groups working with infrastructure management have a common denominator in their interest in the consequences on organizations of mobile work conditions in combination with a widely distributed working area. Examples of occupational groups studied are process engineers (Bertelsen and Bødker 2001), bus drivers (Juhlin and Vesterlind 2001), home-care teams (Pinelle and Gutwin 2003), underground staff (Luff and Heath 1998), and service technicians (Orr 1996; Wiberg 2001). At first glance, the tasks performed by the process engineers (Bertelsen and Bødker 2001) could be seen as individual, but their actions affect the running of the plant, and therefore also their colleagues. To facilitate their work there is a need to share information, but not in the sense of universal access to everything, everywhere. The information cannot be separated from specific action, which in turn is tied to specific places. Accordingly Bertelsen and Bødker characterize the environment as a common information space, and emphasize the importance of being on location to take the correct actions. The work of Nilsson et al. (2000) represents a similar view, highlighting the importance of the physical inspection.

Based on their findings they propose a solution that attempts to smooth the transition between physical and digital interaction. They introduce a non-functional mock-up that can monitor the status of predefined and stationary objects within the workplace. Pointing the device towards the objects is the initial way of adding them to the system. Thereafter they are visible in a list, irrespective of location. Audio notes can be recorded and connected to each predefined object. These recordings are later available on the device. The other studies describing bus drivers (Juhlin and Vesterlind 2001) and service technicians (Orr 1996; Wiberg 2001) reveal certain similarities with the process engineers. A slight difference could be observed in the fact that the latter workgroups perform their work in a broader setting, and coordinate certain activities while mobile. Taken together these studies have increased our knowledge of mobility and collaborative work. But up to now they have mostly considered occupations where people move from one stationary workplace activity to another. When the workspace increases in size, and contains quantities of objects that are neither predefined nor fixed, such as in road inspection, other type of complexities and demands arise. For example, Johansson and Pettersson (2001) present a study illustrating the problems of working while actually moving. They discuss how truck drivers interact with the in-vehicle navigation systems while driving. The study shows how the drivers start interacting with the navigation systems first when they have problems finding their way. Accordingly these occasions are not well suited for providing input to the system.

6.1.2 Road Inspection

We participated in the inspectors' work by following them on their daily tours north of Stockholm. The inspector spends most of his working day alone inside the cab of the truck. It is his responsibility to care for some of the main roads north of Stockholm. He must identify and deal with objects and defects that could disturb traffic. These tasks are all regulated in a contract with the orderer. An inspection tour lasts around 7 h and covers 150–250 km. The inspector patrols the road-network according to a predetermined schedule. The frequency of the inspections of each road type is determined by traffic flow and road size. Main roads in the region are inspected every other day. Minor roads are inspected with less frequency (Fig. 6.1).

A major part of the inspector's time is spent seated in the cab of the truck, where most of the information technology is located. He is surrounded by a large palette

There are three different local offices, each having one or two road inspectors and a supporting staff of 10–20 persons, with several occupational groups represented. Five different inspectors, belonging to the three different local offices, have been studied during a period of 10 working days. We observed their work while sitting in the cabs of the trucks. We followed them out of the vehicle when tasks were performed outside, and also during three morning-meetings at the office. We took extensive field notes, which were transcribed immediately after returning from the inspection tours. The transcriptions were analyzed, and a set of themes was identified. A few themes and a representative sequence are presented in this chapter.

Fig. 6.1 Road inspectors taking care of a defective road sign (*left*). The current reporting-system used by the road inspectors (*right*)

of technological equipment including an FM-radio; communication radio (UHF); a handheld computer; and a mobile phone equipped with a separate microphone and a hands-free speaker.

The ProData-system, consisting of a mobile computer connected to a GPS-receiver, is the main tool for gathering information during inspection. The system was initially introduced as early as 1998, and the functionality has continuously evolved. The GPS-receiver automatically logs the position during the inspection. All defects reported by the inspector are coded and linked to a geographic location. The codes, used to categorize defects, are provided by the organizational body that contracts their work, and they are described in a document placed in each vehicle. The codes are organized into nine main categories, each containing a minimum of five sub-categories of possible defects. In addition, the system allows the users to write their own textual input. The defects should be reported, according to the work manual, irrespective of whether they are repaired or not. The log created by ProData will then verify that the roads have been properly inspected. Mobile phones are used to inform colleagues about local contingencies and to delegate tasks. It is also necessary to communicate with colleagues to stay updated on the status of the road network and to share information regarding their tasks. There are also elements of interaction with people outside their organization, e.g., the police and/or the traffic information central (TIC). Finally, the FM-radio is a source for local traffic information.

6.2 Road Inspection as an Ongoing Practice

In general, the inspectors conduct three different tasks, which are identifiable in the following example. The inspector sees a fox lying dead on the roadway while driving on his daily inspection tour. He identifies it as a defect. He halts the vehicle immediately behind the object of interest, since the truck will then protect him from the surrounding traffic when he is out on the road. Before stepping out of the truck he reports the defect. In this case he fills in the forms provided in the ProData system. He uses a combination of a predefined defect code, which is documented in the manual present in the vehicle, and his own textual input. The positioning system (GPS) forces him to be at the spot of interest when the report is made. Otherwise the automatically generated position-data will differ from the position of the defect, and the report will be incorrect. Finally he leaves the cab of the truck to deal with the defect, i.e., remove the dead animal from the road. This work could be summarized as including the phases of *identifying* a defect, then *reporting* it, and finally *taking care* of it.

6.2.1 Identification as Ongoing Interpretative Work

On many occasions neither the identification, nor the appropriate description when reporting it, are as clear-cut as in the previous example. On the contrary, it often requires considerable skill on the part of the inspector, based on the ability to interpret contingent situations and conduct successful collaborations, to make the appropriate judgment of how to apply the manual in a specific situation. In the following case, the inspector is faced with the problem of deciding if an object (a car) should be understood as a defect or just part of normal road use. We are driving on a motorway north of Stockholm, and the inspector discovers a red Mazda parked by the roadside.

> Inspector: I have not seen it before, so I will report it. If it's still here on Wednesday I'll do it. The owner may have gone to the gas station, but it looked quite nice. Perhaps it will be gone by then. It wasn't rusty. It's troublesome that we cannot remove the abandoned cars. The police have to contact the owner as long as it isn't placed dangerously for the other road users, and the police seldom make this decision.

The inspector is uncertain about the interpretation of the car. He is clear about the object being newly arrived there. Thus, it has not been reported earlier on. But he decides to postpone reporting the object until he receives more information. If the car is still there after 2 days it is more probable that it really is a defect, i.e., an abandoned car. In this situation, he interprets the condition of the car to get an indication of its status. If it is rusty, it is more likely that it is abandoned. New cars are seldom left alongside highways according to this way of reasoning. Thus, the case-by-case identification of defects demands interpretative skill. On some occasions he also has to consider information given by his colleagues. They might be able to tell him if the object has been accorded the status of a normal object rather than a defect.

In other cases, the inspectors struggled with identifying whether a defect was physically located in their area of responsibility. Furthermore, some road signs could either be illegal or have a temporary permit that they were uninformed of. Completely missing signs could also be difficult to identify without genuine local knowledge. Some of the objects in the loosely defined working area are gradually becoming defects, while other defects occur instantaneously.

6.2.1.1 Postponing Reporting and Repair

In most cases inspection is not a three-step sequential activity. Even in cases when identification is made, it normally leads to neither reporting nor repair. Reporting very seldom occurs if the inspectors do not engage in repair or delegation, which depends on their first stopping the truck in the vicinity of the defect. But other traffic in the surroundings limits the possibilities to make an immediate stop, because of the risk of being hit from behind. Furthermore, the possibility of immediately taking care of identified defects could be limited, because of the need for certain equipment or tools. Instead they focus on reminding themselves to bring the proper equipment on a later occasion. In the following example, the inspector stops the truck on the highway, since he caught sight of a gap in the road safety fence:

> Inspector: That gate is open. I do not have a padlock with me. I suppose I have to write it down. [He writes on a Post-it note] "1000 m north Måby traffic interchange junction, road safety fence gate unlocked."

He uses a steel wire to temporary close the gate. He will come back at a later time and lock the gate with a padlock. When repair work needs to be planned inspectors use paper notes as reminders to access earlier reported data. He makes a note of the position of the defect as a reminder of when to plan for stopping the truck, which indicates that they have problems remembering the details of the defects along the inspection tour. In many other cases, where the repairs of defects have been postponed, they just try to memorize the task.

6.2.2 Insufficient Reminders

It follows from the previous case that they need to return to previously identified locations. The problem of recalling the task when approaching the location, or being at the correct location, is obvious in the following two examples. First, while preparing the vehicle for the daily inspection tour, a colleague informs the inspector to take care of a dropped cable in front of a traffic light. He is told of the geographical location, and that the defective cable should be visible. He promises to take care of it since he will pass this area. But by the end of the day he has done nothing to handle the problem. The rich environment makes it troublesome to memorize the specific position, while the focus is on driving the vehicle and continuously searching for other possible defects. The second example shows the importance of the physical object as a reminder. The inspector was reminded of an earlier discussion with a colleague when passing an underground passageway in the vicinity of a highway exit. The discussion concerned broken windows in the underground passageway. He made an immediate call with his mobile phone to remind his colleague to take care of the defect.

Most often the physical object acts as a trigger when recalling a task that has to be taken care of. In most of the cases, it is already too late, since he has already passed the object of interest. In many cases they use Post-it notes to handle the reminders, or even try to memorize the details. It is obvious that these instruments are not sufficient for fitting their driving to the inspection work.

6.2.3 Resources for Delegation

The Post-it notes also give inspectors the possibility to hand information over to colleagues when they meet in person. This might occur at the office, but could also happen on the road. The information could also be useful when discussing with a colleague on the mobile phone. Then the Post-it note reminds him about what to discuss, such as in the following example. The previously observed Mazda is still there when we reach the same place later the same day. This time, the inspector stops his vehicle in order to file a report. Still, he is not absolutely certain what to do. Is it enough just to report the object into his computer or should he delegate the handling of it to someone else?

> Inspector: The car is still abandoned by the roadside. It is probably stolen.
> Researcher: Are you having problems finding the correct code?
> Inspector: No. But I am writing some more details "Mazda 626 LLF657." There is a certain code to use: "abandoned cars." That one is really good. In the same way I can use the code "dropped load." But there is a problem since I can't retrieve what I have reported. For example this car—if I change my mind and decide to call the police I can't retrieve the registration number if I haven't written it on a Post-it note. I don't know what to do.

Excerpt 6.1   Lack of support for delegation

He is not satisfied with his mobile application in this situation. It doesn't support the delegation of work tasks, e.g., in this case, when the police have to be informed. The neglected support for delegation also affects the possibility to share the responsibility for a specific section of road.

6.2.4 Barriers to Collaboration

Furthermore, the system makes it difficult to retrieve previously reported data on the handheld computer. Occasionally this causes data to be reported twice, e.g., both in a file on the computer and on a Post-it note. The problems are apparent in the following example. An inspector, working temporarily during the holiday months, hesitates to report major defects. He believes that, in most cases, they have already been reported. Reporting them once again would only cause problems. He tells me that he usually writes the defect on a piece of paper, and checks with the computer at the office, before he files it into the computer. He will report minor defects, e.g., dead animals, since he takes immediate care of them. In many cases inspectors will report without checking back at the office. When the same defect is reported on several occasions, the quality of the database will decrease. An attempt to avoid this problem is to let the inspectors have their "own" roads to inspect. This will probably increase the possibility for them to be aware of their earlier interpretations and formal reports, but occasionally this is problematic when sharing working tasks, e.g., sharing roads.

6.2.5 *Fitting Driving to Organizational Tasks*

The work of the inspectors consists of several tasks, which are contingent and characterized by constant deviations from the organizational requirements. There are obvious elements of hesitation when applying the administrative rules for identification of defects, as well as appropriate actions to take (as formulated in their work manual). Furthermore, in practice their work involves features which are not accounted for in the system design, such as identification and positioning being temporally extended activities and the need to combine driving and inspection.

First, the identification of defects can be understood as ongoing articulation work (Schmidt and Simone 1996), as in the case of the red Mazda. The red car does not in itself tell the inspector that it is abandoned. The road inspector has to make that interpretation, which in this case demands prolonged engagement, to decide whether it is a defect instead of a random parked car. Second, it is clear that the inspector has to attend to the specifics of working in a vast area. Most importantly, this is visible in the way they work to handle the location and positioning of objects. The difficulty of finding the defects is apparent since they write down their geographical position when they formulate a note. However they still often forget to take care of it, since they forget to look for it while performing the inspection of the area. Third, the driving per se constrains their activities. The mobility of other road users decreases their freedom of action, and the system can not be used while maneuvering their vehicle. Stopping the vehicle is often very difficult and time consuming. Thus reporting and repairing are normally postponed until an indefinite future time. Therefore, they try to remember the defect and its location when they pass by. But it is not easy to remember all the details.

The attempt to provide mobile technology support does not yet account for these constraints. Currently, the driver has to be at the same geographical place as the defect to make a comprehensive report. He also has to stop the vehicle, since it is impossible to report while driving. He has to punch several keys on a keyboard as well as read the manual to find the appropriate code. As a consequence he often refrains from filing a report.

If a report is filed into the system, the inspectors lose all access to the information. It follows that it is difficult to see if the defect is already reported. There is still a need to save information about the defect for a later moment. In these cases the inspectors write Post-it notes to support their memory.

We further argue that memorization tends to individualize the performance of work tasks since it is difficult to share that kind of information with someone else. The inspectors try to identify and repair as an individual task as much as possible and keep all their knowledge in their heads.

This leads to a situation where the databases consist almost entirely of identified defects that have already been taken care of, and where the possibility to use the mobile system to plan future work and delegation is practically non-existent. The sharing of knowledge on the road network is at a minimum in a situation where the orderer and the contractors of inspection, as well as traffic information centers are demanding even more exhaustive information to conduct their work properly.

However, Post-it notes are not sufficient for their work. The good thing about these notes is that you can hand them over to someone when you meet, and you can use them to prepare a future inspection tour. It is also possible to easily describe the situation in the road inspectors' own terms with due sensitivity to the situation. The bad thing is that inspectors cannot drive and write at the same time. They are also difficult to distribute, and lack the qualities of a universal positioning system like GPS. Furthermore, they do not help in planning a stop during an on-going inspection tour. Mobile phones suffer from similar problems since they demand that the driver either stop at the location of the problem to get enough time to get in contact and account for the situation, or rely on a Post-it note if the call is made from somewhere else.

6.3 The PlaceMemo Application

We argue that a system that accounts for the context of use, as described above, could increase the number of reports and amount of communication, and thus strengthen the possibilities for articulation and collaboration. Accordingly, the organization would receive better knowledge of the identified defects and the work could be planned in other ways, e.g., new forms of job sharing and job rotation. A simplified method of creating annotations would probably lead to more reports of defects which have not yet been taken care of. We conceive of a service which could be used as in the following scenario:

> When the infrastructure manager drives his daily inspection tour, he spots a damaged road sign. However, the traffic situation does not allow him to stop immediately. Instead he uses PlaceMemo to save the geographical position and record a voice-memo, so that he won't forget about it. Later the same week, before heading out on the same stretch of road, he listens through the memos. The map gives him a rough idea of where the reported malfunction is situated, and by listening to the voice-memo he knows what equipment to bring. Back on the road he focuses on identifying new faults. When approaching the location of the broken road sign, he can hear the memo just before he reaches the broken sign. He gently decreases the speed of the truck and comes to a halt without jeopardizing other drivers' safety, and then gets out to mend the sign.

To support these issues, we propose the following five design requirements. First, we suggest a system in which voice-memos are associated with geographical positions. Such a system would demand less of the user in terms of activities at the location of the defect, considering that the inspector is occupied with driving and keeping an eye on the surrounding traffic. Still it is essential to save the geographical position of the problem to be handled. Consequently, the interaction with the computer should be limited while driving. We believe that it should be possible to create annotations while driving in the form of voice recordings associated with certain geographical locations. Second, the system should support several work tasks. The current system is designed to support the preparation of administrative documents, i.e., formal reports, which are essential when giving an account of what has been done. This focus leaves out the support for inspection as a dynamically changing and ongoing activity, which also explains the limited usage of the system. We believe that the use of audio-recordings connected to geographical positions has the possibility to become a more integrated tool for inspection work. To fit with current practice, i.e., the articulation work, it is essential that the system should handle different forms of information, such as both situated and contingent ways of representing defects as well as the filing of data according to the formal organizational requirements. Voice-recordings are easier to do and less restricted in terms of vocabulary than predefined coding schemes. Third, the system needs to support the inspectors' individual work tasks, and not just communicate the results. The inspector needs to prepare for the inspection tour by bringing certain equipment. Before heading out on the road, he will have the possibility to retrieve a list of all recorded memos, and choose the ones he wants to listen through. While on the road, he should be reminded about upcoming defects before arriving at the specific location. Thus, the system should include two modes, one for stationary use only, with greater freedom of choice and possibilities for interaction, and a second mode for driving, where the human–computer interaction is of limited scope, with easy reporting and automatic triggering of voice-memos. Fourth, it needs to be very easy to report. To achieve a higher number of reports in the present reporting system, the suggested system should act as a supporting tool in the formal reporting procedure, since the latter will be saved for a better occasion than driving on the highway. The inspector could, e.g., listen through and code the voice messages during a break; i.e., he will import the reported data into the present system. This could be done with the computer in the vehicle, but also between the suggested system and the central database. Finally, we believe that delegation could be performed on more suitable occasions. The recorded information is a support when calling a colleague, as a starting point for discussing the delegation of a task. Alternatively, the voice memos and corresponding coordinates could be shared among chosen colleagues.

6.3.1 Implementation

PlaceMemo (see Fig. 6.2) is a prototype service designed to meet the requirements above. It is based on handheld mobile devices running the Pocket PC operating system. In this specific implementation it uses a handheld computer (a so-called PDA) and a GPS-receiver to achieve the positioning. The configuration allows the users to record voice memos connected to geographical locations. The flexibility of

Fig. 6.2 The functionality of
the PlaceMemo prototype in
map mode

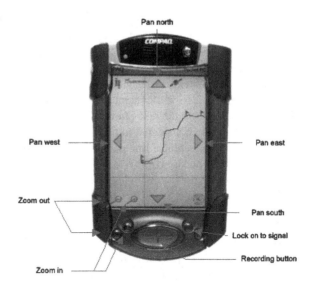

Pan north

Pan west

Pan east

Zoom out

Pan south

Lock on to signal

Recording button

Zoom in

the voice format gives the user the freedom to articulate messages according to the specific situation at hand.

The prototype has two modes: placing and triggering, and memo administration. Placing and triggering are designed to be employed on the road. Administrative functionalities can be far more visually demanding and are conceived as being used in situations where the user can concentrate more specifically on the device, such as prior to an inspection, during a break, or when the inspection is completed. The primary objective for the user in this context will be to remotely access information regarding a certain area.

In order to annotate places outside the vehicle, the user presses the recording-button once (see Fig. 6.2). This normally occurs while driving and inspecting. Looking for defects while driving, requires that the driver stay focused on the outside environment. Hence the device must be designed so that it can be used in these situations with no or only limited demands on the user's visual attention. A geographical position is immediately saved, and a voice memo can be recorded by pushing the button. The system will play the voice memo the next time a previously marked location is approached. Finally, the memos are played just before reaching the precise position, accounting for the speed of the vehicle and the length of the recording.

6.4 Location-Based Information Systems

Our proposed concept is influenced by research on location-based information systems. It has been argued that many context-aware applications apply an inflexible view of context. The focus has been on the challenges of how to use and combine input from different sensors, as well as how to provide the users with accurate information, and how to manage and classify the data (Dourish 2004). A majority of the systems are designed with a proactive approach, where the developers attempt to make the technologies more sensitive to the details of specific settings of use by incorporating contextual dependencies. Many systems rely on information produced by semi-professional content providers, such as in the case of campus and city guides (Abowd et al. 1997; Cheverest et al. 2000), or guidebooks (Grinter et al. 2002). The users are considered to be passive recipients, rather than active producers of content. The technical implementations are mostly too inflexible, and fail to address the users' needs. However, there are a number of applications which are designed to provide the user with high flexibility in the use of the system. Examples include the Cyber-guide (Abowd et al. 1997), comMotion (Marmasse and Schmandt 2000), Guide (Cheverest 2000), CybreMinder (Dey and Abowd 2000), Geonotes (Espinoza et al. 2001), and a reporting tool for fieldworkers (Pascoe et al. 2000).

The comMotion-system is supposed to be used in a geographically extensive area. The geographical coordinates are tagged as recognizable places, such as "home" and "work," with the help of the user. The system thereby attempts to handle the complexity of understanding the abstract figures of longitude and latitude. The main feature of the system is its location-learning agent. Once a location has been defined, a to-do list is associated with it, either by voice or text. The system also provides the possibility to subscribe to different information services (Marmasse and Schmandt 2000).

The CybreMinder-system permits the user to create reminders which can be triggered by more complex conditions including, e.g., relative time, other users' availability, or the status of the stock market (Dey and Abowd 2000). These systems provides the user with a relatively high degree of freedom as to what to augment, both in the sense of locations and content. By locating the user, predefined information is either excluded or made available at the corresponding locations. However, the reminder- and communication-systems rely on the users as active producers of content. Based on a number of variables they provide the users with specified information, and geographical location plays an important role in this provision of data. Current attention is also directed towards generic problems of organizing information (Persson et al. 2002), seeing as it is conceivable that the electronic spaces would be overfilled with information.

In general, available location-based information systems are designed as multipurpose tools, demanding too much computer–human interaction from the user for a driving context. The functionality and the user interface in these systems are heavily influenced by a stationary setting, with the screen as a main source of textual in- and output. The specific activities studied in this case demand a stronger focus on interaction while driving. The main objective of the proposed design implications is not only to handle reminders. The information stored in the intended system should support interaction with specific colleagues. Earlier research has instead focused on design for public broadcast, which is based on central storage of data. The design implications presented suggest a redesign of the current system, to integrate informal actions into the formal reporting tool. We focus on the support of manual work, integrating loosely coupled methods of recalling, delegating, and informing about actual contingencies. The road inspectors will have the possibility to provide an augmentation of the physical environment by recording PlaceMemos and making them retrievable for other people, i.e., colleagues, present in the physical environment. The system does not force the messages to fit into a predefined shape; the limitation lies in the form of voice-messages connected to geographical positions. These positions will be recorded in the form of GPS-coordinates. Thus the messages are easy to access, since all the inspection vehicles are bound to the roads even if their area of operation is widely geographically dispersed.

6.5 The Users' Initial Experiences

Esbjörnsson (2006) has evaluated the prototype. We allowed three professional road users, who were working with various forms of road inspection, to try it out. We wanted their opinions on the usefulness of the system, but also to get feedback on our design assumptions. They were supposed to use the prototype freely for a limited period of time while working on the road in their vehicles. They could choose between having the device on the passenger seat, or mounted in a temporary holder on the dashboard. To increase the volume of the memos an external speaker was connected to the device. We interviewed them in conjunction with the trial. The interviews and the voice-memos have been transcribed and coded, i.e., categorized into a set of themes. The coding scheme evolved while working with the material, and has been a necessary tool for analyzing the material. The level of detail has been chosen with reference to the claims we are making.

We were especially concerned with the possibility of generating place memos while driving. In previous chapters, we have discussed how drivers perform working tasks while driving with their mobile phones, and other studies have shown how navigation systems are used in conjunction with driving (Johansson and Pettersson 2001). However, this application is different, since the task requires focused attention on the physical surroundings as well as on the maneuvering. However, the test person, John, felt safe using it.

> Whatever you are doing I consider this to be really safe to perform while driving, in comparison to other solutions, where you have to focus on the device while pushing several buttons. You just push one button and talk. . .On the highways you have to follow the traffic flow, which means that you have to go at 90 km/h. Like on the E4 through Stockholm, there are no possibilities to stop to report the position. You must do it on the move.

John also argued that voice recordings provide him with a greater freedom of expressiveness than systems with predefined codes: "In comparison to writing a memo, the chance to say something is greater."

We were also concerned with the possibility of retrieving memos, irrespective of being at the geographical location or not. The system relies on the general idea that users will benefit from creating and listening to personal memos. These are played automatically when in the proximity of the position of the recording, but are also possible to browse while at remote locations to give an overview of upcoming tasks. Peter was driving at 80 km/h when a memo was played.

The sound starts so early that I can decrease the speed and take a closer look.

He is satisfied with the timing of the memo playback. The memos were played in their entirety before the vehicle arrived at the position where they had been recorded. The calculation of message length and current speed fitted with the driving situation. This gave him time to react: either to stop, or, as in this case, at least to lower the speed and take a closer look. After passing a few more memos, he commented on the precision.

The memo is played approximately 200 meters in advance; that's reasonable. I don't think the precision is so important, because you are always describing the position in the voice-memo.

He is not so concerned about the accuracy of the triggering of the audio files. It does not need to be just ahead of the location, since he gets leeway from his own geographical referencing in the audio recording.

Peter is not as satisfied, however, with the administrative support for the memos. The simplicity of creating new memos leads to a large stock in the database, which can make the next inspection tours rather tedious, with recurring presentation of old files.

It's a bit so-so. When you record all these memos, there is a signal every time you pass the position. In some cases you pass the areas quite often, and it is really annoying hearing these sounds.

The handling of old messages, e.g., deleting them, is more complex in the system than creating new ones. This is done while stationary, since the memos must be marked in map-mode, and thereafter deleted in list-mode. Additionally, during the trial we found that identifying each memo in map-mode was a complicated task. Despite having said they were easy to find, Tomas had obvious problems doing so during the interview.

In general, the ways in which the memos map onto the geography are another crucial aspect of the design. The concept of associating voice-memos with geographical locations appealed to the participants in the field trial. Two users had previously been using tape-recorders to save voice-recordings while driving, however with no geographical connection. This was helpful to how they perceived PlaceMemo as a tool for associating voice-memos with geographical positions. Accordingly, there were no difficulties for them to understand the concept. In practice, some problems occurred with the underlying model of memos being linked to a single GPS-position mark. We had expected them to be interested in delimited road-side objects, such as a small hole in a fence or an abandoned car. But it turned out that they were sometimes interested in much larger objects, such as in the following example, and had to find workarounds to use our system. They also reflected on the appropriate geographical referencing when sharing the memos with other people. Here, the GPS coordinates were not sufficient. They argued that colleagues need additional information to locate the defects.

To sum up, the test subjects used the system for personal reminders as well as for formal inventories. This disparity in incentives for usage led to a variation in the levels of detail in their recorded memos. The system lacked support for the current practice of filing standardized forms. Nevertheless, it supported the users by reminding them of previously reported defects. The feature of playing the memos in advance of the geographical positions was appreciated. Unfortunately, when located elsewhere the ease-of-access to memos was insufficient. The memos were difficult to identify without the use of a proper detailed map providing an overview, and the controls for zooming in and out were difficult to handle. Nevertheless, an important aspect was that the test subjects used the system in the car while driving, either with the device on the passenger seat, or with a temporary holder on the dashboard. The design seemed to fit with their practice, seeing how they used it for a wide variety of tasks. The recording of, as well as the listening to geographically bounded voice-memos took place as intended. The users understood and benefited from the positioning functionality. They all seemed to agree that it was possible to record and save data while on the move. The level of acceptance of the system varied according to the level of formalized procedures in their current organization of work. The trial displayed the different reasons for performing inspections, in which the level of precision, and description of places, vary depending on the task.

6.6 Conclusion

The study of road inspection provides an interesting window on our design space. Road inspectors constitute an advanced form of road users who spend a considerable amount of time on the road. They are equipped with mobile technologies and have the road context as the object of their work. However, our close study reveals interactional adaptation of mobile device use and driving in a very rudimentary form. They just park their large vehicles before interacting with the computer.

Road inspectors are both similar to and different from everyday drivers. Like an ordinary commuter they scan the roadside to identify obstructions. They do this as part of their work tasks, thereby differing from ordinary drivers who just want to avoid accidents. The inspectors' interpretations of the road context are also situated, which is in line with our study at the driving school. For example, the inspector was unsure regarding the interpretation of a red car as either abandoned, and therefore an obstruction, or just parked for a while. The study also showed how this interpretative work was done in collaboration with colleagues within the organization. Hence, although the interpretation of roadside obstructions can be seen as an individual work task, it includes collaborative articulation. Furthermore, there was an ambition to share their knowledge on the state of the highway system. Thus, systems that support the sharing of information on roadside obstructions might gain from supporting both flexible articulation among several people and the vague and undecided phases where the individual inspector makes his interpretation.

Technically, we have shown that it is possible to design a system which supports such articulation. More important, by allowing simple interaction with the device by clicking on a button, and focusing on voice interaction, we have made it possible to use at the same time as driving. Thus, we support a form of interactional adaptation in conjunction with driving that is similar to the way many people use their mobile phones. This greatly expands the benefits of the technical support for road inspection. In the following we will show how these experiences could be extended to much broader road-user groups.

References

Abowd GD, Atkeson CG, Hong J et al (1997) Cyberguide: a mobile context-aware tour guide. Wirel Networks 3(5):421–433

Bertelsen OW, Bødker S (2001) Cooperation in massively distributed information spaces. In: Proceedings of the seventh European conference on computer supported cooperative work, ECSCW'01, Bonn, Germany, pp. 1–17

Cheverst K, Davies N, Mitchell et al (2000) Developing a context-aware electronic tourist guide: some issues and experiences. In: Proceedings of the SIGCHI conference on human factors in computing systems—CHI'00, The Hague, The Netherlands, pp 17–24

Dey KA, Abowd GD (2000) CybreMinder: a context-aware system for supporting reminders. In: Proceedings of the second international symposium on handheld and ubiquitous computing, HUC'00. Bristol, UK

Dourish P (2004) What we talk about when we talk about context. Personal Ubiquitous Comput 8(1):19–30

Esbjörnsson M (2006) From ethnography on infrastructure management to initial user feedback on PlaceMemo. Personal Ubiquitous Comput (Theme issue on Interactive Mobile Information Access). 10(4):195–204

Esbjörnsson M, Juhlin O (2002) PlaceMemo—supporting mobile articulation in a vast working area through position based information. In: Proceedings of ECIS'02—the 10th European conference on information systems. Wydawnictwo Uniwersytetu Gdanskiego, Gdansk, pp 1185–1196

Espinoza F, Persson P, Sandin A et al (2001) GeoNotes: social and navigational aspects of location-based information systems. In: Proceedings of the third international conference on ubiquitous computing—Ubicomp'01, Atlanta, Georgia, USA, pp 2–17

Grinter RE, Aoki PM, Hurst A et al (2002) Revisiting the visit: understanding how technology can shape the museum visit. In: Proceedings of the 2002 ACM conference on computer supported cooperative work—CSCW'02, New Orleans, LA, USA, pp 146–155

Grudin J (1994). Groupware and social dynamics: eight challenges for developers. Commun ACM 37(1):92–105

Johansson M, Pettersson M (2001) Activity and artifact: the symbiosis of truck drivers' work and navigational systems. In: Proceedings of interact'01—IFIP TC. 13 international conference on human–computer interaction. IOS Press, Tokyo, pp 399–407

Juhlin O, Vesterlind D (2001) Supporting bus driver collaboration: new services for public transport management. In: Proceedings of eighth ITS world congress. Ertico, Madrid

Luff P, Heath C (1998) Mobility in collaboration. In: Proceedings of the 1998 ACM conference on computer supported cooperative work—CSCW'98, Seattle, WA, pp 305–314

Mantovani G (1996) New communication environments—from everyday to virtual. Taylor & Francis Ltd, London

Marmasse N, Schmandt C (2000) Location-aware information delivery with comMotion. In: Proceedings of the second international symposium on handheld and ubiquitous computing—HUC'00, Bristol, UK, pp 157–171

Nilsson J, Sokoler T, Binder et al (2000) Beyond the control room—mobile devices for spatially distributed interaction on industrial process. In: Proceedings of the second international symposium on handheld and ubiquitous computing—HUC'00, Bristol, UK

Orr J (1996) Talking about machines. ILR Press, Ithaca

Pascoe J, Ryan N, Morse D (2000) Using while moving: HCI issues in fieldwork environments. ACM Trans Comput Hum Interact–(TOCHI). 7(3):417–437

Persson P, Espinoza F, Fagerberg P et al (2002) GeoNotes: a location-based information system for public spaces. In: Höök K, Benyon D, Munro A (eds) Readings in social navigation of information space. Springer, Berlin, pp 151–173

Pinelle D, Gutwin C (2003) Designing for loose coupling in mobile groups. In: Proceedings of the international ACM SIGGROUP conference on supporting group work. Sanibel Island, FL pp 75–84

Schmidt K, Simone C (1996) Coordination mechanisms: towards a conceptual foundation of CSCW systems design. Comput Support Coop Work J Collab Comput 5(2–3):155–200

Suchman L (1987) Plans and situated actions: the problem of human–machine communication. Cambridge University Press, Cambridge

Wiberg M (2001) In between mobile meetings: exploring seamless ongoing interaction support for mobile CSCW. PhD thesis, Umeå University, Department of Informatics, Sweden

Chapter 7
Road Talk: A Public Roadside Location-Dependent Audio Message System

Previously we have discussed how social interaction among drivers is strongly connected to the vitality and access of urban life.[1] Drivers need to find ways to agree on how to share specific sections of the road, both to avoid accidents as well as to ensure that they will reach their destinations. In Chapter 2 we argued that the way people agree on how to share the road space could be understood as a negotiation which depends on the contingencies of every situation. Such interaction occurs in encounters which are often short, due to the speed of the vehicles. Further, the interaction is also influenced by the drivers' being inside their cars made of steel and glass. This somewhat constrains the possibility to look at each other, but most importantly the possibility for aural interaction. We have also argued that new technologies might make it possible to transcend current practical restrictions of time and place, that is, expand the interaction to situations where drivers are out of sight of each other, and provide new media by which they can communicate. Since the social interaction occurs as a situated activity, system design should recognize the drivers as experts, and not enforce any specific way of settling the social negotiations on road space. In the following we will discuss a specific problem in driving concerning how the current restrictions make it difficult to share information between drivers, and how new technologies could be used to support such activities.

Drivers wish to have adequate knowledge about the state of upcoming stretches of road before getting there. During any trip the driver moves forward into unfamiliar situations. Take, for instance, a bend in the road followed by a section which is suddenly obstructed. Most of the time the driver would safely travel beyond this bend assuming that nothing unexpected will appear. But this assumption might be a mistake if the oncoming section has undergone a drastic change. The driver could be heading towards the tail of a traffic queue, or road construction work, instead of an open and unobstructed highway. A hazard could also be less dramatic, e.g., when children are playing dangerously close to the road. All of these situations can have a negative impact on traffic safety, and the driver can more easily deal with the situation if he or she is forewarned.

---

[1] An expanded version of this chapter has been published as Östergren and Juhlin (2005). Reprinted from the publication with permission from Rinton Press.

O. Juhlin, *Social Media on the Road*, Computer Supported Cooperative Work 50,
DOI 10.1007/978-1-84996-332-9_7, © Springer-Verlag London Limited 2010

Here the limitations of beneficial social interaction are particularly salient. Every driver who passes the bend has to make the same discovery for herself, even though she has probably passed several drivers coming the other way who already knew about it, but were unable to tell her. Here we see how emergent mobile technologies provide new resources to enable the sharing of information. But it also provides possibilities for improving on such systems, drawing on our experiences when we developed the previously discussed PlaceMemo application.

7.1 The Use of Speed Trap Message Systems

Our work is further motivated by a statistical study of commercially available message systems. As discussed in Chapter 4, car drivers already communicate by various means to achieve smooth coordination. The most obvious is the use of turn signals. Occasionally they also communicate by other means, e.g., by blinking the headlights to warn oncoming drivers of a hazard. Still it is not evident that drivers would use mobile technologies to help each other in more elaborate ways. Nor is it obvious that they would require any new technology to do it. The statistical analysis of existing speed trap message system gives an initial understanding of the needs of drivers to communicate roadside events using mobile technologies. It also gives a rough impression of when and where these messages occur, which in turn tells us where roadside events worth communicating happen.

The purpose of the commercially available systems is to let subscribers warn each other about speed traps with short text messages. A speed trap is an activity taking place by the roadside, where the police monitor compliance with speed limits by manual means. They stand by the road and measure the speed of passing vehicles with radar or laser equipment. The purpose of the *speed trap message systems*, which are available in many countries, is to allow drivers to warn each other of their occurrence. Drivers can report through various means, e.g., SMS, wap, the web, or by phoning to a call center. A subscriber to such a service receives these warnings on his mobile phone as text messages.

Our concern is not to improve speed trap systems per se. In a sense these particular services are counter-productive to police work and therefore immoral. Instead we are interested in these systems as a particular, and peculiar, example of services aiming to help drivers help each other. They are of interest since they are message systems allowing people to communicate knowledge about roadside events. Besides, warning of speed traps is not always counterproductive to traffic *safety*. Occasionally, advance knowledge of a speed trap complies with the intentions of the police. This is obvious since the police themselves reveal the time and location of the speed trap on their website, and on local radio. Finally, it must be stressed that it is not illegal in any of the countries studied to report or subscribe to speed trap messages.

In the following, we present a brief overview of four speed trap services and the messages they contain. The statistics provide us with an understanding of the quantity, location, temporal distribution, structure, and content of the messages. We collected messages from the public web pages of the service operators over a period of roughly 5 months, from 10 October 2003 to 3 March 2004. In total we downloaded 6,140 messages. This data does not accurately tell us how many people who actually received the messages. Nevertheless we believe that the speed trap message systems were actually used for receiving messages in this period. For instance, the number of subscribers of one particular service was about 1,500, according to one operator's website.

A user subscribes to messages about speed traps that occur in a specific region. We have found that the messages were located in no less than 644 such regions of Denmark, Norway, and Sweden. The messages are unevenly distributed, and the top 20 regions have about 31% of all the messages. At the very top we find urban regions corresponding to larger cities in Scandinavia: Bergen/Hordaland (198), Göteborg (186), København (170), Stockholm (154), and Trondheim/Sør-Trøndelag (141).[2]

The messages are *temporally distributed* over a day as shown in Fig. 7.1. The analysis yields a pattern where the most frequent activity occurs between 9 a.m. and around 6 p.m. There is a distinct peak at noon. The message frequency seems to decrease from about 6 p.m. and vanishes altogether at four in the morning. The average number of messages per days is 42, but the average number is higher during workdays than on weekends.

We have also more closely examined the wording of the first 416 messages. The messages had a common three-part *structure*. The first part is a brief description of the activity, e.g., stating the occurrence of a police checkpoint. At times, the activity description includes a description of the type of checkpoint, e.g., whether the police are enforcing speed limits, safety-belt use, or permitted vehicle weight. The type is sometimes implicit in the reference to the particular instrument the police are using, such as "laser" or "photo-vehicle," which are used for enforcing speed limits. Second, the message provides a reference to the location where this activity occurs, such as "Roskilde street in Vipperød beside gas station 100–150 meters after city sign." Finally, the message occasionally includes the impact of the activity,

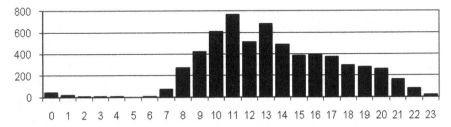

Fig. 7.1 Temporal distribution of messages over 24 h

[2]It may seem surprising not to find Oslo in the top five. After all it is the largest city in Norway. The reason is that it was divided into smaller regions. Accordingly, there are six smaller regions that together cover Oslo, and collectively they had 173 messages.

Table 7.1 Examples of speed trap warning messages

Original message	English translation
HOLBÆK FOTOVOGN PÅ ROSKILDEVEJ I VIPPERØD LIGE VED TANKSTATION 100-150 METER INDENFOR BYSKILT	Holback photo-vehicle at Roskilde street in Vipperød beside gas station 100-150 meter within city sign
Laser på E4 i höjd med Bölesjön	Laser at E4 around Lake Böle
KONTROLL PÅ E39 CA 2 KM ETTER SØYLANDSKIOSKEN RETNING STAVANGER.	Inspection at road E39, about 2 kilometers after the kiosk at Søyland heading Stavanger

e.g., informing drivers that a particular road is closed. Further, we found that as many as 12% of the messages do not concern speed traps at all, but report accidents, weather conditions, etc. This is a surprisingly high rate since the members pay to receive speed trap warnings and are probably averse to messages concerning other topics. Nevertheless people do post such messages and they get through the system. We believe this indicates that users also perceive a need to share information about other topics than speed trap warnings (Table 7.1).

The messages are most frequent during the daylight hours on weekdays and occur mostly in urban regions. The messages coincide more or less with the times and places where traffic is most intense. However, a closer look at the distribution over the day reveals that they are not especially frequent during morning and afternoon rush-hour traffic, when people commute to and from work. Thus it seems that the users of the speed trap message systems are not ordinary commuters, but people who do work by driving, e.g., delivery and taxi drivers.

To sum up, our statistical study of such messages shows that people are interested in sharing information about this particular type of roadside events using mobile technologies but also concerning other topics than speed traps. We also found that messages are most frequent during the day in urban areas.

7.2 Message Systems in Research

The work presented here is related to research on *message systems*, i.e., research on technologies that enable people to send and receive messages *asynchronously*. A message is a piece of information in some particular form, for example, text, graphics, sound, or a combination of all three (Borghoff and Schlichter 2000). We use the term "messaging" to refer to the actions of sending and receiving messages, and otherwise engaging with such systems.

Messaging occurs in many shapes and contexts from stationary to mobile systems using a wide set of technologies. The most widely spread messaging applications today are based on Internet technology. It is undeniable that e-mail, instant messaging (Isaacs et al. 2002; Nardi et al. 2000), blogs, and chats (Bradner et al. 1999;

Norton and Bass 1987) have contributed to its popularity. The work presented here is particularly related to mobile message systems, which today are also a widespread phenomenon. In Europe sending messages with the Short Message Service (SMS) available though GSM mobile phones is a huge phenomenon (Grinter and Eldrige 2001). Similarly, in Japan, using mobile phones to do e-mail messaging is a widespread practice (Masui and Takabayashi 2003).

Mobile message systems allow messaging anytime and anywhere when the users are away from their desktop PC. However, many mundane messages concern a particular spatial context and the location accordingly gives additional meaning to them. For example a sign outside a grocery shop stating "buy strawberries here!" obviously indicates that "here" should be interpreted as that grocery shop and nothing else (see Chapter 10). As we discussed in the previous chapter, there are several research projects in the context-aware computing domain that aim to bring such context information into mobile messaging (Burell and Gay 2002; Espinoza et al. 2001; Griswold et al. 2002). Typically, these systems explore an extension of the notion of the message and couple a physical location to a body of text. This, in turn, lets the user interact with the messages in a literally mobile fashion. When users roaming the physical world happen to coincide with the location of a message, it becomes available. Typically the message "pops up" in the graphical user interface. This is still an emerging field and the benefits are still questionable. For instance, in the evaluations of E-graffiti (Burell and Gay 2002) and GeoNotes (Persson and Fagerberg 2002) it was found that the users often mistook the systems for chats, and entered messages with no significance to actual places. This might be due the systems being so similar as to be mistaken for standard chats and blogs. This is most obvious with the GeoNotes application, where positioning was based on access to wireless base stations. Such positioning could not discriminate between locations within the base station range, and the users had to specify the particular location with so called "place labels," i.e., textual descriptions entered in a specific field. Messages in discussion forum often have structural information fields too but for other purposes such as "subject," "topic," or "group," etc. Consequently the place-label field was used to indicate a topic not necessarily concerning a place, which indicates that GeoNotes was basically approached as a forum.

Furthermore, mobile location-dependent messengers of the context-aware domain are primarily designed for pedestrians. These systems are intended for people walking around, whereas our intention is to design for car driving. Walking and driving are, of course, related. In both cases you have to plan ahead and make sure you remain on the decided course to avoid bumping into others. However, they differ greatly in terms of how and at what speed movement occurs. Hence, a driver has to pay more attention to how and where he or she is moving than a walking person.

Finally, common to all of the above-mentioned systems is that the users always have access to the messages and rely on the assumption that opportunities for networking and distributing messages are ubiquitously present. However, there are many other research projects, similar to Road Talk, which investigate situations where communication opportunities are expected to be intermittent for various reasons. Pollen Networking (Glance et al. 2001) is an example of mobile messaging where distribution is achieved by people's physical movement, typically in an office, and messages are transferred through physical contact or at very short ranges between devices.

7.3 The Road Talk Concept

Road Talk is designed to distribute knowledge on the state of the roads from one driver to another. With Road Talk an obstruction would hopefully only surprise the first driver to the scene (see Fig. 1.1 and scenario in Chapter 1). She could then record a warning which would be automatically spread to other drivers that she encounters. It is a message system for car drivers enabling them to annotate the roadside with voice messages. A message in Road Talk is constituted by audio recordings, or voice memos, together with a location reference, in a similar way to the previously discussed PlaceMemo application. When a memo is recorded, it is simultaneously associated with a GPS position (Fig. 7.2).

The statistical analysis of speed trap systems yielded that messages roughly occur when and where traffic is dense. Therefore the Road Talk concept is a good candidate for using wireless *mobile* ad hoc *networking* (MANET) and *epidemic diffusion* to distribute the memos. First, we can use the physical movement of cars and wireless networking of limited range to perform transfers when cars meet to distribute data. In this way, messages move in traffic with the cars, and "hop" from car to car when networking becomes available in those encounters. The use of such MANET technology is appealing for distributing messages in Road Talk, as it requires very little infrastructure to operate. In fact, it only needs the PDAs and the networking interfaces they contain to form a fast and cheap distribution method. Second, the message distribution in Road Talk can be classified as an epidemic information diffusion process (Khelil et al. 2002). Such a process shares some similarities with how diseases like influenza spread among populations. Viruses spread when an infected

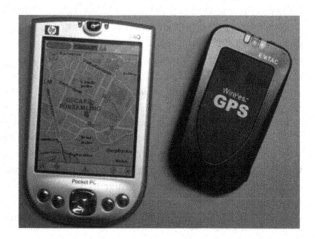

Fig. 7.2 An HP Ipaq 4,150 PDA and a Bluetooth GPS Receiver (**a**). Screen shots of Road Talk. (**b**) Map with squares indicating locations of memos

person encounters someone who is not yet infected. The spreading becomes epidemic when a large number of people are infected. Epidemic processes are well understood and describe many phenomena besides diseases, for example the adoption of high-technology products (Norton and Bass 1987) and information diffusion in MANETs (Khelil et al. 2002). What is particularly interesting about epidemic diffusion in MANETs is that there exists an optimal node density yielding an optimal diffusion speed. Khelil et al. (2002) found, through a simulation of a distribution scheme that resembles Road Talk, an optimal node density of 620 nodes per square kilometer. Their findings are not directly applicable to Road Talk as they are based on "artificial" simulations that only vaguely resemble traffic flow and wireless communication on streets. Nevertheless, this metric gives a crude estimate of the density of Road Talk units needed to achieve a satisfactory spreading of memos, and considering actual statistics on the number of cars in an urban region, the number is surprisingly low. For example, in 2003 there were about 278,500 cars registered in the municipality of Stockholm (Stockholm 2005) and the municipality is responsible for roughly 16 square kilometers of streets. This being the case, there would be about 17,400 cars per square kilometer, if the cars were evenly spread out on the streets. Hence only about 3.6% (or about 10,000) of the total number of cars would need to have Road Talk to achieve an optimal node density of 620.

7.3.1 Design that Accommodates Driving

The speed trap message systems have been somewhat successful among people who drive for a living. Still, there is room for considerable improvement, especially concerning the possibility to adapt the interaction with the device to the interaction with other road users. Existing speed trap systems are not well adapted for in-vehicle use. It is almost impossible, and definitely unsafe, to write an SMS on a mobile phone when driving. Thus, as in the study of the road inspectors' present systems, the driver needs to stop the vehicle to communicate. Since that will probably not happen until the driver reaches her destination, the information will be lacking in temporal accuracy. The temporal and spatial distance between identifying an event and reporting it, will also affect the possibility to remember details of the event and report them adequately. Thus, the design of the Road Talk message system must specifically accommodate driving in order to be useable.

The design approach we have taken is guided by the principles that governed the design of infrastructure management support for driving road inspectors: the PlaceMemo prototype, which was presented in the previous chapter. This prototype shows that it is possible to create a user interface that allows audio messaging while driving.

7.3.2 Design Requirements for Road Talk

The arguments above are summarized as a set of requirements for an improved service for messaging about roadside events between drivers in traffic. We suggest that sharing messages should *concern roadside events*. The quantity of speed trap messages indicates that there are location-dependent topics interesting for drivers to share with the use of mobile technologies. The system should support the creation of messages concerning a *broad span of topics*. We interpret the fact that other types of information occurred in as many as 12% of the examined messages as an indication that there are many other roadside topics of interest for drivers. An improved service should allow for as many types of messages as possible in a flexible manner. The messages should be *distributed epidemically* among drivers. Speed trap messages use SMS and GSM mobile phones. SMS communication is costly and does not provide any service guarantees. However, based on mobile ad hoc networking technology we may achieve epidemic distribution that would be free and potentially very efficient given a certain level of deployment. The system should *accommodate driving* as well as handling the system, i.e., lend itself to interactional adaptation. Speed trap message systems are text based, which conflicts with driving. It is thus paradoxical that a service that distributes information about the roads is practically inaccessible while driving. The PlaceMemo prototype is an example of a design that allows interacting while driving. Essentially it shows that audio-based interaction is clearly feasible when driving and much preferred over text-based. Finally, the messages should be *accurately positioned* in the vicinity of the reported events. Text-based messages are appropriate for planning a trip in advance, but can hardly be used to provide accurate warning when the driver is approaching a place where a roadside event is occurring. A design similar to PlaceMemo would also be applicable for Road Talk. Still, giving users an opportunity to plan ahead and avoid hazards altogether is an important aspect and should be taken into consideration.

7.4 Implementation

The RoadTalk prototype is implemented on a Pocket PC operating system. Most importantly, the application consists of the *Monger library*, which deals with the recording, playing, and sharing of memos. Memo sharing is accomplished over wireless single-hop ad hoc networks using popular standards such as XML and HTTP. It is carefully designed to react to fleeting connection opportunities and transient links caused by the rapid motion and the limited range of wireless radio transmitters. The application relies on a peer-to-peer system architecture, which means in practice that each node is equally capable of exchanging and processing information. Furthermore, the system is fully distributed; that is, it requires no external infrastructure to operate. This approach allows a peer to establish network connectivity autonomously, which fits the brief constellation of nodes of the wireless ad hoc network. The links over which these information exchange transfers are performed are furthermore not expected to be persistent or predictable. Nodes are not expected to stay in range of each other's transmitters for long. However, sometimes they do, which would allow for extended networking opportunities.

The implementation of memo sharing has in itself two key components: Rapid Mutual Peer Discovery (RMPD), and the Monger Diffusion Scheme. The RMPD module is responsible for monitoring the presence of other nodes in wireless reach and is designed to rapidly discover changes. Furthermore the aim is to provide mutual discovery. In other protocols, such as Jini, UPnP, and SLP, discovery is strictly one-sided. These protocols are designed for a client discovering some resources, but not the other way around. The resources are never assumed to be interested in discovering the clients. The RMPD is based on repeated pings, and whenever it hears a new ping a node echoes a "pong."

The Monger Diffusion Scheme synchronizes memos among peers in a wireless ad hoc network as a two-step process. First, whenever RMPD discovers a peer it downloads a database of the memos stored on that peer. Second, the monger downloads each memo it is not currently storing.

7.4.1 Initial Prototype Performance Evaluations

It is not obvious that Road Talk is technically feasible. After all, the hardware we used here is intended for indoor office settings where people at most walk about. Therefore, we decided to examine the prototype performance in terms of sharing memos in mobile situations. First we recorded 22 memos together with the memo database constituting 92 kb of data. We kept one PDA with Road Talk stationary and drove by at various speeds with another installed in a car. The PDAs were used "as is" and *no* extra equipment, such as range-extending antennas, was used. In the first ten drive-bys we kept a speed of about 50–60 km/h and cleared the stationary PDA of downloaded memos for every second run. Altogether we had five complete downloads and one failure. This also means that for four drive-by runs there was no download operation simply because the synchronization was complete. We then increased the speed to about 80 km/h and cleared the stationary Road Talk of memos for each complete download. At this speed the download immediately failed once. At the time, we believed this was due to some signal path problems caused by an elevation in the road. When we moved the stationary PDA about 100 m to the crest, downloading worked for three straight runs at this velocity. We then increased the speed to about 100 km/h and performed a successful download.

7.5 Discussion

We have demonstrated how a mobile message system can be designed to let drivers communicate about roadside events such as hazards or situations that deserve extra caution. The Road Talk prototype meets the specific requirement we have set up. It is designed to allow sharing of messages concerning roadside events. The initial prototype performance evaluation indicated that sharing is possible at a wide range of speeds. Memos consist of voice recordings, which are distributed in their original form. There is no discrimination of topic and a user may mediate any issue, such as warning for hazards, to fellow drivers. It draws on epidemic distribution, which in this case means that the application supports the exchange of memos immediately, from one car directly to another, and also indirectly, i.e., from one car to another via a third car. In this way the memos would spread epidemically, following the physical movements of vehicles and spreading quickly wherever and whenever traffic is dense. Road Talk accommodates interacting while driving in a similar way as the evaluated PlaceMemo prototype. The application plays memos automatically when approaching the location associated with it and requires no other intervention besides driving. Finally, Road Talk also makes use of accurate GPS positioning to capture the location of a memo and continuously tracks the car's position to determine when it is approaching a memo. In addition, Road Talk supports planning ahead as the application also features a zoomable map on which all the memos (stored on the local PDA) are plotted as squares. A user may click on the squares to hear the corresponding memos.

The prototype is also an inspirational pattern for the ways in which new technology can be introduced to overcome some of the practical limitations of social interaction in this setting and provide support for "expert" drivers. Road Talk provide a possibility for drivers to interact even when they are out of sight of each other, and means for audio interaction even though they are enclosed in the shell of the car. The current use of speed trap message systems indicates that social interaction goes beyond negotiating the right of way, and Road Talk extends the opportunities for sharing information of various kind. Such activities can provide for a better vitality of future life on the streets, where people collaborate to increase safety as well as to more efficiently reach their destinations.

References

Borghoff U, Schlichter J (2000) Computer-supported cooperative work: introduction to distributed applications. Springer, Berlin

Bradner E, Kellog W, Erickson T (1999) The adoption and use of 'babble': a field study of chat in workplace. In: Proceedings of the sixth European conference on computer-supported cooperative work, Copenhagen, Denmark, pp 139–158

Burell J, Gay G (2002) E-graffiti: evaluating real-world use of a context-aware system. Interact Comput. doi:10.1016/S0953-5438(02)00010-3

Espinoza F, Persson P, Sandin et al (2001) Social and navigational aspects of location-based information systems. In: Proceedings of Ubicomp, Atlanta, Georgia

Glance N, Snowdon D, Meunier JL (2001) Pollen: using people as a communication medium. ComputNetworks Int J Comput Telecommun 35(4):429–442

Grinter R, Eldrige M (2001) y do tngrs luv 2 txt. In: Proceedings of European conference on computer-supported cooperative work, Bonn, Germany

Griswold W, Boyer R, Brown S et al (2002) Using mobile technology to create opportunistic interactions on a university campus. Presented at Ubicomp 2002 workshop on supporting spontaneous interaction, Göteborg, Sweden

Isaacs E, Walendowski A, Whittaker et al (2002) The character, function and styles of instant messaging in the workplace. In: Proceedings of computer supported cooperative work, New Orleans, LA

Khelil A, Becker C, Tian J et al (2002) An epidemic model for information diffusion in MANETs. In: Proceedings of symposium on modeling, analysis and simulation of wireless and mobile systems, Atlanta, GA

Masui T, Takabayashi S (2003) Instant group communication with QuickML. In: Proceedings of the 2003 international ACM SIGGROUP conference on supporting group work, Sanibel Island, FL, pp 268–273

Nardi B, Whittaker S, Bradner E (2000) Interaction and outeraction: instant messaging in action. In: Proceedings of computer supported cooperative work, Philadelphia, PA

Norton J, Bass F (1987) A diffusion theory model of adoption and substitution for successive generations of high-technology products. J Manag Sci 33(9):1069–1087

Östergren M, Juhlin O (2005). Road talk: a roadside location-dependent audio message system for car drivers. J Mobile Multimed 1(1):47–61

Persson P, Fagerberg P (2002) GeoNotes: a real-use study of a public location-aware community system. Swedish Institute of Computer Science Technical Report T2002:27, ISSN 1100-3154

Stockholm 2005 sifferguide (2005) http://www.uskab.se/index.php/component/docman/doc_download/42-sifferguide-2005.html. Accessed 12 November 2009

Part III
Sense and Social Interaction

Chapter 8
The Automobile Flâneur—Joint Music Listening in Traffic Encounters

Previously we have discussed how people find car traveling to be a positive experience in itself, beyond just getting to their destination.[1] We will now examine the characteristics that make up this feeling, which Kevin Lynch refers to as the sense of driving. Following Lynch (1981), we argue that the experience depends on the particular identities of what we experience and the clarity with which we perceive them. We take drivers' curiosity about their fellow road users in a traffic jam, or during an overtaking, as a starting point for the investigation of social life in traffic, beyond access, fit, and vitality. People tend to peek into other cars when opportunities are given, which demonstrates that something more is going on than just avoiding physical accidents.

Donald Appleyard and Kevin Lynch have performed several studies on the driving experience. In their 1964 book *The View from the Road* they made an important contribution regarding how drivers and passengers experienced the passing landscape. Even though their intention was to inform architecture and urban planning, and they therefore did not investigate how drivers experienced the company of others, they suggest that traffic per se is the most influential factor on our emotions in that situation. They claim that:

> Most impressive of all is the motion of the accompanying traffic, to which he is forced to be attentive, and which even passengers will watch with subconscious concern. (Appleyard et al. 1964)

Thus, drivers take an interest in the other drivers and vehicles they encounter. We suggest that this experiencing is characterized by the same qualities as what appealed to the classic nineteenth-century figure called the "flâneur." The flâneur was a figure invented by the poet Charles Baudelaire to capture a way of being that occurred in the modern city life in Paris. According to Baudelaire:

> He marvels at the eternal beauty and the amazing harmony of life in capital cities...He delights in fine carriages and proud horses, the dazzling smartness of the grooms...the sinuous gait of the women, the beauty of the children, happy to be alive and nicely dressed. (Baudelaire, quoted by Mazlish 1994)

---

[1]The chapter draws upon a previously published paper by Östergren and Juhlin (2006). Reprinted from the publication with permission from Springer Verlag.

Baudelaire describes how the flâneur strolls along the street and makes up small stories about the identities of the people and what they are doing. Obviously, Baudelaire does not base this description on scientific observations. Still his ideas about flâneuring seem to have relevance today and particularly as concerns modern drivers. For instance we find in the sociologist Michael Bull's recent investigation of sound and automobility that one interviewee claims:

> When I'm sat in a traffic jam or at traffic lights, in town especially, to ease the boredom, I quite enjoy watching what's going on around me. I look in other people's cars, and watch people walking down the street. I like to see what they're doing and where they're going. As I am in my car a lot, I do need something to take away the boredom. (Anonymous driver quoted by Bull 2004)

This driver engages in the same kind of enjoyment as the flâneur. He takes an interest in the visual appearance of the social interaction in the vicinity. At the same time, it should be stated that sociologists who discuss flâneuring, like Bull (2004), Bauman (1994), and Tester (1994), see driving as a threat to the possibility of having such experiences. Driving is detrimental to the experiences of the social life on the street.

We, on the other hand, suggest that a modern driver-flâneur would not mind sharing music listening, which currently is a private matter, with fellow road users. More so, she would particularly enjoy prying into the music being played in other cars. Here the visual appearance would be complemented with personally selected sounds. Such an approach would draw upon the things the driver pays attention to anyway, namely encountering other fellow drivers and their vehicles as part of the collaborative and situated work of moving the vehicle, and add a novel flavor to it to tease the driver's curiosity and thereby enrich the experience of being in traffic.

More precisely, Sound Pryer draws on two appreciated activities that drivers already engage in to entertain themselves in traffic. First, it is about in-car music listening. Such music listening is very popular; e.g., in a recent study concerning the habits of a group of music enthusiasts, it was found that they listened to music 82% of the time they spent in cars (Brown et al. 2001). The reason for music listening being popular is that it can easily be combined with driving, but also that the car is a good place for listening. The selection or volume level rarely disturbs others, and a driver can unconcernedly sing along (Bull 2004; Öblad 2000). Second, drivers appreciate looking at the surrounding cars not just for practical purposes.

The purpose of this chapter is twofold. First, we would like to investigate whether ordinary driving has the experiential qualities here suggested. Second, we would like to make driving more interesting than it already is through the generation and implementation of a collaborative car stereo . Evaluating the drivers' experiences of using the prototype application is important to answering both these questions. In order to get realistic feedback from a small group of users we decided to conduct a field trial. In the trial, we restricted the drivers to a particular route to increase the number of encounters, and we set up individual starting points to keep the users separate and anonymous. We also decided to follow each participant to learn about the users' immediate reactions to the concept. We learned that listening, or providing music for others, was enjoyed the most when the user could see the "other end." It was also enjoyable to look around for the source of the music, which compensated for hearing only snippets of sound with poor audio quality.

8.1 Music and Social Interaction

Our concept was influenced by research on music sharing, which occurs in areas such as computer–human interaction and computer supported collaborative work (Brown and O'Hara 2006). Collaborative music listening has been a topic in CSCW and research within computer–human interaction . In 1998, McCarthy and Anagnost presented the MUSICFX system, which enabled members to influence the music selection in the fitness center as they exercised. It is one of the first examples that draws on a social practice surrounding music listening, namely selecting appropriate music that fits the taste of a group. The system uses a set of stationary computers to collect feedback from the members and select a track. The tracks are grouped in genres and then selected randomly. More recently, in 2001, following the growing popularity of Internet peer-to-peer applications, Brown et al. examine music sharing. Based on their findings from a study on enthusiasts' general music habits, they draw some implications for design and suggest a system that re-introduces tangibility to music stored digitally on a "CD sized book" that connects to an online copy of the music as well as enhancing the socialization that emerges around music sharing.

Music files have also become increasingly available away from the desktop with the growing number of mobile devices capable of storing and playing digitally stored music, such as MP3 players, mobile phones, and car stereos. A number of research projects in the mobile computing domain have begun to investigate sharing music files between such devices. An early investigation of *mobile music sharing* is Kortuem et al.'s (2001) mobile peer-to-peer platform, which was explicitly intended for music file sharing. Mikael Wiberg's FolkMusik prototype (2004) addresses how walking and mobile music sharing could be combined. This prototype contains functionality that lets a user select any song on the play list of any other user within a certain distance. The FolkMusic prototype demonstrates an interesting development in mobile music sharing as it uses proximity to filter the available music selection.

Through a series of field-studies and workshops with a group of commuters, Åkesson and Nilsson (2002) found that they are often bored while driving and long for alternative entertainment. They propose ShoutCar, a mobile music player that allows interaction while driving, to help meet this demand. The prototype consists of a text-to-speech play-list browser, a music player, and a wheel-shaped input device. The play list is prepared in advanced and made available through a web interface. The browser is installed in the car and reads out the items that the user cycles through using the input wheel. ShoutCar does not concern music sharing per se, but is a relevant example of a mobile music application designed especially for the driver. Sound Pryer extends this research in two ways. First it focuses on sharing the experience of music listening, rather than sharing music files. Here, the way in which awareness of other users is provided through the system is an important issue.

Second it investigates joint listening experiences while driving, where most mobile music-sharing research concerns people walking around.

8.2 The Sound Pryer Concept

Sound Pryer can be thought of as a collaborative car stereo. A user can listen to his or her favorite music much like a regular stereo. However, he or she can also "pry" into what *other users* in *other cars* are currently playing on *their stereos*. Hence, Sound Pryer provides joint listening experiences. Access is limited to a certain distance; that is, only stereos in close proximity may be overheard. Furthermore, while playing someone else's music, the Sound Pryer interface also gives a sketchy graphical impression of the vehicle where the music is coming from (Fig. 8.1). If the driving situation permits, the stylized icon, vaguely resembling the vehicle, will help the user determine the source of music. We envision a usage scenario as presented in Chapter 1.

8.2.1 The Sound Pryer Prototype

The Sound Pryer prototype is an application-based, wireless, mobile, ad hoc networking tool, similar to the Road Talk application presented in the previous chapter. Networking between cars moving in traffic is limited to the range of the transmitters. Generally this is considered a disadvantage. But we use this to provide joint music listening only when cars are physically close, i.e., when they take part in a mutual traffic encounter. The user interface of the prototype is carefully designed to safely entertain the driver (Fig. 8.1). The interface combines two modes of music playback: *local play* and *remote play*. Local play allows the user to listen to his or her most wanted music. It cycles through a play list pointing to MP3 files stored on the PDA. At the same time as the music is being heard, it is also broadcast on the wireless network. Remote play, on the other hand, allows a user to listen in on what someone else is listening to at *exactly* that moment. In this mode Sound Pryer captures and plays the music being broadcast by another PDA within networking range.

Fig. 8.1 The Sound Pryer Prototype. A PDA and speakers on the dashboard (*left*). The Sound Pryer Interface: Local play (*middle*) and remote play (*right*)

The interface is also designed to automatically switch from local play to remote play whenever a broadcast is detected in the network. It negotiates switching to ensure that in a group of PDAs one will remain in local play guaranteeing music provision for the others. The interface also gives awareness of other users and helps in the interpretation of the source of music. Whenever remote play is activated the interface shows a stylized icon and the color of the other user's vehicle.

8.3 The Field Trial

We wanted to acquire realistic feedback on the concept and on our assumptions about being in traffic. There are some practical challenges that needed to be addressed to obtain useful data, for instance, ensuring that the drivers who took part in the evaluation were *anonymous* and only met very *briefly* in traffic. Sound Pryer is intended for encounters among unacquainted drivers. Most joint listening situations will be brief and could potentially occur anywhere along the vast road network. A study where we hand out devices to a limited number of drivers would not be successful, as the likelihood of a small number of unconstrained drivers encountering each other is very low. In such a case, opportunities for making observations would be scarce, brief, and hard to predict. Therefore, we decided to conduct a field trial where the subjects use the prototype during a limited period of time and restrict the users' movement to one particular route (Fig. 8.2). We conducted three separate trials, which engaged 13 test subjects in all. With our set-up we could follow each individual user throughout the test to be able to watch and video record their immediate reactions and activities, and then interview them on their experiences.

Fig. 8.2 Still captures of the video material

8.4 Video Analysis

The purpose of the video analysis is to study how the drivers behave during Sound Pryer events and interpret how they experience them. We have found four main categories of how the drivers observably relate to their experience of Sound Pryer, i.e., where they put their focus of attention and how they express themselves. The first category is for events where drivers show the visible behavior of intensely *looking around.* The second category comprises the observable behavior of showing interest in *remote music*, but not looking around. The third category comprises both of these observables, i.e., *looking around* and *paying attention to music.* Finally, we will discuss situations where Sound Pryer events were *disregarded* and elicited no observable reactions from the driver. We will present the transcripts for the first case, but then omit them for brevity.

We could see in the video that there were a number of occasions when the drivers were looking around intensely. In the following we will discuss an event occurring when Eric is driving on a straight section of the road (Table 8.1).

Here Eric is gazing forward and suddenly says "green car!" Local play is then interrupted by 4 s of silence (23:05) which is caused by the application's negotiation of which device that should play music and which device should receive music. As the two cars pass in opposite directions he smiles and then takes a quick look at the screen. Remote play starts, continues for 3 s, and then stops as the parties leave wireless range.

We interpret his smile as a consequence of him spotting the car shown on the screen in the oncoming traffic. It is clear that his comment "green car" is about identification, and his smile comes before the music has begun to play. It seems that he recognizes the car and that he looks at the screen for confirmation. Given his smile, it seems that looking around and identifying the car seems to be an enjoyable experience. Interestingly, the same kind of emotional attitude was displayed in situations where the driver believed that someone was listening to their music, as in the following example, which is presented in brief.

Ruth is waiting for a green light and her vehicle is standing still. Sound Pryer starts to negotiate at the same time as she adjusts her seat. Local play comes back on after a few seconds of remote play. She looks out the window trying to identify the source of the music she just heard. However she says to the researcher that she is not sure where it was coming from. She starts smiling and then laughing. She tells

Table 8.1 Transcript of Eric looking for a source of music

Time	Sound pryer	Facial expression	Attention	Comments	Road context
	Local Play		Looks ahead		Going straight
23:04				Green car	
23:05	Silence, 4 sec.	Smiling	Looks at screen		Two cars pass in opposite lane
23:08	Good remote play, 3 sec Silence, 2 sec		Hits turn signal	We're entering here? Right? Res: You said before event.	
23:14	Local Play		Looks at intersection	Res: mmm right . . . we should enter there	
23:15					Turns

the researcher she realizes that the other driver is probably listening to her music. Here, her emotional reaction is about realizing that she is playing music for someone else. Although she fails to accurately locate the listener, this example shows that doing identification work is an experience for "both sides" and that providing music for others also triggers interest in the surrounding drivers. Being "listened to" is a fun experience when one knows that someone close-by is receiving the music. We found that two kinds of emotional attitudes were displayed in "looking around" events. In 30 events, the subjects showed facial expressions of positive appreciation and in 61 events they had a neutral face. Having a neutral face does not necessarily imply that the subjects were indifferent, but it is hard to interpret their emotional experience. Still, these cases show that the concept was understood and the subjects were engaged.

We could also identify a number of events where the drivers' observable behavior relates to receiving music from someone else, but without their looking around. In one of these events, Mark is waiting for a green light at a junction. Sound Pryer starts negotiation and his local play is paused; a second of remote play follows and then there is another a pause. Sound Pryer then plays nine more seconds of remote play (snappy Latino music) and Mark whistles along. The remote play continues and Mark then starts talking to the researcher. During this event Mark is visibly "whistling along" and he seems to do so when hearing the remote music. It is clear that Mark is not concerned with locating the provider. Still, we interpret the event as a positive experience for Mark. Thus, Sound Pryer could provide an interesting experience without subjects taking an interest in knowing the source of the music. But such occasions were few. There were only six examples where the drivers enjoyed listening to remote music *only* and did not engage in identifying the source at all. This could, of course, be explained by the fact that it is hard to tell whether a subject is listening and enjoying music. It could very well be the case that he or she would do so without showing it. The rather poor audio performance of Sound Pryer was probably another reason why there were so few such events.

The most complex behavior occurs in events when the driver looks around in conjunction with displaying some emotional attitude vis-à-vis the music. In the following example, John approaches a junction with traffic signals and stops his car. His local play jumps to the next song on the play list. Then remote play commences and jazzy music fills his vehicle. He takes a quick look at the screen and in his inner rear-view mirror. He smiles and says, "now we don't get to listen any more," as his own music is interrupted. John leans forward to get a look in the mirror, and continues to look carefully in the rear-view mirror as the light turns green and his vehicle advances. He looks out towards the other lanes. After half a minute of remote listening, John says "strange tune" and laughs. Here we interpret his comment "strange" and him laughing as some sort of engagement with the music. Furthermore, we cannot be sure that the provider was identified, but he is looking for it. Hence, he is showing some sort of attitude towards the music and curiosity about its source. All in all there are 15 such events. This indicates that Sound Pryer is not only about looking for who is providing music, which was the dominating category of events. Knowing the source, or at least looking for it, contributes to the experience of listening to someone else's music.

There were also many events in which Sound Pryer was ignored. This was due to two principal reasons. First, we suspect there were occasions where the driver did not look at Sound Pryer due to poor prototype performance. In some events the negotiations were "lost"; i.e., local play was interrupted by a couple of seconds of silence instead of music from a remote source. This occurred mostly in situations when the cars quickly traveled in and out of wireless range, e.g., when meeting in opposite lanes. In any case, the silence was probably experienced as a long pause in local play rather than failure of joint listening with some remote source, and users did not bother to look at the screen. Second, drivers interactionally adapt their attention to mobile technologies and traffic. Naturally driving had top priority and Sound Pryer was ignored when the driver was performing complex maneuvers, such as turning or coordinating with other drivers. Furthermore, in several cases the drivers did not bother to look at the display when they were talking with the researcher. Hence, the drivers prioritize their focus of attention much like how previous research has described the way drivers handle and talk in mobile phones, as we discussed in Chapter 3. The design of Sound Pryer apparently allows drivers to leave it unattended if other things are prioritized.

8.5 Analysis of Interviews

The questions in our interview concerned the capability of the prototype; concept comprehension; experience of the service; and traffic safety.[2] Of the 12 interviewed drivers, a discouraging 10 complained about the quality of the audio in the remote play sessions. Also, in line with such criticism, another two users were negative in more vague terms towards the technical performance of the prototype. Thus, the prototype was marred by some deficiencies in sound reproduction. All in all, five users commented that they wanted to hear more of the music they actually received in some traffic encounters. On the other hand, from the video analysis we know that almost all users had at least one remote play of acceptable quality that yielded a good enough listening experience of appropriate length. And although only four users explicitly stated that they also experienced transfers with good quality in conjunction with talking about performance, we are confident the prototype was able to

---

[2]Twelve drivers were interviewed directly following the field trial. The interviews were loosely structured and performed by five different researchers. A loose structure interview has the advantage of letting the researcher investigate issues as raised by the individual participant. In this case, we wanted to acquire as many comments as possible about the system, rather than acquiring comparable results from the interviewees. All the researchers had a common set of topics to cover, but also had the freedom to skip some if they found them irrelevant to the test subject's experience. This means that not all the participants answered all the questions, and we therefore show the answer frequency in conjunction with each question.

demonstrate the concept well enough for them to give constructive feedback on its design.

It seems that the users understood the idea of a shared car stereo. All the users expressed they could determine when remote play commenced. Furthermore, five users could also describe that it happened when in the proximity of another car with Sound Pryer. Finally, four users made reference to when the eavesdropping commenced by describing which cars they had encountered.

> Red station wagon, yellow station wagon, silverish station wagon, small blue car. I think they were the ones I noticed.

Three users stated that they quickly learnt which other cars were part of the test and could therefore determine the music source quickly without looking at the display. However, 10 users had experienced some situations where this was difficult and where they felt unsure where the music was coming from, for example:

> Yes, absolutely! Several times. The first time I thought it was the car behind me, but it was probably the car in front. Then, since I didn't know whether there were three or more cars in the trial I was, of course, uncertain.

When asked whether the display was helpful in understanding the source of the music most users were ambiguous. They noted that it was helpful in most situations. But some users had experienced or thought of situations when it did not help much such as in the following:

> Yes, a little. I mean, if I'm in dense traffic then "red car" is not enough because there are so many around.

The users also commented upon the experience of Sound Pryer usage. Nine drivers enjoyed listening to other Sound Pryer players. A typical comment was as follows:

> I liked one tune. I don't know the band, but it was rap. I found it groovy when we entered the last turn. It was cool to listen to some rap music. I found that really cool.

In addition, four users also claimed they enjoyed trying to determine the source of the music, for instance:

> It was a little choppy in the beginning, but then when you could hear the music it was fun to listen to somebody else. It was fun to be able to see on the display what the car should look like, because then you could look and see if there was anyone in the vicinity: yes it has to be that car! Then you could figure it out.

However, because of the prototype's technical deficiencies, three users stated they could not really discuss their experience of the concept.

> It can't be done really. The experience was exciting as soon as you were approaching somebody. Since it didn't work the way it was supposed to or the way I suspect it should work, it is a little hard to say.

Remote play interrupted local play whenever there was an external source available, and in line with the comments above, eight users found this principle fun.

However, six of them also wished to have a little more control, for instance the possibility to override the automatic selection and only hear songs from the play list. Remote play also means that sometimes others can hear what you are playing. When asked about how this felt, four users claimed they did not think about this, either as being fun or intimidating, for example:

Didn't think much about it. On the other hand, don't know. Nothing that I care about really.

Another six users expressed that they enjoyed this aspect. For instance, a user describes his feelings when he realized he was streaming music to another user as follows:

It was really a spontaneous reaction, I must say. It was not like I was sitting there thinking: I wish my music would come on soon. Rather it was like: "yes" now we are listening to mine.

A closely related question we asked the users was whether they would be willing to distribute music to surrounding cars as demonstrated by Sound Pryer. All the users who were asked this question, who were as many as eight people, had no problem with this at all. One user explained:

Because music is nothing controversial. You're not sitting there listening to something others won't feel good about.

Finally, we asked the users whether they found the Sound Pryer concept interesting. Out of the 12 answers we collected, an encouraging nine said it was a fun concept. As one user noted:

Absolutely, I believe so. If you just get it properly organized, why not? It is completely new and I haven't even heard that it was possible to do it before.

Only three users rejected the idea. Their objections were to entertainment as such, and they were looking for something that would make obviously useful—in a functionalistic sense—improvements in their lives.

When asked if the Sound Pryer prototype interfered with the users' driving, seven subjects said it did not. On the other hand, three of them said that there was some sort of impact while they were driving, but that "interference" was too strong a word. Similarly, another three users stated they felt an impulse to drive a little differently than they would normally do, for instance:

One time I drove to try to get away from it just to see when you'd lose contact with that car.

Finally, only three users objected to Sound Pryer and claimed their driving was impaired. To sum up, despite a somewhat artificial field trial with a flawed prototype we were able to collect valuable insights and feedback on its design as well as the general concept. The video analysis and the interviews reveal that the users understood that Sound Pryer is about providing joint music listening in traffic and at the same time creating awareness of other users. It seemed that both listening to remote music and providing it were enjoyable when the users were able to see who was receiving or broadcasting it. They also enjoyed looking around for the provider of music, and this seems to compensate hearing only snippets of songs with poor audio quality. Many users used vehicle shape and color "hints" when looking for the source. Hence, providing awareness of users contributes to the experience of mobile music sharing. On the other hand, Sound Pryer was not appreciated just for the music experience, i.e., when there was no way of understanding which driver was playing it. Some users experienced situations where the graphics were insufficient to determine the source of music. Such situations occurred when, e.g., there were many similar cars around and when it was dark. In those cases Sound Pryer was experienced as playing remote music from sources that were out of sight. This means that the range of the wireless transmitter sometimes did not reflect that users were near each other. Sound Pryer is not dangerously distracting and the drivers seemed to be able to adapt the interaction to the use of this new application. The video analysis showed that drivers did sometimes ignore the prototype to cope with driving, e.g., when turning in a busy intersection. And the interviews confirmed that Sound Pryer did not interfere with driving. Furthermore, it does not seem to invade privacy in any serious way. In the interviews no users stated that it was particularly intimidating to reveal the shape and the color of the car, and a majority of the users were willing to distribute music in this manner. Technically, the prototype needs improvements in order to better implement the concept. These improvements concern technical audio issues, e.g., switching between local and remote sources and transferring music data. Poor switching performance when, e.g., meeting cars in the opposite lane was particularly detrimental to the experience of the implementation.

8.6 Driving as Flâneuring

Our work on Sound Pryer draws on two activities that drivers already do to entertain themselves. The first is listening to music. The second is the type of flâneuring behavior that it is our conviction that drivers occasionally engage in, namely enjoying visual impressions of fellow drivers and their vehicles beyond the needs of just coordinating traffic flow. Despite a flawed prototype, the field trial showed that users often wanted to know the source of music and that engaging in such an endeavor was particularly enjoyable. We argue that hearing someone else's music gives an additional reason to look around. Therefore this experience is still very much visually oriented; the kicks are in *seeing* who is providing music. Similarly, flâneuring, as we have described it above, is also essentially visually oriented. Thus, we have good support for our hypothesis that drivers enjoy getting impressions from other drivers and their cars.

This conclusion is somewhat contrary to contemporary social theory on listening to music and driving. Michael Bull recognizes that driving (in traffic) is essentially an *accompanied* enterprise, but puts particular emphasis on *solitude* as being much desired (2004). More precisely, he argues that the car realizes the "desire of urban citizens to maintain a sense of privacy, to create a mobile bubble, while on the move." Furthermore, driving a car is the "dominant means of escaping the streets." This being so, he argues, the places that are traveled through become uninteresting and music listening "appears to bind the disparate threads of much urban movement together." We agree that driving is an accompanied solitude, but the emphasis is on "accompanied" and not so much on "solitude." Driving is a social practice and the fellow drivers with their vehicles constitute an ever-changing scene which gives practically endless inspiration and delight for the modern driver-flâneur. Joint music listening adds to his or her experience, and in a sense bursts the "mobile bubble" making driving less detached, but never invading privacy.

Sound Pryer demonstrates that drivers take an interest in and look into the surrounding cars and the activities that go on there. Hence present-day flâneuring occurs in traffic-encounters in which the surrounding vehicles and the people in them are appreciated. But there are also two principal differences. First, the object of appreciation is different from the people in the arcades, and the carriages, horses, etc. of the streets of nineteenth-century Paris. Second, the car-borne flâneur does not aimlessly wander about, or linger to the same degree as the pedestrian.

Furthermore, Östergren argues (2006) that contemporary social theory regards flâneuring as a lost street-art (Tester 1994). According to Bauman (1994), the flâneur can no longer be found in the streets. He describes the flâneur as a person who wanders "without aim, stopping once in a while to look around." Flâneuring is accordingly defined as strictly a pedestrian activity. Streets are no longer places which require "nothing more than being watched and fantasized about." Road use has become an instrumental way of going from one place to another as quickly as possible, and with as little distractions from the surroundings as possible. Automobility has taken the hunting ground away from the flâneur who has to move into shopping malls, theme parks, etc., where he or she has turned into a simple consumer. Similarly, Tester (2004) argues that flâneuring is challenged by the cars in a very concrete way.

> If the flâneur does not pay attention when he crosses the road he … will become a victim of the lorry. (Tester 2004)

Vehicles prey on the flâneurs to the degree that they becomes extinct. What Bauman, Tester, and others overlook is clearly what is uncovered with the Sound Pryer case. The hunting ground has perhaps been taken away from the pedestrian flâneur, and streets may no longer be the place for them, but the activity is still exercised by others. The roads are now instead populated by the automobile flâneurs.

Finally, we have identified what Kevin Lynch referred to as sense, in highway city life, in that drivers recognize and dwell upon differences among their fellow road users. Variations in the identities of people in traffic provide for an interesting experience. Such distinctions are publicly communicated between them at a glance, in the way that sociologist Goffman (1963) called "unfocussed interaction." The drivers send such messages through the visual appearance of their vehicles and their personal behavior. Lynch's (1981) expression " legibility" denotes the degree to which such communication is possible. Here it must be said that, although traffic provides for legible social interaction, the means for expressing identity are very slight. However, as we have argued, new mobile technologies provide new means for increasing the sense of street life. Sound Pryer is, in this regard, an inspirational pattern showing how other means for interaction, such as sound, could be used to increase the communication between unacquainted people who have no relation to each other beyond their co-visiting of a specific section of road. We have displayed how research within the area of human–computer interaction, could partly be extended to the domains of transportation research. In the next section we will continue the investigation of the design space. There, we will focus on road users who have both a common identity and technology as a starting point, to support their social life on the highways.

References

Åkesson KP, Nilsson A (2002) Designing leisure applications for the mundane car-commute. Personal Ubiquitous Comput 6(3):176–187

Appleyard D, Lynch K, Myer JR (1964) The view from the road. MIT Press, Cambridge

Baudelaire C (1994) The painter of modern life, written 1859, quoted from Mazlish B, the flâneur: from spectator to representation. In: Tester K (ed) The Flâneur. Routledge, London

Bauman Z (1994) Desert spectacular. In: Tester K (ed) The flaneur. Routledge, London, pp 43–60

Brown B, O'Hara K (eds) (2006) Consuming music together: social and collaborative aspects of music consumption. Springer, Berlin

Brown B, Geelhoed E, Sellen A (2001) Music sharing as a computer supported collaborative application. In: Proceedings of ECSCW'01, Kluwer, Bonn

Bull M (2004) Automobility and the power of sound. Theory Cult Soc 21(4–5):243–259

Goffman E (1963) Behaviour in public places—notes on social organization of gatherings. Free Press, New York

Kortuem G et al (2001) Wheen peer-to-peer comes face-to-face: collaborative peer-to-peer computing in mobile ad hoc networks. In: Proceedings of international conference on peer-to-peer computing, Linköping, Sweden

Lynch K (1981) A theory of good city form. MIT Press, Cambridge

McCarthy J, Anagnost T (1998) MusicFX: an arbiter of group preferences for computer supported collaborative workouts. In: Proceedings of CSCW'98, Seattle, WA, USA

Öblad C (2000) Using music—on the car as a concert hall. (Att använda musik—om bilen som konsertlokal.) PhD dissertation, University of Göteborg, Sweden

Östergren M (2006) Traffic encounters—drivers meeting face-to-face and peer-to-peer, Doctoral dissertation, IT University of Göteborg, Studies in Applied Information Technology

Östergren M, Juhlin O (2006) Car drivers using sound pryer—field trials on shared music listening in traffic encounters. In: O'Hara K, Brown B (eds) Consuming music together: social and collaborative aspects of music consumption. Springer, Berlin, pp 173–190

Tester K (1994) Introduction. In: Tester K (ed) The flaneur. Routledge, London, pp 1–21

Wiberg M (2004) FolkMusic: a mobile peer-to-peer entertainment system. In: Proceedings of HICSS'37, Honolulu, HA

Chapter 9
Motorcycling and Social Interaction—Design for the Enjoyment of Traffic Encounters

There are road users whose driving habits and other activities on the roads are constitutive of their identity and membership in communities.[1] Among them, we have chosen to study motorcyclists. Here, the ways in which social interaction occurs are more elaborate than among the automobile flâneurs. They spend lots of time on their vehicles, partly for the road experience per se. Driving is a highly motivating factor, including the strong tactile experience of the roar and vibrations of the engine as well as the exposure to wind and weather. By studying this group we can learn more about the relation between sense in driving and social aspects of road use.

Motorcyclists are also explicit about their interest in other road users, which is visible in the way they often greet other bikers they meet along the road. They appreciate riding even more if they are likely to encounter other bikers. But they also engage in several other forms of social interaction with their peers on the road. These include meeting up at specific places, going on planned trips, or, more recently, hanging out together on internet web forums. Among all these forms of social interaction, we argue that the brief and random encounters with other people on motorbikes along the vast road network, are fundamental for their experience.

The role of such interaction in traffic in the bikers' community life has not yet been accounted for in other sociological studies in this area (e.g. McDonald-Walker 2000). However, its importance is easy to miss from a sociological standpoint. Two bikers passing each other at high speed along a highway may not seem like much of a social event. The meetings are very short, and at best include a quick acknowledgment through a nod or a wave. Additionally their clothing and the design of their machines are calculated to convey at a glance an image of themselves to people they encounter in traffic (Goffman 1963). Nonetheless, we argue that the extreme nature of a traffic encounter between bikers—considering the strong focus on driving, high speed, and the motorcycle—is both a prerequisite and a limiting factor for a highly cherished form of interaction. The short meetings on the road are somewhat exciting, which generates an urge to get more out of the encounters. Sometimes they want to prolong such interaction, and sometimes they want to get more out of each encounter.

---

[1]This chapter draws upon two previously published articles. Esbjörnsson et al. (2003, 2004). Reprinted from the publication with permission from Springer Verlag.

O. Juhlin, *Social Media on the Road*, Computer Supported Cooperative Work 50, 127
DOI 10.1007/978-1-84996-332-9_9, © Springer-Verlag London Limited 2010

We argue that the other ways in which they interact with each other, e.g., going on planned trips and meeting on the internet, can be understood as attempts to get more traffic encounters and overcome some of the experiential constraints. They organize motorcycling to prolong meetings through group rides and by circling around in certain geographical places. Finally the use of public message boards on the web provides a new way of hanging out with other motorcyclists. However, these alternative forms of social interaction are all compromises in comparison with the central experience of traffic encounters. First, continuous meetings with a small group of acquainted bikers are predictable; second, meetings at certain locations compromise the driving experience; and finally, the use of Internet involves no driving at all.

9.1 Social Interaction Among Motorcyclists

The *driving experience* is central to motorcycling. The bikers spend time on the road to experience the feeling of acceleration and the centrifugal forces when taking turns. Accordingly bikers can crowd winding roads far from built-up areas just for fun. During the fieldwork we observed many other bikers on these types of roads. Additionally, in the videos published on the website, these winding roads appeared more frequently than others. Here it is of great importance to control the bike, e.g., to be able to maintain a high speed when taking the turns. These roads are often very popular and well known in the biker-community. Knowledge of the location of "enjoyable" roads is passed around by word of mouth, posted on motorcycling web-sites, or, in some cases, is marked up on special road maps sold by motorcycle clubs.

In general, many motorcyclists see themselves as being outside of society, and driving their vehicle provides them with a feeling of freedom and individuality (McDonald-Walker 2000). Nevertheless, it gives them many opportunities to express an identity and interact with other road users.

The bikes are designed to provide impressive performance and appeal, beyond the logistical demands of a transport vehicle. The bikers expressed themselves in their driving performance. It was important to handle the bike in an impressive manner, for example by doing "stoppies" where they brake hard with the front wheel in a way that makes the back wheel lift up in the air (Fig. 9.1). In addition, they spend considerable resources to modify their bikes to stand out from the rest. They not only attempt to diverge from other types of road users, but also within the group of bikers. During the fieldwork we noticed the popularity of discussing and displaying motorcycle modifications. This standpoint is expressed in interviews conducted at the large organized events, but is also observable in the weekly informal meetings and on the message board. One person expressed it in the following way:

> It is rather interesting if there is something out of the ordinary. It doesn't need to be a special bike. It is interesting enough if they have made some modifications . . . On this one [pointing at his own bike] there are always discussions concerning the high performance exhaust pipes and how to increase the motor power.

Fig. 9.1 Pictures from the weekly meeting at the "The Yellow Café" (*to the left*) and motorcyclists performing stunts (*to the right*)

Modified bikes receive attention and comments irrespective of whether they appear at the meetings, or in a picture-gallery on the web. The importance of expressing the "right" attitude also influenced the choice of personal equipment. This should not only protect from injuries, but also provide an accepted appearance, or display one's belonging to a certain group. For example, we observed how some bikers wore a sweater with a URL to a public message board printed on the sleeve. This phenomenon was not very widespread in the initial part of our study, but gained in popularity during the summer. Consequently the number of visits to the message board, to which the URL belongs, increased throughout the summer.

Many of the bikers express their identity on the web with pictures or movie clips displaying their bike or demonstrating their skills. They use thumbnail pictures in their signatures to show off, and take an interest in giving and receiving recognition for each other's performance. This is similar to what they do on the roads. There are greater possibilities for lengthy interaction on the message board than during the brief traffic encounters. Here, the onlooker can delve into the details as long as she wants. Besides, the asynchronous use of the website compensates for the difficulties in reaching an audience. On the road, it can be tricky to find all those who might be interested in a newly attached exhaust pipe. The thumbnails also facilitate making connections between individual members of the message board and bikers one has previously encountered. Thus they reconcile the on-line and the physical realms. However, interaction on the web is different from all other forms of biking interaction in that it lacks the driving experience.

Traffic encounters are an ordinary feature of biking all over the road network. However on some roads they occur with a higher frequency. In Stockholm, motorcyclists especially like the winding roads northwest of the city center. During the weekends large numbers of bikers drive along these curvy routes and consequently numerous encounters occur. The possibilities for direct communication with each other while biking are scant. Still, we argue that most bikers engage in weak forms of interaction in encounters with other motorcyclists, beyond what is necessary for traffic coordination. This is observable in the ways in which they greet each other and interact with a wave or by flashing their lights. Their appreciation of traffic encounters is also expressed in our interviews. One motorcyclist said that he greeted almost every biker he met on the road.

This interest in traffic encounters is also obvious since it often occurs as a topic on their message-boards on the web. Out of 91 excerpts from the message board, 23 concern earlier encounters along the roads. Often, the web is used to identify a person they have met on the road, and find people with similar interests to have discussions with.

This mutual interest in traffic encounters is evident in the excerpt given in Table 9.1. In this specific case, a group of bikers make an effort to identify a motorcyclist someone saw being stopped by the police. The discussion is held during the evening, after a day filled with activities on the roads.

At the end of the evening, Alex has seen a white/red/blue "CBR900," which was stopped by the police, at the exit to the town of Uppsala. After returning back

Table 9.1 Excerpt from the message board, displaying the collaborative effort to identify a biker

(23:28) Alex: Saw a white/red/blue (?) CBR 900 which had been stopped at the Uppsala exit on the Stockholm highway southbound this evening around 11 pm. Was that one of "us" and if so how'd it go? I buzzed by at a steady 70 km/h and felt bad for you . . . think it was the dark blue unmarked 850 seen earlier that evening which stopped the bike in question . . .

(23:31) Michael: Sounds like Eric unfortunately!!! ☹☹☹ He rides that way anyway, really hope it wasn't him, in any case that's really too bad. ☹ Hope he doesn't lose his license!

[excl. transcript of one posting]

(23:34) John: They just never give up. Saw him waiting there on the on-ramp right when I was getting ready to go for a wheelie. After that it was 70 all the way home. Almost forgot how slow that is . . .

(23:36) Peter: Sh** man . . . that sounds like Eric . . . he dropped me off here in Gävle then he took off for home . . . do you have to go by Uppsala if you're going to Västerås?

(23:39) John: Heck of a detour via Uppsala from Gävle. Can't have been Eric unless he was really itchin' to ride . . .

(23:39) Richard: Nope you don't go by Uppsala if you're going to Västerås . . . that was probably someone else unless he went the wrong way . . . Keep your fingers crossed for whoever it was anyway. Also I think we should take it a bit easy with names and the like from this evening . . . it seems we've stirred things up tonight . . .

[excl. transcripts of two postings]

(23:48) Peter: There's a real chance Eric got lost on his way to the freeway tonight . . . ☺ He ought to be home soon and be able to answer..

(10:07) Alex: I dunno . . . probably wasn't Eric . . . was a little newer bike than what he's got . . . I'd guess between 97–00 but I only saw it for a sec and it was dark so I could be wrong . . . well, just hope things turned out all right

(11:23) Eric: Nope! It wasn't me . . . whew! Lucky. There was a lot of the back wheel going home. Thanks for the kind thoughts anyway. I only got stopped by the police at The Yellow Cafe at 0 km/h.

home to his computer, he logs on to the message-board and initiates a discussion by asking whom the police had stopped. Michael (23:31) guesses it is Eric based on the description of the bike. Peter (23:36) agrees, saying that he was probably the one who met Eric last. Later postings oppose the conclusion that it could be Eric, since this would not be the ordinary route for him to drive. The mystery remains unsolved until Eric ends the discussion (11:23) 12 h later. Luckily, he was not the one who got caught by the police.

This excerpt illustrates both the special character of these meetings as well as the participants' interest in the encounters. First, even though the bikers had actually met during the day, and there was a source of concern about the welfare of one of them, the bikers were even unsure about who they actually had encountered. Second, the encounter only gave a short glimpse of the activities that occurred, which called for elaboration.

There is a great deal of interest in a specific traffic encounter, in this case identifying the motorcyclist stopped by the police, since they think it could be a member of the group. This is evident at 23:28, where Alex asks if the biker was one of them. Also the number of postings, that is, 10 messages during the course of 20 min, displays their interest in sorting out the issue.

Finally, during the brief encounters they look for icons and messages on the clothing, as well as characteristic features of the bikes to identify the other person. It is important to correctly name a biker in order to give credit, or to place him or her as a part of a specific group. This argument is supported by how they discuss issues of identification on the web, rather than what is possible to observe in their behavior on the roads. In the excerpt above it is evident how they benefit from the details picked up during the brief encounter. At 23:28 the biker is described by means of the model and color-scheme of his bike. Later in the discussion (10:07), the same person adds some details regarding the age of the vehicle. He also refers to the confusion caused by the brief interaction and the darkness. Further, the encounters play an important role since they cause the web site to increase in popularity, with a growing number of visitors. This could be explained by the group's wearing of sweaters with a URL printed on the sleeve during encounters on the road.

9.1.1 Arrangements to Increase Social Interaction

Social interaction among bikers takes place in even more forms and settings than brief and random traffic encounters. As we have previously stated, we argue that these forms of interaction, which include using web forums, are ways to get more out of the brief traffic encounter. The chances for social interaction with unacquainted bikers are rather low since the roads constitute such a vast public space. Moreover, even if a biker wants to meet an acquaintance, it is improbable that he or she will randomly come across that person. Consequently, the bikers have developed many ways to increase the likelihood of enjoyable social interaction.

Moving around a specific site, known among a community of drivers, is a way of increasing the possibilities for social interaction. When revolving around a small geographical location they always return for another encounter. The setting is often given by tradition, i.e., places where bikers usually meet. However, the site can also be selected through contingent negotiation, for instance, by mobile phone communication. During the summer there is a weekly gathering at a specific place, here called the "Yellow Café," on the outskirts of Stockholm (Fig. 9.1). Approximately 300–400 bikers turn up at this specific place each Wednesday to show off and socialize. They impress each other with newly modified bikes or show off their driving skills. During the evening motorcycles are constantly approaching or leaving the place. Towards the end of the evening smaller groups leave the place and head towards more quiet areas such as industrial sites, where they race against each other.

During these informal meetings, they use their motorcycles, or themselves, to carry information. They benefit from the number of bikers present, by equipping their bikes with for-sale ads, or with stickers expressing their membership in various groups. At the "Yellow Café" they also park their bikes alongside the road and walk around watching and commenting on other bikes. They often show interest in bikes, either similar to their own, or ones they find spectacular.

Another way of increasing interaction is to travel together on joint rides. Bikers organize trips, for example to explore untried roads, with familiar bikers. They teach each other how to maneuver on familiar ones, or simply go together to enjoy the bends on a particular route.

Meetings at certain places and joint rides do not give full satisfaction to the demand for a good driving experience. Since the activity is concentrated to walking around between the parked bikes, it contains little driving except by the drivers who are showing off and performing stunts in front of other bikers. Joint rides have the opposite quality. They provide a decent driving experience. But the increase in interactional events is restricted to acquainted bikers, and does not add to the experience of interacting with unfamiliar drivers.

9.1.2 Planning a Joint Ride

As we have shown, motorcyclists have come to embrace the web to further increase interaction. Several motorcycling web sites have recently evolved in Sweden. On the web, they not only discuss previous encounters, but also plan and organize upcoming trips. The site we have studied further hosts a number of other discussions related to motorcycling such as expressions of identity, negotiations of appropriate behavior, and arranging rides.

In the following we will discuss the message-board as a way of increasing the likelihood of interactions on the road by arranging a ride. The excerpt from the message board depicted in Table 9.2 illustrates how a group of bikers organize a joint ride. It indicates the problematic issues that arise when deciding on a time and place for them to meet:

Table 9.2 Excerpt from the message board, displaying the collaborative effort in organizing a joint ride

---

(09:03) Richard: I CAN'T TAKE IT ANY MORE! We have to get out and ride on wed again . . . who's coming? come on now, there should be more of us than ever . . . after all I'm going to show you what I've learned . . . I'm going to fall on wed . . . muhahahahahahaha!!!!!

[excl. transcripts of eight confirmations]

(22:30) Bill: Couldn't we meet at mcd in Tyresö instead? Maybe we could race a few times before all the "Bike-haters" go to bed. It'd be so f**ing great if we could do it before the cops arrive. ☺

(22:43) Eric: I guess I'll be there and it doesn't matter to me where we meet. If we meet in Tyresö then we could take a ride on curvy and nice roads down towards Nynäshamn ☺ Bill, you want a revenge race, right? ☺

(22:45) Bill: Any time!

(23:18) Peter: If I get my piston rings like promised tomorrow, then I'll probably be able to take a ride with you! In any case I want to go to the Yellow Cafe first . . . .

(09:38) David: Coming later, have to work at a race first. Ought to be in at Svea by about 21. And you guys who are out earlier, be sure to let loose properly, preferably right by Chairman Bluelight on one wheel.

(14:40) Richard: Awesome!!! but I'll probably go to Donk's on Sveavägen . . . 18:15.18:45 C U WHEN YOU GET THERE

(15:46) Ralph: F**, is it raining up there in Stockholm? Here in Gothenburg we're suffering from brilliant sunlight . . . well ok some cumulous clouds ☺ I'm in the best mood there is because my buddy's gonna drive me my 22 km home from work on his new fireblade ☺☺☺☺ oh believe me if you don't have a bike and have only passed the theory test then this is the closest thing to total happiness you can get!!!

[excl. transcript of one posting]

(16:35) Steve: Coming, absolutely . . . ☺

(16:37) Steve: Forgot . . . was it Tyresö or Svea????? ☺☺

(03:45) Steve: Okay I'll swing by Tyresö first hope there's some carrots there, otherwise I'll/we'll come to Svea . . . .☺

(08:48) Michael: I'll come sputtering into Ronald's Place except in the event of precipitation . . . Seems like there's some mixed signals about where to meet and what time but I vote we just ride like usual, it doesn't get so complicated that way . . . .☺

(16:52) Phil: McDonalds right??? What shitty weather we got!!!!! The Weather gods must love us carrots!!!!!

(17:05) John: In at the last minute, are you guys going out to the yellow cafe or will it be some other local route? I won't be coming to the M, am sitting at work in Solna, will probably ride directly to the cabin and have a look then we'll see if I find any carrot peels.

(17:11) Robert: McDonalds we'll be driving at between 18:15–18:45 . . . . . . (like usual that is) . . . .☺☺

(17:14) Paul: Have to see if you all are still around when I get there. Have to go home and get the bike first. Otherwise see y'all somewhere else along the way.

Richard initiates the discussion by inviting others for a joint ride two days later. The interaction goes smoothly during the next eight turns, i.e., while people only accept the invitation. It starts to get complicated when Bill (22:30) starts to negotiate the invitation and suggests another meeting place. This suggestion is explicitly confirmed by a second person. Then follows a series of short confirmations, which do not make it explicit whether they mean the first or the second geographical location. Then David confirms the first place (09:38). Thereafter Richard, who made the initial request, acknowledges all those confirmations without commenting upon the discussion of a possible second place (14:40). The confirmations and the discussions continue, but nothing more is heard from Richard, Bill, or Eric. John (16:35) raises the question as to which place he has agreed to go to. He gets no answer for 11 h and then puts up a message saying that he will go to both locations. Michael (08:48) complains that they have not come to any conclusion regarding either time or place, and instead suggests that they should do it the traditional way.

Much effort is put into deciding the specific place and time, but it is still not obvious when and where to meet, and who will turn up. We think that the struggle to decide on a place to meet is due to two issues. First, it is difficult to reach consensus since the participants step in and out of the forum in unpredictable ways. When a message is posted it is not immediately obvious who receives it. This is the case when the objections to where to go (22:30) are left uncommented. The cause may be the initiator (Richard) already having left the forum and thus not being available for negotiation. It is also difficult to repair misunderstandings, as visible in the 11-h delay after the request for clarification made by Steve (16:37). Second, the process of achieving mutual agreement is flawed by the website being public. People not familiar with the context may confuse the discussion. This is visible in the digression made by Ralph (15:46), where he posted a comment on the weather in a different city. There could also be a case of subtle digression (22:30). The objection by Bill is perhaps ignored due to the fact that he is on the fringe of the group, lacks context awareness, and is unacquainted with what he may suggest. This may explain why Michael (08:48) and later Robert (17:14) state what the group usually does on Wednesdays, i.e., where and at what time they meet.

To conclude, the web message-board serves the purpose of simultaneously reaching a number of likeminded persons, e.g., when organizing joint rides. However, some deficiencies are visible. It is an asynchronous message exchange, which makes it difficult to negotiate the activities. Discussions are lengthy, occasionally spanning several days, and participants are not present all the time. Consequently, all participants are not aware of the decisions taken during the discussion, not even the initiator. Since the message board is public, much confusion is also caused by the different interests and situated practices among the participants.

Thus, the biker community has embraced the web. But there is room for improvement of this new technology. The web is only available in stationary settings, and not in the extremely mobile situations of traffic encounters. A stronger linkage between the Internet and the interaction on the road network could lead to improved interaction, i.e., more enjoyable biking. This linkage should not focus on providing wireless connectivity to the web anytime and anywhere. It should rather somehow exploit the benefit of the mobile activities, i.e., the traffic encounters.

9.2 The Hocman Prototype

Our work is also related to existing mobile services supporting social interaction, such as interpersonal awareness devices, since we explore a community relying on the alternation between activities in the physical and on-line realms.

There are several research projects that propose badges and devices providing interpersonal awareness or supporting various other aspects of mobile ad hoc collaboration based on personal technologies and wireless systems. Examples include the Hummingbird device (Holmquist et al. 1999), GroupWear Tag (Borovoy et al. 1998a), the MemeTags System (Borovoy et al. 1998b), and Proxy Lady (Ljungberg et al. 1998). They vary in their ways of mediating personal expression from emitting a humming sound when friends are close by to making it possible to send shorter text messages. However what they all have in common is that they are designed for semi-stationary settings. The users must be in close range, standing still or moving slowly relative to each other. Systems designed for such settings are not applicable for bikers that move at high speeds over large areas. Moreover, these systems share rigid and highly structured data, both in terms of content and format.

We designed the Hocman prototype (see Fig. 9.2) to improve social interaction among motorcyclists, with a special focus on their traffic encounters. It is a web-based peer-to-peer application for handheld computers capable of wireless ad hoc networking. It works as an automatic web client to be used in the background of the user's attention. Upon detecting a new peer entering the ad hoc network, it plays a sound icon and downloads the index page of the main web directory on the newly discovered peer. In this sense, the networking functionalities are very similar to those of both the Road Talk and Sound Pryer applications. But it provides mobile web servers and web browsers, instead of enabling the sharing of various kinds of audio.

The HTML language, which is basic to web services, is a flexible format that can contain various media formats such as tagged text and images. Since the user controls both content and format, it allows the service to mediate a personal expression.

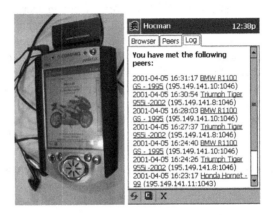

Fig. 9.2 The hardware used (*left*) with a typical biker's page on the screen. Screenshot of the log (*right*)

We designed Hocman to be used as in the scenario presented in Section 1.2. Upon encountering another Hocman-user, the user hears the sound icon informing him about the upcoming meeting with its sharing of web pages. Later on, for instance at home, the biker can browse these pages. We argue that being able to share HTML documents containing embedded sounds, pictures, or texts, enhances the brief experience during an encounter. For example, when browsing the shared material, a biker may enjoy increasing his knowledge about some other biker. By sharing images, a user may communicate his personal identity with a wide range of representations, e.g., acceleration graphs or pictures of modifications. Audio clips that contain engine roars, ambient sounds, conversations, or music, also add value to this experience. Finally, the biker can take contact with the person encountered through other prevalent media to set up future rides with the bikers he or she met. The contents of their pages may provide contact information such as phone numbers, ICQ number, or e-mail address, that may be helpful in planning and organizing biking trips. Thus, this will increase the likelihood of future meetings along the roads.

9.3 Hocman in Use

Hocman has been used by motorcyclists to give us feedback on the concept. We conducted a field trial very similar to the Sound Pryer test described in the previous chapter. Several unacquainted subjects used the prototype for a limited period of time, which was immediately followed by a semi-structured interview.

Fundamentally, all the bikers recognized that the sound icon alerted them to the presence of other Hocman users. About half of the subjects could also account for where and when it was heard, which indicates they had plenty of time to react, look around, and let the experience sink in. More importantly, almost all of the bikers enjoyed hearing the sound icon to an extent that was surprising to us. For instance, some bikers changed their driving behavior, e.g., waved more or less than what is customary when otherwise passing a biker. Besides remembering where they heard the sound icon, most users were also able to associate a particular log entry to it. In one case, an entry and the associated web page were helpful when recognizing an acquaintance. The feedback we got on hearing the sound icon, and being able to inspect the log, indicates that Hocman was able to enrich traffic encounters.

The users found it interesting to read the information on the downloaded pages we prepared for them. Collectively they also had many suggestions on what other data the pages could contain, which suggests that Hocman provides ways for bikers to express identity. On the other hand, there was no consensus on the matter of sharing pages with all users or a limited group. Nevertheless, all agreed that some sort of user-defined filtering or sorting mechanism would improve the concept.

Most of the bikers we interviewed claimed that they took an interest in which bikers they rode together with. They found it plausible that they could contact somebody on the premise of reading a page someone shared. Moreover, a few users recognized that Hocman could also be used for a variety of other purposes, such as ads or dating. This tells us that Hocman may increase the likelihood of interaction among bikers.

In summary, the field trial indicates that Hocman is able to add to the enjoyment of driving. It was evident that the bikers did not think that using Hocman would overly rationalize biking, but that hearing the sound icon, inspecting logs, and browsing contact information, etc., would instead add something positive. Furthermore, we are confident that Hocman could be used while driving. However some details could be improved. Lowering the volume of the sound icon playback, a less bulky device, and more comfortable earphones, perhaps integrated with the helmets, would have been appreciated.

9.4 Conclusion

Mobile interaction includes experiences of very brief meetings between motorcyclists on the road. Here, they share some of the enjoyment of the urban flâneur, who strolls the pavements of the modern city to cherish the richness of unpredictable occurrences. But motorcyclists go beyond the brief encounters to create a sustained community life. Our fieldwork reveals the importance of accounting for highly transient forms of mobile social interaction, in order to understand motorcycling as a social phenomenon. Bikers appreciate traffic encounters, which is observable in the way they wave to each other and in their engagement with the web. But the highly transient meetings provide them with only a glimpse of the identities of others and the activities going on. This leads to an urge to fill in the sketchy encounter. Furthermore, the chances for social interaction with unacquainted bikers are rather low since the roads constitute such a vast public place. Bikers attempt to organize their driving to increase the likelihood of meetings on the road. The other forms of social interaction have different strengths and weaknesses in terms of providing for richness in traffic encounters and driving experience.

The motorcyclists are somewhat remarkable in the way they mix traffic encounters and community life. Still, we have seen how they struggle with what Kevin Lynch terms the sense qualities in city life. Most importantly, the brevity of the traffic encounters reduces the bikers' transparency, i.e., the ways in which they can show who they are and what they do. Although the roads are public and there is no hindrance to showing who you are and what you do in principle, the practical constraint of their relative speed makes this form of urban interaction unlikely to lead to their experiencing each other beyond a very superficial level. There are severe limitations of legibility, i.e., the ways in which they can communicate via symbolic features.

With Hocman we attempt to introduce a tool to support social interaction among bikers. New information technologies based on handheld computers and ad hoc peer-to-peer networks fit with current practice since they will provide mobile services in the situations where encounters occur. The purpose is to expand on the individual encounters, as well as increase the likelihood of their taking place.

Hocman will integrate the extremely mobile activities on the road with the stationary activities on the computer, and thus enhance the road as part of a "good city life" (Lynch 1981).

References

Borovoy R, Martin F, Resnick M et al (1998a) GroupWear: nametags that tell about relationships. In: Proceedings of CHI'98, Los Angeles, CA, pp 329–330

Borovoy R, Martin F, Vemuri S et al (1998b) MemeTags and community mirrors: moving from conferences to collaboration. In: Proceedings of CSCW'98, Seattle, WA, pp 159–168

Esbjörnsson M, Juhlin O, Östergren M (2003) Motorcycling and social interaction—design for the enjoyment of brief traffic encounters. In: Proceedings of the 2003 international ACM SIGGROUP conference on supporting group work. ACM Press, New York, pp 85–94

Esbjörnsson M, Juhlin O, Östergren M (2004) Traffic encounters and hocman—associating motorcycle ethnography with design. Personal Ubiquitous Comput 8(2):92–99

Goffman E (1963) Behavior in public places: notes on the social organization of gatherings, The Free Press, New York, NY

Holmquist LE, Falk J, Wigström J (1999) Supporting group collaboration with inter-personal awareness devices. J Personal Technol 3(1–2):13–21

Ljungberg F, Dahlbom B, Fagrell H et al (1998) Innovation of new IT use: combining approaches and perspectives in R&D projects. In: Proceedings of PDC'98, Palo Alto, CA

Lynch K (1981) A theory of good city form. MIT Press, Cambridge

McDonald-Walker S (2000) Bikers—culture, politics and power. Berg, Oxford

Chapter 10
Legibility and Public Road Signs

The legibility of social interaction in traffic is also mediated through such public road signs as are made and posted by private persons along the roads. These differ from official road signs that are sanctioned and administered by a road authority.[1] This chapter introduces an ethnographic field study of the social practice of designing and posting private signs along public roads in Sweden and Canada. It is a large and global, yet vernacular practice, where people present various messages in a multitude of ways. In general, the signs are made to tell passing drivers something about the current location. They are a means for members of the community to communicate accurately with others via symbolic physical features, and they therefore contribute to legibility (Lynch 1981). They can be mounted along the road to inform drivers of local characteristics, e.g., small children living near the road, or to promote local products, events, or establishments. Signs can also be used to express opinions or just state the existence of local activities. The styles and materials of signs vary considerably, from the most cheap paper posters to costly installations in concrete.

In this chapter we will particularly focus on how these signs support different forms of communities; on the practical work of making and placing them at appropriate places to get the message across to swiftly passing drivers; and finally, on the activities that occur to avoid removal by authorities. First, we see that this practice has relevance for the work of keeping, showing, and maintaining a local neighborhood. There is always a need to be able to express the identity and belonging of a group of people (i.e. a locality or sense of place). These expressions and signs aid the ongoing work of defining, among the people, what their interaction is about. But the signs also introduce, as a label, the community to those who pass by the location. Second, we have also studied the practical achievements of the people who design and mount signs, hereafter referred to as the posters. As argued by Garfinkel (1967) and Suchman (1987), we need to study not only the signs or systems themselves but also the people involved with them and the practicalities on which the signs depend, to understand how this practice works. Third, road spaces and highways are

---

[1] The chapter draws upon the article Juhlin and Normark (2008). Reprinted from the publication with the permission from Sage Publications.

heavily supervised and regulated. Driving on them requires a driver's license and several regulations restrict and limit their use. The roadside and the messages that are posted there are no exception. Official signs are part of a strict socio-semiotic sign system (Krampen 1983). They are made and designed by a national authority and are constrained by international standards. Changes in this system can be explained as the result of interaction between, on the one hand, internal linguistic possibilities, and on the other, social and technical factors which affect decisions made by international standardization bodies. But here we are concerned with signs that exist in parallel to, or alongside these official signs. There are also rules for personal or local signs, which postulate where to place them as well as procedures to follow and permits required before one may place them along the road. However, the posters of the signs we are interested in lack such permits. Still, their signs seem to dwell in an ambiguous state of uncertainty as to whether they are illegal or not, as well as whether there are other considerations that legitimate their existence. All in all, these signs witness of local communities and their sign practices, in a similar fashion as Merriman's (2004) critique of Augé's (1995) description of road life as detached and placeless.

10.1 Communities and Communication Technology

As we have argued earlier, technology mediates social interaction and thus contributes to making social life transparent and legible (Lynch 1976). These interactions are situated, mediated, and interrelated with the context—in our case consisting of buildings, pathways, villages, telephones, discussion-boards, and mobile phones, not to mention public road signs. From each situation to the next, the context varies, as do the modes of interaction that are facilitated or inhibited by it.

Our interpretation of the posters' use of public road signs is linked to recent discussion in sociology on community life and its relation to communication technology. The concept of communities predominantly refers to groups of individuals whose sense of belonging, social identity, support, locality, culture, and shared knowledge tie individuals together. As technologies are enmeshed with everyday life, they are consequently entwined with communities. However, among sociologists, transportation and communication technologies are considered to have an external impact on community life, yielding a debate on whether transport and communication technologies destroy or increase the vitality of such communities (Wellman et al. 2002). For example, sociologist Barry Wellman (2001a, b) argues that different modes of interaction facilitate or inhibit different forms of communities. He identifies three forms of communities: neighborhood networks (door-to-door); networks of nodes (place-to-place); and networks of persons (person-to-person). These communities are distributed along a spectrum from geographically limited groups to people whose communities are totally independent of place.

Interpersonal interaction depends on sustained or re-occurring physical proximity and a shared sense of belonging to a place in a neighborhood. It is a traditional form of community which is geographically bounded and spatially compact, with regular interaction and limited movement occurring within walking distance. Networks of nodes are generally far-flung, loosely-knit, and fragmentary; and the individuals comprising them are connected to loosely bound networks of shared interests, work, practices, and locality. Thus, networks of nodes rely to a greater extent on technologies that bridge the gaps between these places such as phones, highways, and mail service. These technologies make it possible to meet and stay in touch despite physical distances. A network of nodes depends on interaction between places rather than within a place, such as a network consisting of households and places for work, living, and leisure time activities. Networks of persons are further detached from place and are based on interaction mediated by technologies like mobile phones. The community becomes totally detached from any sense of belonging to a place. Maintaining such a network is only a personal responsibility.

Seen in this perspective, roads are an external factor that either facilitates or inhibits communities. On the one hand, transport technologies have compressed distances and enabled networks of nodes and persons to develop—automobility being the paradigm of everyday mobility (Beckmann 2001; Pooley et al. 2005; Urry 2000). We use roads daily, dwell in them, and use them to meet each other. In Sweden, over 60% of our travel consists of car travel (SIKA 2003), which is consistent with statistics from other western countries (e.g. Urry 2004). On the other hand automobility and roads have in many cases inhibited neighborhoods and the interaction between residents (Lynch and Southworth 1974). As a consequence roads are often described as in-between communities—as placeless, history-less strips of asphalt and concrete, a super-modern non-place (Augé 1995). As we have discussed earlier, this view of the road as a non-place is further accentuated by the focus of urban and traffic politics on accessibility, with the road being presented as a mono-functional space meant exclusively for transportation (Buchanan 1964; Fotel and Thomsen 2004; Gunnarson and Lindström 1970; SVOW 1997).

However, the focus in this book has been about identifying and augmenting prevailing social interaction on the road. We argue that road use and traffic are not external to social life, but are part and parcel of it. For example, social interaction is essential to the coordination of traffic movements, and we have also identified groups or communities of road users, such as motorcyclists, whose sense of belonging, social identity, and shared knowledge tie individuals together. In these cases, the categories and research focus suggested by Wellman and others seem to miss our target. Still, when it comes to posters of public road signs, such concepts as neighborhood networks and networks of persons seem to be more applicable.

10.2 Studies of Road Signs

The practice of posting unofficial road signs does not sit well with the perspective of road use as a mono-functional transport activity. People present, express, and form descriptions of their location as a complement, or in opposition to official road signs.

Road signs, and their relation to communities, were initially studied in the 1960s and 1970s by architects such as Donald Appleyard, Kevin Lynch, Michael Southworth, Robert Venturi, Denise Scott Brown, and Steven Izenour. Kevin Lynch and his colleagues were among the proponents of measures to regulate public signs. He urged an organization of the presentation of road signs to favor messages that were connected to the local context: "Signs might be used for something more than giving directions or pressing a sale. And those advertisements that are most connected to the location should be favored" (Appleyard et al. 1964, p. 17). They advocated a design of road signs that preferred a strong connection between the sign and its neighborhood. The signs should in various ways explicitly reflect the local communities and make their social life transparent. According to Lynch (1976, p. 35), the "liveliness of a place is influenced by... the transparency of the setting (that is, by how it makes visible the activity it contains); the way people can leave perceptible traces of their presence; the manner in which things express their action and purpose; the patterns of ownership, which always have sensory consequences; and the mix and density of movement and activity" (see also Francis 1991).

Venturi et al. (1972) instead saw the possibilities in maintaining the weak connection between the driver and the roadside. The loose connection between driver and road context provides an opportunity to playfully experiment with new roles and heightened symbolism. They saw the de-contextualization along the roadside as not necessarily implying a decline of communities. The use of signs enabled the creation of the imagery of the pleasure-zone, and conveyed "lightness, the quality of being an oasis in a perhaps hostile context, heightened symbolism, and the ability to engulf the visitor in a new role" (Venturi et al. 1972, p. 53). For Venturi the signs could express nodes of interests in a network of nodes. Thus, the signs along the roads enable more powerful ways of communicating between roadside inhabitants and passing drivers, e.g., expressing communities of interests.

Roadside memorials, which can be seen as a type of public road signs, have recently received attention in folklore studies and social studies of death. Most scholars report that this practice has become increasingly common in the USA (Everett 2002; Reid and Reid 2001), Australia (Hartig and Dunn 1998), and Sweden (Petersson 2005). The memorials are secular commemorations of the absence of lost family members, relatives, and friends. They provide a personalized place at a publicly available location. Thus the roadside memorials complement cemeteries, which are the authorities' appropriate (or proper) places for grief and remembrance, since the structure of cemeteries inhibits personalization (Petersson 2005).

Like other public signs, roadside memorials do not fit well with current policies of the road authorities. Still, researchers on roadside memorials report a tolerance on the part of authorities towards the signs. As Hartig and Dunn (1998, p. 10) remark, "there are two reasons why some of these institutions have accepted the proliferation of roadside memorials. The first revolves around the way in which these artifacts of death possess a reverence, and the second is related to the hope of policy makers that these memorials may serve as warnings to careless or carefree drivers." For example, in Texas the authorities have created guidelines regarding where roadside memorials can be mounted and how big they can be. But these shrines are only allowed if the fatalities are caused by drunk or drugged drivers, i.e., in order for the signs to function as a warning. Few comply with these guidelines. Paradoxically, objects such as empty or full beer-cans are even placed at the sites, which could be interpreted as contradictory to the objective of roadside memorials as a safety reminder (Reid and Reid 2001).[2]

10.3 Analysis

The analysis of the ethnographic data reveals, first, how signs express identity and belonging among communities, both as a form of interaction within communities, and as a mode of intermediate interaction between forms of communities. Second, the fieldwork unveils the detailed ways in which signs are made and posted. Third, the data reveal tactics and strategies by which the practices of posters and civil servants adapt to each other, which in the end establishes a second geography of public signs.

10.3.1 Communities and the Public Road Signs

Communities are made, shaped, and sustained through interaction. We suggest that interaction through public signs has a role in "doing" communities. Some signs are used to interact within a network of neighborhoods, others within networks of people. Furthermore we discuss the more prevalent practice by which signs are used for interaction outside of such communities.

Interaction within communities. Public signs are used to communicate with other members of a community. A bulletin board, adjacent to mailboxes, is a common feature in small neighborhoods (Fig. 10.1). It fits for interaction within a neighborhood community, where people spend time at a particular place and also revisit the same location, for example when they pick up mail. This type of sign seems to support "neighborhood networks" or "door-to-door" communities. However, the bulletin boards we passed were often empty or scarcely used.

We also found road signs that supported networks of nodes as well as networks of people. Here people used signs to interact with fellow members of a specific network by addressing a group in the message on the sign. For example, signs were put up that were understandable by members of the group even though the object or symbol was cryptic, or simply odd, for a larger audience. One informant had a large

---

[2]The study presented in this chapter was generated from ethnographic field work including observation of public signs, interviews with posters of signs, as well as observations and interviews with civil servants who are responsible for maintenance of the roadside. We have gathered more than 2000 pictures of signs while traveling with road inspectors in Stockholm and Toronto, as well as between Gothenburg in the south of Sweden and the village of Vilhelmina in the north. We also conducted seventeen interviews with posters during the journey through Sweden. Third, we also approached road inspectors who maintain the roadside in Sweden and in Canada.

Fig. 10.1 Bulletin board

collection of old records that he wanted to sell. Therefore he mounted a large iconic record on his flea-market sign. He argued that it attracted interested collectors.

> They recognize the old 78 record hanging outside by the road and that is why they stop and enter... it's a specific community of interest that I want to attract and it works...Of course I get good contact with other collectors, many from Norway... and many of them return a couple of times every year.

Other collectors could find his place and his second-hand store through the disc. It was a well-known sign among collectors. By mounting the record on the sign, the store became a node for collectors who now and then pass by.

Similarly, persons can establish temporary relationships, or networks, assisted by the interaction of road signs. The occurrences of such signs are empirically available as obscure messages, which are hard to understand for non network members, but also in the way the meanings are strongly linked to specific activities that are bounded in time. For example, the sign in Fig. 10.2 consists of an arrow-shaped

Fig. 10.2 Obscure sign

Fig. 10.3 Presence of children

piece of wood which is posted on a stick. It is painted yellow and there is a text which says "CAT." By interviewing the posters we learnt that it was mounted to give directions to a person on a particular occasion. A house-builder had contracted a manual worker to dig in his yard. The worker in turn mounted a sign along the road to inform a truck driver of the direction to the place where he should dismount a Caterpillar. Thus the text "CAT" refers to the object he was supposed to bring, and the arrow to where it should go. The purpose and use of the sign was limited to one particular situation, and the communication occurred within a "network of persons" consisting of a house-builder, a worker, and a truck driver. But the sign was then left at the crossing, and it was still there at least half a year later.

Intermediate interaction with non community members. Road signs are mostly used to interact with people outside of a neighborhood or personal network. We will refer to such messaging as *intermediate interaction.* Such interaction occurs for various reasons. Signs can be posted to inform drivers of local characteristics, e.g., small children living near the road (see Fig. 10.3), or to promote local products, events, or establishments. In general, they are used to reach out to other people to make them relate to the neighborhood networks, e.g., by slowing down to avoid accidents or by buying goods. We will in the following argue that these signs go beyond these forms of use and also have an effect on people's community membership.

During our observation of signs, we encountered several small gatherings of houses whose inhabitants had mounted their own road signs to name their location. One example is the sign with the text "Slut" (Fig. 10.4) that was made a couple of years prior to the study, after disputing for 8 years with the road authorities.

Fig. 10.4 Neighborhood sign

The authorities found it unwarranted to label the setting, since the road was too small and there were too few houses. For the people living in the houses, the sign was important for two reasons. First, it was of importance for helping people navigate to commercial activities in the village and thus for sustaining the community economically. An informant argued as follows:

> We have an entrepreneur in the village who rents out forest-machines and farm-equipment, and it's very important for him that his customers can find the way to Slut.

Second, the sign was important for people to sustain a sense of neighborhood community. As a poster argued:

> There are many people that do not know that this village is called "Slut". . . and now at least those who pass by know of us, and there are many people that pass by.

The posting of the sign is not discussed solely as a way to support navigation. Rather it is about establishing an identity of "us" through interaction with anonymous people passing by. The name of the village, as the informant pointed out, is known to all the residents, but unknown to others. The sign can be seen as strengthening the neighborhood community by expressing this "we" to non-members.

Thus, intermediate interaction, which occurs between members of different forms of communities, supports activities between unacquainted people as well as existing social networks. Granovetter (1973, 1983) has argued for the importance of such interaction when studying what he describes as weak ties. He claims that occasions of bridging weak ties are "of special value to individuals. . . It should follow, then, that . . . groups making the greatest use of weak ties are those whose weak ties do connect to social circles different from one's own."(italics in original, 1983, p. 208) Wellman's apparatus makes visible the way in which signs are used to mediate interaction within forms of communities. But we also need concepts that refer to the abundant forms of intermediate interaction which occur between different forms of communities.

10.3.2 Posting Signs as Practical Achievements

Our observations and interviews also reveal the detailed ways in which signs are made and posted to get the message across, given the awkward situation for potential readers. This includes accounting for the location where the drivers read the signs as they pass by, and the time available for reading, which depends on the speed of the car. The posters adopt a repertoire of themes to send the message in a favorable way. We will, in the following, discuss some of these, referred to as boldness, location as index, repetition, personalization, and dynamic messaging.

Boldness. Posters tend to make their signs audacious to get the message across to those passing the place in their vehicles. These drivers and passengers will have to read the sign from quite afar during a brief moment. Boldness is achieved by working with the size, shape, color, iconic features, and material of the sign. In the

Fig. 10.5 A bold and simple food sign

following example, a restaurant owner utilizes both the text and the color to make a strong impression (Fig. 10.5). He said that:

> Considering that they [the drivers] drive ninety kilometers per hour, they have to read it from a distance to be able to slow down and turn. You have to use letters they can see from 100 to 150 meters ahead.

In this case, he used a bright red color to make the sign stick out. Furthermore, the restaurant owner minimized the word length, reducing the message to the blunt concept of "food" ("*mat*" in Swedish) since the drivers have to be provided with big letters. He said "All you need to see is that there is food." More detailed information was provided in proximity to the restaurant (Fig. 10.6). However, the restaurant

Fig. 10.6 Sign beside the restaurant

Fig. 10.7 The sign on the
left is placed as an index for
the turnoff to the greenhouse,
while the side road continues
by turning to the right

owner argued that it was the "food" sign that attracted customers, and not the more elaborate sign.

Location as index. Public road signs get some of their meaning from the location in which they are posted, e.g., a village or a work site. There are also other ways by which the signs become indexical. A vast number of posters extend the index of a sign by making it into an arrow, either through its form or by painting it (see Figs. 10.2 and 10.5). Other posters carefully select the location to provide directions to viewers and help them navigate (Fig. 10.7). For example, a family-run greenhouse had several signs along a road close to their business. They had one official sign, posted by the road authority, on the main road, but the crossing was peculiar. The side road at the crossing swung right after the junction, while the greenhouse was located along a gravel road turning off to the left on that road. While we, the informant, and one of the authors, stood at this crossing, the interviewee argued that:

> We placed it here so that it shows that this is the entrance, so that it's not that one here [pointing at a formal sign and the asphalt road turning right] and then drivers come and start wandering around to the neighbors and so on.

The informant placed a large metal sign beside a gravel road connected to a side road. The location was chosen to direct potential customers off the main road and onto the gravel road, instead of following the side road that diverged to the right and continued in parallel to the main road. Thus, the position of the sign was used as an index.

Repetition. Occasionally, posters multiply signs so that drivers gradually understands the meaning of them, even though their speed, direction, or perspective limits the perception of the signs. Such signs can even play on being small, to draw attention. For example, one poster placed several almost identical small signs (Fig. 10.8) along a stretch of around a kilometer leading up to a bigger sign (Fig. 10.9).

Multiple signs can also be a way of notifying the driver about, for example, directional information. The text on some signs describes how far ahead an activity, a turnoff, and a subsequent sign are (Fig. 10.10). This is particularly useful when, e.g., the official sign is obstructed by a curve or a hill. A person posting such signs (Fig. 10.10) explained as follows:

> The first signs are there so that they [the drivers] will react to the other sign.

Fig. 10.8 Small sign repeated over a long stretch

Fig. 10.9 Big sign by turnoff

Fig. 10.10 Sign in front of curve, notifying the driver of a flea market 100 m ahead

By posting a public sign at the beginning of a curve the owner of an antique shop wanted to alert passers-by that the turnoff to her store was located less than a hundred meters ahead.

Personalization. Public road signs attract drivers' attention because they are unique and distinguished from official signs. One interviewee commented, "you need something more alluring." Thus, in addition to the official signs that the interviewee purchased from the road administrators, he also posted four handwritten signs made of plywood, which, according to him, attracted more customers.

I don't know if it is because they look more amateurish, but the signs work.

Fig. 10.11 Public road-sign
hidden underneath carpet

Thus, a personal and unofficial style was more successful for the interviewee's business than signs that copied the style of official road signs.

Dynamic messaging. Sometimes a message concerns a topic where a static road sign is less appropriate, e.g., shops whose business hours have to be conveyed for some reason. One informant commented that customers arrived at "odd" times unless he provided the hours along the road. One strategy is to hang a specific "open" sign on the other sign every morning. Another approach is to hide the sign altogether when it is not applicable, e.g., by putting a carpet over it (Fig. 10.11).

10.3.3 Adapting to Road Authorities

The life of public road signs is also in the hands of a road authority and its inspectors. We argue that whether a sign should stay or go depends on formal rules about posting signs; organizational procedures; its material form and location; and its content. We will, in the following, discuss first how the administrators actively work with "strategies" to manage the road as an "orderly" place, and second how the posters adapt to the inspectors.

Road inspectors possess the authority to remove public signs, in accordance with a set of formal regulations. But the specific interpretation of them has to be made with reference to a specific situation (Suchman 1987). The signs are first and foremost treated as material objects. The inspectors interpret the need to remove signs in terms of where the signs are placed, how big they are, the material they are made of, etc. The legislation for national roads in Sweden states that messages should be taken away if they are posted inside the "road area." Thus, road inspectors have to decide where these physical boundaries go. On the highways into Stockholm this is defined as the area up to the game fence. Road inspectors also interpret whether a sign is a direct or indirect threat to traffic safety. A direct threat should be taken away immediately, whereas it is less urgent when the sign is understood as an indirect hazard. The interpretation is made with reference to the location and physical form of the sign. Banners are often posted above the road on overpasses, and are considered especially dangerous since one end can fall down. It will then hang all the way down to the road surface, becoming a physical obstruction for drivers.

Their work is complicated by rules which state that removal of signs should be handled with respect towards the owners of the signs in order to maintain the State's "goodwill" and further ensure that they act in a way which is "service oriented" (SNRA 1999). For example, they have to be more careful with removal of expensive signs. If the signs are considered to be litter they are removed because they pollute the road scenery. For example, graffiti can be perceived as un-aesthetic and the writing of it is a criminal offence, rather than a safety hazard.

But it is not always clear if an object beside the road is a sign or not. Citizens are allowed to mount a mailbox along the road. But mailboxes also have the function of telling the road users where the box owners live (Fig. 10.12).

Fig. 10.12 Ambiguous mailbox

Decisions are also affected by content and meaning. Directional signs and signs that warn of hazards seem to get a milder treatment. No civil servant seems to have anything negative to say about, e.g., community signs warning about the presence of children. Signs that inform passers-by about various events are also occasionally accepted since the event is limited in time. The organizers are then trusted to remove the signs afterwards. Commercial signs are occasionally accepted when the removal of them might ruin a small business, e.g., a café. Ideological and political expressions are also allowed in conjunction with elections. And memorial signs marking where a person was killed in a traffic accident, are seldom removed.

The identification and removal of non-allowed road signs is also affected by the organizational procedures of the road inspectors such as regular nine-to-five working hours; routines as to when and where they travel to look for signs (see Chapter 6); or available funding for the task.

To sum up, road-inspectors not only act as maintenance workers, but also as a form of editors of public signs.

Testing the limits of inspectors' interpretations. Posters take into consideration the road authorities' practices when they make and put up signs. Road-inspectors have the authority to remove signs and discipline posters, making them adopt several tactics to keep the sign up as long as possible. The most common strategy is to test the limits of the roadside regulations given the ambiguous practice of the administration. The posters vary the positioning of signs, their appearance, and the times that they are up. For example, one poster placed a sign just beside the road, but it was regularly removed. Then he started to post signs close to a nearby tree on the outskirts of the roadside.

Fig. 10.13 A tractor parked beside the road, or a sign attracting attention to the antiquities store?

In the end I mounted the sign so far out on the roadside that I guess it's no longer the responsibility of the road administration, and the sign has been left alone there.

Posters also vary the times, such as by placing signs along the road during weekends when the road inspectors are not working. Some posters enhance the formal signs, e.g., by attaching flags or additional signs to them. The combination provides legitimacy to the sign, whereas the decorations enhance and complement the official message. Another strategy is to use an ambiguous object that can be understood as a sign but also as, for example, a vehicle that could legitimately be parked along the road (Fig. 10.13). Thus, posters can be seen to display tactics to make use of the gaps in the surveillance of the road authorities. This is tolerated by the inspectors who are sensitized to the specifics of the posted signs, which in the end enables this second road-sign system, or rather sign-posting practice, to exist alongside the official one.

10.4   Discussion

With reference to sociologist Wellman (2001a, b) we argue that most public road signs should be understood as an important mode of interaction between members of different forms of communities. Such road signs are often placed in proximity to settlements or work sites. But the messages are rarely directed to other members of these local communities. Instead they are made for passing drivers, who are themselves more engaged in interaction with people in several other loosely related localities. Here, we needed to go beyond Wellman's categories which account for communities and mobilities. We use the term intermediate interaction to account for this social practice, which is used to strengthen the identity of the neighborhood or the network, and to make it economically sustainable by bridging between different communities, and even different forms of communities.

The posters have developed strategies to enable communication with people who pass on the road. They do not have much time available to get their messages across. Therefore, the messages have to be brief, bold, and easily understood. The driver might have to be notified in advance that there is something ahead for them to read, for example by means of a series of signs. It must also be clear what the sign refers to. Posters of unofficial public signs exploit the locality, indexicality, and context in which they are posted to account for the ways in which signs are perceived by drivers who pass by during a brief moment.

Road authorities struggle with this practice. On the one hand these signs are incompatible with the road administration's view of the road and its proper use, and most of them are removed. On the other hand, they have an informal practice of preserving messages which are considered to have a special value. For the posters, it is essential to develop a repertoire of "tactics" that account for these practices.

However, road administrators' removal of this kind of public signs is not only a problem for this socio-semiotic system; in fact it is a vital recourse for the success, or potential success, of public signs. The roads we visited were remarkably uncluttered by community road signs, with the exception of some roads in Toronto. This is probably due to the road inspectors' maintenance work, but also to the posters restricting themselves as an adaptation to the authorities. A roadside without any restrictions would soon be overcrowded with signs. Hence the role of the road inspector is important to how the public signs are seen. Specifically, we are thinking of how the road inspectors interpreted the content of the signs in a sophisticated way. Their practice is best understood as a form of editing, rather than a mechanical, routine process that could be automated without the loss of important signs. Thus, the roadside is a vital element which makes local life transparent for passing drivers as a form of intermediate interaction. But that geography cannot be seen as in conflict with road authorities and the official state. Rather, it is an intermediate geography also in the sense of something occurring in between communities and the official state.

Kevin Lynch suggested that the "transparency of the setting" made it interesting and meaningful. We have shown how public signs can, and do, provide legibility to the road-space. The signs are used to provide clues in relation to what happens on them, who the abutter to a particular segment of the road is (i.e. who "owns" it), what road-users can do along the road, where children play, where someone is mourned, etc. The roadside, authored by people living on and beside the road, is available, even in the view from the road—as we are driving through the road network.

Further, Venturi pointed towards the opportunity to use the weak tie between the driver and the poster to create a fictitious interpretation of a locale. However, in our studies such use of signs seems much less present than indexical signs with strong links between the sign and local activities. Additionally, Lynch's call for the regulation of such an order was found to be answered by road authorities. Thus, a more postmodern or narrative view on signs has to find other ways into this social practice.

References

Appleyard D, Lynch K, Myer J (1964) The view from the road. MIT Press, Cambridge

Augé M (1995) Non-places: introduction to an anthropology of supermodernity. Verso, London

Beckmann J (2001) Automobility—a social problem and theoretical concept. Environ Plann D Soc Space 19(5)593–607

Buchanan C (1964) Traffic in towns—the specially shortened edition of the Buchanan report. Penguin Books, Hammondsworth

Everett H (2002) Roadside crosses in contemporary memorial culture. University of North Texas Press, Denton

Fotel T, Thomsen TU (2004) The surveillance of children's mobility. Surveill Soc 1(4):535–554

Francis M (1991) The making of democratic streets. In: Moudon AV (ed) Public streets for public use. Columbia University Press, New York, pp 23–39

Garfinkel H (1967) Studies in ethnomethodology. Polity Press, Cambridge

Granovetter MS (1973) The strength of weak ties. Am J Sociol 78(6):1360–1380

Granovetter MS (1983) The strength of weak ties: a network theory revisited. Sociol Theory 1: 201–233

Gunnarsson OS, Lindström S (1970) Vägen till trafiksäkerhet. Rabén och Sjögren, Stockholm

Hartig KV, Dunn KM (1998) Roadside memorials: interpreting new deathscapes in Newcastle, New South Wales. Aust Geogr Stud 36(1): 5–20

Juhlin O, Normark D (2008) Public road signs as intermediate interaction. Space Cult 11(4): 383–408

Krampen M (1983) Icons of the road. Semiotica 43(1/2):1–203

Lynch K (1976) Managing the sense of a region. MIT Press, Cambridge

Lynch K (1981) A theory of good city form. MIT Press, Cambridge

Lynch K, Southworth M (1974) Designing and managing the strip, In: Banerjee T, Southworth M (eds) City sense and city design—writings and projects of Kevin Lynch. MIT Press, Cambridge pp 579–616

Merriman P (2004) Driving places: Marc Augé, non-places, and the geographies of England's M1 motorway. Theory Cult Soc 21(4/5):145–167

Petersson A (2005) The production of a proper place of death. Paper for the seventh conference on the social context of death, dying and disposal, in Bath, UK, September 2005

Pooley C, Turnbull J, Adams M (2005) A mobile century?: changes in everyday mobility in Britain in the twentieth century. Ashgate, Aldershot

Reid JK, Reid CL (2001) A cross marks the spot: a study of roadside death memorials in Texas and Oklahoma. Death Stud 25:341–356

SIKA (2003) Transport and communications—yearbook 2003. http://www.sika-institute.se/Templates/FileInfo.aspx?filepath=/Doclib/2006/ars03en.pdf. Accessed 19 November 2009

SNRA (1999) Handläggningsrutiner för borttagande av otillåten reklam inom vägområdet. (In English: Routines concerning the removal of illegal advertisements within the road area). Report, Swedish National Road Administration, Region Stockholm 1999-02-01

Suchman L (1987) Plans and situated actions. Cambridge University Press, Cambridge

SWOV (1997) Sustainable solutions to improve road safety. Research activities 8.SWOV Institute for Road Safety Research, Leidschendam

Thrift N (2004) Driving the city. Theory Cult Soc 21(4/5):41–59

Urry J (2000) Sociology beyond societies: motilities for the twenty-first century. Routledge, London

Urry J (2004) The automobility system. Theory Cult Soc 21(4/5):25–40

Venturi R, Scott Brown D, Izenour S (1972) Learning from Las Vegas: the forgotten symbolism of architectural forms, MIT Press, Cambridge

Wellman B (2001a) The persistence and transformation of community: from neighbourhood groups to social networks. Law Commission of Canada, Ottawa

Wellman B (2001b) Physical place and cyberplace: the rise of personalized networking. Int J Urban Reg Res 25(2):227–252

Wellman B, Boase J, Chen W (2002) The networked nature of community: online and offline. IT Soc 1(1):151–165

Chapter 11
The Road as a Stage in Journey Games

We suggest that the delight and playfulness of road use can be drastically enhanced through the design of computer games that in various ways include encounters with other drivers and roadside objects, hereafter referred to as Journey Games (Brunnberg 2008). But the success of such games depends on balancing Kevin Lynch's (Lynch and Southworth 1974) demand that local geography and social life be made transparent and legible, with the possibility to transform and play with the meaning of spatial properties in the landscape. As we have previously discussed, Lynch himself favored an adaptation of roadside architecture, to make local community life transparent to the mobile visitors. Venturi et al. (1972), on the other hand, agreed on the distracting effect of high speed, but instead saw it as an advantage that should be preserved. The speed provides the architect with an opportunity to engulf the traveler in a new role by designing roadside objects with heightened symbolism, e.g., the bold signs in Las Vegas that are reminiscent of Roman culture. Signs and architecture can be used to enable the imaginary, and appeal to the tastes and values of "common" people. The speed of the vehicles erases the ordinary local meaning of individual geographical objects, which is then transformed into something completely different through the large-scale roadside architecture. We will in the following investigate whether it could be possible to design for the cursory experience of people in traffic by utilizing emerging digital technologies. We suggest that this new design material, which was not available to the architects in the 1970s, provides opportunities to design for delight and play beyond the possibilities inherent in the physical materiality of roadside objects.

Children traveling in the back seats of their parents' cars are the intended players in our design experiments. They spend time in the back seats of cars for various reasons such as routine trips back and forth to school, or to pursue their leisure activities. Kids go with their families to shopping centers, visit relatives and friends, and follow their parents on longer trips on vacations and weekends. In the UK children younger than 5 years of age travel in a vehicle as much as 45 min per day (DFT 2005; Hu and Reuscher 2004). They have very limited control of where the car is moving, and there is no demand on them to take part in the maneuvering. There is no other option than to sit still for some time, and possibly try to enjoy the journey by looking out the windows, reading, or daydreaming. However, this period of

O. Juhlin, *Social Media on the Road*, Computer Supported Cooperative Work 50,
DOI 10.1007/978-1-84996-332-9_11, © Springer-Verlag London Limited 2010

physical inactivity is sometimes considered boring, which makes transit a common use-context for mobile games (Andersen 2002).

Currently, the fight for their attention between looking out at local communities and looking in at symbolic digital illusions on their computer screens is being won by the latter. The children in the back seats focus on the digital worlds of the computer game characters on various game consoles. Many passengers attend to their avatars and their movements through digital landscapes, at the same time as the vehicle in which they sit moves through the road network without them paying any attention to it. We acknowledge such experiences, but suggest that the local context could provide for a new type of thrill in game play. We learn from Las Vegas that their isolated position could be used to provide fictitious experiences, but suggest that we should learn from Kevin Lynch that these could be more interesting if they are linked to the local. Thus, the game application should make the geographical objects more transparent and communicate local meanings of geographical objects over distance and during a very short interaction span. Then those meanings could be *transformed*, that is, referenced as geographical structures but with associated fictitious content.

The idea of providing mobile game play which draws upon the geographical surroundings of a car journey is related to the concept of pervasive games. This term originates from the research field of pervasive computing with its focus on computing "anywhere, anytime" (Brunnberg 2008; Lindley 2005; Montola et al. 2009). The games surround the player everywhere, all through the day, which makes them tightly interwoven with the player's everyday life. The term is today often seen as a broad genre arching over subgenres such as augmented reality games and location-based games. Augmented reality is generally seen as a mixture of real and digital environments, but often specifically refers to people who put on techy glasses, or so-called "see-through" displays (Cheok et al. 2003; Milgram and Colquhoun 1999; Nilsen et al. 2004; Thomas et al. 2000). The players walk around within an outdoor game-space and see digital objects overlaid on the surroundings. A number of industrial and academic research projects explore the idea of using geographical locations as a resource in computer-generated game play. This possibility is, for example, exploited in an SMS game (Stroud 2002) where players move around and fight opponents using cell-phone positioning. In research, several other games have been developed for pedestrians. They might chase after virtual coins in teams (Bell et al. 2006) or chase each other (Flintham et al. 2003). Basically, these location-based pervasive games relate to geography for navigational challenges, and manual work is often utilized to enrich map data and make the game scale over space. The way in which our games have been designed and investigated has also been informed by the game theoretician Eskelinen (2001) and his use of Espen Aarseth's theory of cybertexts (Aarseth 1997, p. 64). Aarseth argues that there are three main user functions in a game. The player needs to interpret a game, just as when she reads a traditional text. She needs to figure out how the game works and what she is supposed to do. This aspect is close to what would be called usability aspects in other domains of digital technology. When it comes to hypertexts the player also has to choose which way to go, which Aarseth calls the explorative function. This is tied to narrative aspects, though specifically concerning texts with multiple optional reading paths such as on the internet, or recently, in interactive storytelling. The reader herself has to choose which way to move through the text, and in that sense has some control over the narrative aspects. Finally, games have a configurative function by which it is possible to add to the content through manipulative actions. This is the most essential part of a game, according to Eskelinen. It is when the player engages in configurative manipulations, and actively changes some game states, that she really engages in game play.

Taken together, we need to balance how much transparency we give to local life with the necessary fictional transformation, when we design a game which should be able to be interpreted, explored, and configured in an interesting and challenging way. The ways in which such connections should be made have been investigated by designing three different games. These are called the Backseat Game, Backseat Playground, and Road Rager. The Backseat Game was the first attempt to explore how specific roadside objects could be tied to a digital game in order to provide interesting manipulative challenges, enjoyable explorations, and ease of interpretation. Specifically, we made efforts to provide salient configurative challenges along with narrative and explorative features. Backseat Playground added to the investigation by accentuating interactive storytelling and exploration, as well as providing scalable game play with the inclusion of a complex series of road objects. Finally, Road Rager investigated the possibilities for game manipulation in very brief traffic encounters, which accentuated the interpretative aspects of journey gaming.

References

Aarseth E (1997) Cybertext; perspectives on ergodic literature. Johns Hopkins University Press, Baltimore

Andersen (2002) Mobile multimedia study. Report from European Commission Directorate-General Information Society

Bell M, Chalmers M et al (2006) Interweaving mobile games with everyday life. In: Proceedings of the SIGCHI conference on human factors in computing systems, Montréal, QC, Canada, pp 417–426

Brunnberg L (2008) Playing with the Highway experience – pervasive games on the road, Ph.D. Thesis, IT-University of Göteborg, Gothenburg

Cheok AD, Fong SW et al (2003) Human pacman: a mobile entertainment system with ubiquitous computing and tangible interaction over a wide outdoor area. In: Proceedings of mobile HCI—the fifth international symposium on human–computer interaction with mobile devices and services, Udine, Italy, pp 209–223

DFT DfT (2005) Focus on personal travel. Department for Transport, DFT, London

Eskelinen M (2001) The gaming situation. In game studies. Int J Comput Game Res 1 (1), http://www.gamestudies.org/0101/eskelinen/. Accessed 15 July 2010

Flintham M, Benford S et al (2003) Where on-line meets on the streets: experiences with mobile mixed reality games. In: Proceedings of CHI 2003, pp 569–576

Hu PS, Reuscher TS (2004) Summary of travel trends: 2001. National Household Travel Survey. U. D. FHWA

Lindley CA (2005) Game space design foundations for trans-reality games. In: Proceedings of ACM SIGCHI international conference on advances in computer entertainment technology, ACM, New York, pp 397–404

Lynch K, Southworth M (1974) Designing and managing the strip. In: Banerjee T, Southworth M
    (eds) City sense and city design—writings and projects of Kevin Lynch. MIT Press, Cambridge,
    pp 579–616
Milgram P, Colquhoun H (1999) A taxonomy of real and virtual worlds display integration.
    In: Ohta Y, Tamura H (eds) Mixed reality-merging real and virtual worlds. Springer, Berlin,
    pp 1–16
Montola M, Stenros J, Waern A et al (2009) Theory and design pervasive games: experiences on
    the boundary between life and play. Morgan Kaufmann, Burlington
Nilsen T, Linton S, Looser J (2004) Motivations for augmented reality gaming. In: New Zealand
    game developers conference NZGDC'04, Dunedin, New Zealand
Stroud M (2002) Have cell phone, will shoot wired. http://www.wired.com/gadgets/wireless/news/
    2002/02/50205, Accessed 20 November 2009
Thomas B, Close B et al (2000) ARQuake: an outdoor/indoor augmented reality first person
    application. Personal Ubiquitous Comput 6(1):75–86
Venturi R, Brown DS et al (1972) Learning from Las Vegas: the forgotten symbolism of
    architectural forms. MIT Press, Cambridge

Chapter 12
A Game for the Backseat Experience

The Backseat Game consists of a framing story and five geographical game locations where local stories are told and manipulative challenges are provided.[1] The game locations are situated along a 4-km stretch of road in the periphery of downtown Stockholm, separated by a distance of approximately 800 m. The children have to find virtual objects at these locations, which are only visible when using the screen of a handheld computer as a small virtual window onto this magic world.

A framing story is told whenever the player launches the game, which provides the player with an understanding of the goals of the game. They are told of a scientist who works in a laboratory at the edge of the town. He has succeeded in inventing a special kind of energy. Unfortunately he gets locked out of his lab and finds himself in a parallel world inhabited by other life forms. The player's mission is to carry a virtual key and give it to him as soon as he is located. When the scientist is provided with the key, he can get back into the lab and get rid of the ghosts from the parallel world.

The player can see the parallel world through a special device (Figs. 12.1 and 12.2). It works both as a virtual window that reveals objects in the fictitious world, and as a collector of these objects. Many of the game's characters are malicious creatures which attack the player in order to grab the key. But the player is safe as long as she has enough energy. If the creatures' attacks on the player are successful they get hold of the key and then the lab, and eventually they would invade our physical world.

The game is designed to make it possible to reach game locations in any sequence without limiting the possibility to interpret and engage in a series of manipulative activities. This is done through provision of abstract and self-contained local stories. When the car approaches a location (Fig. 12.3) it will first trigger a local story (Fig. 12.4), presented by means of pictures of the particular roadside object overlaid with animations and a narrator voice. The story is initiated well before the roadside object passes beside the vehicle, in order for it to be completed before the manipulation begins. It provides instructions about upcoming configurative challenges, which

---

[1] This chapter draws upon research presented in Brunnberg and Juhlin (2003). Reprinted from the publication with permission from IOS Press.

Fig. 12.1 Game device with "virtual window"

Fig. 12.2 The game was implemented on a handheld computer (PDA) equipped with a GPS receiver and a digital compass module

Fig. 12.3 Conceptual description of a manipulative event

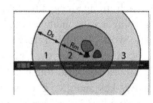

Fig. 12.4 Screenshot from a local story

is important since the player is only located near the game location for a very short time. The manipulative event is triggered when the player comes very close to the location. The device automatically changes to a window-mode (Fig. 12.5) where the player can aim at objects in the physical environment to find virtual objects.

Fig. 12.5 Mode for manipulation

12.1 Selecting Roadside Objects

The geographical objects have been selected with reference to the way they can be interpreted, explored, and configured. An object is selected from an interpretative perspective. It should be easy to recognize and single out from the surroundings when passing by in a car. The chosen objects are either single items, such as a tree or a house, or an area, e.g., an allotment or a gas works. Areas are easier to distinguish than smaller items. But the choice of objects must also be considered in terms of suitability for manipulation. The player has to know where to look when aiming. A virtual object can be more difficult to find if the player is uncertain where to look on the physical object. The player has to find exactly the right spot in the area to identify the virtual object. We believed that it would not add to the gaming experience to search the whole area just for one virtual object. We have therefore chosen to add multiple virtual objects on large physical objects. This is hereafter referred to as a *patch event*, since the virtual objects can be seen as a number of patches on a large roadside body. Examples include an allotment area (Fig. 12.6) inhabited by several virtual creatures, or a gas works area containing virtual tools. *Wrap events* consist of singular virtual objects tied to a physical object, such as a virtual document dropped at an old oak tree (Fig. 12.7), or a ghost inhabiting a cottage (Fig. 12.8). They provide for different configurative challenges when finding the virtual objects at a specific area and aiming at them.

Second, the objects chosen were located about 10–50 m away from the road, which adds to the sense of motion which is central to the highway experience (Appleyard et al. 1964). However, the time for identification and manipulation is

Fig. 12.6 An allotment

Fig. 12.7 An oak tree

Fig. 12.8 A little cottage

Fig. 12.9 A gasometer

decreased, which makes game manipulation hard. Furthermore, most of the real roadside objects chosen were located on one side of the road, rather than on both sides. The allotment was an exception, with the player traveling through the object and being surrounded by virtual objects. According to Lynch, objects which communicate some social practice create a specific sense of drama. Again, the positive experience of exploration can make game manipulation more challenging. Third, the objects were chosen to convey a specific meaning. It had to be attractive and fascinating for the player to locate them by the roadside. We assumed that players would easily understand the meanings of concepts such as "old oak tree," "red cottage," and "power plant." The game would also benefit if the objects were interesting elements even within the traditional highway experience. There is an element of prying involved in looking out of car windows. Appleyard et al. (1964) argue that "the sight of activity, or a sense of the meaning and use of areas, is an important pleasure of the road." Therefore, we chose objects like a power plant, a cottage, and a gasometer (Fig. 12.9), which evoke questions concerning their everyday use. Finally, the objects are provided a meaning in the game stories. Here, it is possible to either emphasize the object's spatial attributes and then provide a fictitious meaning to it, or try to draw upon a common socially recognized meaning. In this game, we choose to employ everyday recognized meanings of objects, and make the game story fit with them. The magic of the objects is created in the way the objects' traditional meanings are used as elements in the game stories. We have only invented new meanings for objects if the players almost certainly lack a clear understanding of what the object is, e.g., when making a gasometer into the lab of the main character.

12.2 Children's Appreciation

Two girls and two boys, between the ages of five and ten, were invited to evaluate the game. Initially, all of them hesitated a bit before accepting roadside objects as part of a computer game and instead constantly focused their gaze on the screen. One of the boys, who was only five years old, never quite understood the idea of connecting the game play with real-world objects. The three older children changed their behavior after a while. Two of them understood the game concept rather quickly; that is, they made a connection between the game-content and the physical surroundings outside the car, while the third player had to struggle a bit. Their understanding of the game, which included roadside objects, was visible in the ways in which they looked for objects outside the vehicle as soon as they were referred to in the local story. The oldest boy became most immersed in the game. He even avoided aiming the device towards the supposed object if any other physical entity, e.g., the car seats in front of him, were blocking the line of sight. This indicates that he thought of the virtual creatures as really being on the roadside. The three oldest children managed to find and hit virtual objects at least a couple of times during the game. We concluded that it was possible for the older children both to understand the game concept, as well as manipulate the device effectively.

In general, the players managed to find and interpret roadside objects correctly. But some mistakes were made, e.g., when one boy tried to interpret the meaning of "old oak." He found it difficult to decide which of all the trees that was the oldest one before he had seen them all.

The ease by which a player identifies a geographical object indicates the possibility of understanding and interpreting the game. The players managed to find virtual objects at wrap events with minimal effort, but it was more difficult during patch events. We expected them to scan both sides of the area with their virtual window when the local story declared the virtual objects to be all around. But instead they sighted in a fixed direction out of the right side window of the car and used the movement of the car to sweep through the area. Possibly they missed information presented in the local story telling the number and location of virtual creatures.

There was a noticeable difference between the ways two players moved the device, and how they fixed their gaze, during the two types of manipulative encounters. During wrap events, such as the old oak and the cottage, they identified the physical object and then aimed straight at it. The angle of the device was continuously adjusted to the position of the car to fine-tune the direction. Their gaze moved back and forth between the screen and the physical object to make sure that they were aiming in the right direction. At patch events, they adopted a different strategy. They either aimed the virtual window at a fixed point inside the car, making it sweep through the large roadside object, or at a specific point outside of the car. Further, they fixed their gaze either on the device or out through the window. We suggest that this behavior could be explained by the larger virtual space to explore in order to find the virtual object. They had to investigate the roadside continuously during the whole event, which was cumbersome. Therefore, they focused either on the screen, waiting for objects to show up, or out through the window, peppering the environment, without checking whether there were any virtual objects on the screen. In all, we argue that it is possible to build on different relations between physical roadside objects and digital objects, where physical objects provide clues as to what imaginary objects there could be, and where they are located.

12.3 The Enjoyment of the Game

The players' facial expressions differed between the first and the second round. Two of the children looked concentrated and serious during the first tour but relaxed during the next. The older boy became active and involved, which was visible in his expressive facial expressions and body movements. The other child was generally calmer in appearance during both rounds. But there was a noticeable difference as soon as she had understood the game. She said that it was hard in the beginning when she tried to hold the device like a normal portable game, but became fun as soon as she understood what to do. The second girl looked tense all the time, even though she made very positive comments afterwards.

The children's level of engagement varied between different events. The older boy got excited during several manipulative encounters, and seemed to favor the old oak tree the most. He also said that he enjoyed the wrap events most. It was easy to figure out where the virtual object was at the old oak tree. At the same time, it provides a strong sense of motion (Appleyard et al. 1964), since one of them is located in a corner close to the road. The girl, who scored most, displayed a more relaxed attitude, smiling gently during many of the manipulative events. The less successful girl looked stressed and did not seem to enjoy the game at all. Second, the children also showed varieties of emotions in relation to the exploration of the journey as different local stories played out along the way.

In general, they all displayed amusement with many of the stories, including the framing story. The allotment event, which is a patch event, where the car passes right through the game space, caught most of the girls' attention. This is supported by the research on the highway experience, which suggests that objects surrounding the road generate a special sense of drama (Appleyard et al. 1964). In terms of game research theory, we might think of this appreciative game function as an explorative part of the game. It is not game exploration in the sense that the children control their movement, but rather the appreciation of being taken along on an exploration.

To sum up, the first attempt to produce a Backseat Game proved to be rather successful. But it is complex game and the players differ in the way they appreciate exploration and manipulation. The roadside objects must be highly distinctive. The choice of ambiguous objects, such as a specific oak tree from among several, has negative effects. This could be a problem on monotonous sections of roads. Basically the fun of use differs depending on whether the players prefer exploration or manipulation. Manipulation is most fun at wrap events. Furthermore, it is more fun if it provides a strong sense of motion. All of them enjoyed the stories in the game. Eskelinen's argumentation (2001) for a focus on configuration, or manipulation, in game research should be understood as a part of the game experience and not the whole experience. Storytelling is most fun at roadside objects that in themselves evoke interest, such as places that display activity or evoke a sense of drama.

References

Appleyard D, Lynch K, Myer J (1964) The view from the road. MIT Press. Cambridge
Brunnberg L, Juhlin O (2003) Movement and spatiality in a gaming situation—boosting mobile computer games with the highway experience. In: Proceedings of interact'2003—IFIP TC 13 international conference on human–computer interaction. IOS Press, Zurich, pp 407–414
Eskelinen M (2001) The gaming situation. Game Stud Int J Comput Game Res 1 (1), http://www.gamestudies.org/0101/eskelinen/. Accessed 15 July 2010

Chapter 13
Locative Interactive Storytelling Along Vast Road Networks

Our first attempt, described in Chapter 12, to design a context-dependent game for passengers inspired us to make another attempt.[1] In order to further elaborate our design space we have designed another game which expands the narrative elements in the game, as well as increases the scale to cover vast geographical environments. Recent advances within the interactive storytelling area are promising (Crawford 2005; Mateas and Stern 2003; Szilas 2003), and show how stories adapt to players' or readers' engagement in various ways.

The issue of providing for multiple readings of a designed experience is a topic in the emerging field of interactive storytelling. This is a research area that has come into focus in the area of computer games, where better stories could provide more interesting experiences (Charles et al. 2004; Laaksolahti 2003). Charles et al. (2004) defined it as the "real-time generation of narrative action that takes into account the consequences of user intervention, by 're-generating' the story as the environment is modified by the user's intervention." Research has aimed to resolve the tension between interactivity and the traditional demand of linearity in a plot, to provide dramatic effects such as conflicts and resolutions. Furthermore, the focus has been on providing believable characters with depth and complexity, e.g., emotional behaviors (Crow et al. 2003). Although, it is too early to say that interactive storytelling has settled the issue of how to balance linearity and user control, the available systems are sufficiently developed that we can expand the area of research.

There is a also a genre of mobile, location-based storytelling applications of interest for the generation of journey games. A number of locative mobile games (Charles et al. 2004; Crow et al. 2003; Jakl 2004) present individual static stories when the players access specific geographical locations. The total travel experience becomes a random collection of visits to locations with embedded stories, which in terms of a reading experience could be described as an anthology, rather than a novel. We would like to see a game where a single and interesting story unfolds independently of where the players go and how they move through the road network (Malaka et al. 2004). Appleyard et al. (1964) argue that since the

---

[1]This chapter draws upon research presented as Brunnberg et al. (2009). Reprinted from the publication with permission from ACM Press.

O. Juhlin, *Social Media on the Road*, Computer Supported Cooperative Work 50,
DOI 10.1007/978-1-84996-332-9_13, © Springer-Verlag London Limited 2010

traveler moves in physical space, the view changes from one moment to the next generating various sequential *experiences*. The experience is composed of a series of objects, which might provide a dramatic experience where the arrangement or type of objects abruptly changes, or a more stable and soothing experience where a homogeneous arrangement of objects gently moves against a large background or slowly passes in the far distance. The sequence of the objects depends on how the passenger moves through the road network. A road can normally be followed in two directions. Traveling along the road in one direction leads to the objects appearing in a different order than following it in the opposite direction. It follows that a critical challenge when designing for the journey experience is to account for the multitudes of possible readings of the landscape. This poses a design problem at any specific section of road. To use a more computer-centric vocabulary, it can be argued that the journey experience is interactive vis-à-vis the road users' movements. It is therefore a challenge to design for dramatic effects, for example escalation and relief, when the designer cannot know in what order they will be experienced.

Furthermore, several mobile, location-based storytelling applications provide narratives rich in detailed references to the specific locations where they are being told. Our challenge lies in generating content for very large geographical areas. The genuine mobility of vehicles, and their abundant use, make them move over large territories and in very complex patterns. Since it is not likely that game designers will manually cover such areas with game content, we also have to investigate ways in which to provide game events over vast territories with minimal effort.

Our challenge is to develop a narrative engine that utilizes the movement of the vehicle and the path of the journey to form a sequential story rather than a random anthology. The concept of a journey through a computer-generated environment has been used in several interactive storytelling systems to enforce linearity (Crawford 2003). But then the journey is a pre-designed backdrop which determines the unfolding of the story. There is a major difference between such a use of a journey, to provide narrative rigor in a computer game, and using a journey as it unfolds in real time through a physical landscape.

Finally, we saw that the children struggled to pay attention to both the digital device and the passing landscape. Thus, the design of the interface seems to need further attention to make it fit with the context of use. Again, we return to Appleyard et al. (1964) study of looking at the roadside from a passing vehicle. They argued that a passenger's *visual focus of attention* is affected by the speed of the vehicle, which makes each object appear during a very short time span. Motion, as well as spatial geographical arrangements, structures certain forms of interaction. The direction of the gaze is likely to change with the speed of the vehicle. At high speed the visual attention tends to be directed forward. A slower speed allows a broader gaze where the viewer is likely to pay more attention out to the sides. The shape of the road itself might contribute to directing the attention of the viewer. A curvy road would, for example, direct the viewer's attention in an outward angle. A viewer is more likely to attend to nearby objects in the immediate environment, which appear to be "moving," rather than distant stationary ones.

13.1 Design Concept and Implementation

The game-play scenario presented in Section 1.2 is made possible through the system presented below (Gustafsson et al. 2006). It consist of a device which provides the player with a hardware interface, as well as a back-end system. The players' device consists of handheld hardware in the form of a directional microphone (Fig. 13.1) and a pair of headphones. The directional microphone metaphor is used in order to superimpose an aural landscape onto the outside view. For this task it contains a Pocket PC and an advanced module containing magnetometers and gyros capable of sensing the users' gestures. The display of the Pocket PC is used to represent a number of virtual tools, e.g., a walkie-talkie and a phone. The phone and walkie-talkie provide audio conversations through synthetic voice generation with in-game characters. The player responds by making selections on a list presented on the screen.

The back-end of the game consists of a laptop, which hosts the server, a GPS receiver, and a local wireless LAN. The server contains commonly available digital maps, game scripts, sound effects, several voice libraries for speech synthesis of the in-game characters, as well as story and map engines. As the passenger moves through the landscape a soundscape is automatically generated using the information provided by the maps and the motion data provided by the GPS. This is done by first filtering the maps for suitable information, which is then translated into geographical encounters that can potentially occur along the road. The encounters are then provided to the game engine which compiles story events with local geographical references. The player interacts with the soundscape by pointing the directional microphone at audio augmented objects.

The choice of audio-centric interaction is motivated by the experiences we had with our first attempt. Passengers have no means of controlling their velocity and direction in order to make time to visually attend to both the landscape and a screen. Furthermore, even minimal graphical interaction diverts passengers' visual attention from the outside environment onto the computer screen. Taken together, it would be much better if the passenger could focus as much possible on the passing

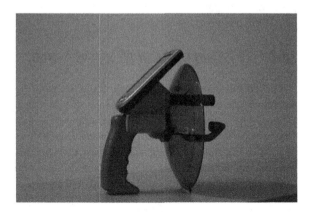

Fig. 13.1 The Backseat
Playground handset

environment, which leaves it up to us to find other ways to interact with the game. Audio-centric interaction gives the player the ability to listen to fictive activities taking place in the surroundings while at the same time looking out the windows.

As we have previously argued, a journey game should make the meaning of geographic objects more transparent (Leshed et al. 2008; Lynch and Southworth 1974), as well as transform the meaning (Venturi et al. 1972). Here we draw upon digital maps based on commonly known classification schemes of geographical objects such as houses, public buildings, mansions, churches, sports grounds, lakes, and fields. That data enables us to present the roadside objects in somewhat greater detail than is normally available to the passenger (Leshed et al. 2008). The game allows us to transform local meanings of objects.

Furthermore, the velocity of the passenger causes the experience of an individual geographical object to be influenced by passengers' previous encounters; i.e., the exploration is a sequential experience. The application should be designed to fit into a series of encounters with geographical objects, rather than just a single location. Therefore, the game engine pauses the progression of a story line until a requested geographical object emerges. As a player's intended route is unknown to the game, the sequence of physical objects that appear is highly arbitrary, and a specific object might take time to become visible. A single story line, with specific local objects, might not provide sufficient sequential experiences. Hence, the prototype is implemented with six concurrent and interconnected story lines. Each story line includes a set of story events—each triggered by a particular set of objects—that advance the narrative. Furthermore, the choice of objects changes over time. When the game starts, an event might only be triggered by an infrequent object, such as a church. It might also accept a more commonly occurring object, such as a private house, if no church appears for a set period of time.

13.2 How Did It Work?

We conducted a field trial where the subjects used the prototype for a limited period of time in its intended setting. In total, 10 players, three girls and seven boys, participated in pairs.

13.2.1 The Geographical Origin of Sounds

We asked the players whether they could identify the geographical source of the sounds. Michael and Daniel (Fig. 13.2), said that they knew the origins "to some extent." For example, they linked the sound of a submarine to the surface of the water they had seen. They also connected sounds of a tennis game to a sports hall. Other players linked the sounds of boats to the view of the sea. They connected various sounds to map objects such as a golf course, houses, and a road junction.

But the objects they reported were only a minority of all those that were executed during the field trials. Furthermore, the objects they recalled seemed to be rather

Fig. 13.2 Michael and
Daniel testing

large, as compared to non-reported objects. The prevalence of oversized objects can
be explained either by insufficiencies in mapping the digital to the local, due to deficiencies in the precision of the gyro, or by the way the sounds are presented. They
could also have failed to actually see the geographical objects, since these might
have been occluded by other objects in the landscape. But then they would instead
recall other geographical objects than those referred to in the digital map data. It
could also be explained by the motion of the user vis-à-vis the object, providing only
limited time to identify and then remember it. Geographical objects such as forests,
golf courses, and enclosed pastures allowed for more time to identify and interact
with them. Thus, similar to what Lynch and Venturi (Lynch and Southworth 1974;
Venturi et al. 1972) argued regarding architectural roadside objects, it seems that
size does matter, even in the case of passengers interacting with audio-augmented
objects. Although some game experiences occurred as a combination of visual sight-
ings and audio effects, it seems that the soundscape did not sufficiently foreground
smaller objects for visual identification.

13.2.2 Imaginary Visual Experiences

The interviews reveal another interesting aspect of how the landscape was experienced. The difficulties in recalling what they had seen led them to remember what
they had seen inaccurately, such as in the following two interview transcripts:

Table 13.1 Was there really a church?

Researcher: Where, more precisely? Which church are you talking about?
Michael: Mmmmm, don't know.
Researcher: What did it look like.
Michael: Like an ordinary church [Daniel: Yes]
Researcher: You actually did see the church?
Michael: No [Daniel: No]

Michael talks about a church he has seen. He even describes it as "ordinary" and Daniel agrees. Upon further questioning they both reconsider and claim that they did not see the church. Interestingly, the interviews with Steve and Bob reveal a similar confusion as to what they have actually seen.

Table 13.2 Overhearing some burglars

Steve: We heard the robbers a couple of times talking about 40,000. What was it? 40,000 dollars? [Bob: 40,000 dollars]
Researcher: Okay. Where were they?
Bob: We had just turned into a road by then.
Steve: It was in a church, wasn't it? They were in a church.
Bob: Yeah, later on. But we had just made a turn.
Researcher: How did you see that it was a church? How do you know that they were in a church? [Bob: First, we heard. . .]
Researcher: Bob, how do you know that it was a church. I wasn't there you know.
[Bob: I guess you said so.] Steve: How did it go... This leader, the one who is our main boss said that they had. . .
Researcher: She said so, but did you see it yourself? [Steve: No]
Researcher: Okay, you didn't see it.
Steve: Or wait! I heard it. Yes, I could hear the bells.

They recalled overhearing a conversation between burglars. When asked where it occurred they first referred to a junction, where the car made a turn, and then to a church. They claimed that the conversation could be heard "in a church," which was the location given to the sound effect by the game engine. Upon further questioning it turned out that the reference was not to a sighting of the church, but to the sound effect of church bells. In both those cases, they spoke about the objects as if they had seen them, whereas after further discussion it turned out that they had not. It follows then that the design of the system did not support them well enough to make the church itself noticeable. The system failed to overcome the interactional challenges posed by the motion of the passengers, which make it hard to single out specific geographical objects and link them to the game events. However, the cursory experience might also explain why they thought they had seen the church. This is interesting since it tells us that there are opportunities to lure the players into a fictitious understanding of not only what is going on outside the car, but also what they are actually looking at.

13.2.3 Sequential Experiences

The passengers' motion brings them to many different places during a game session. The game is designed to account for that motion and provide a serial location-dependent narrative. The game execution varied between all trial runs, even though the evaluation took place along the same route. This was due to variations in velocity, game play, and occasional system errors. Our video recordings and the interviews give more details as to how the velocity of the vehicle affects the players' alignment of game events into sequences.

In the following we will discuss the "dead body" scenario (see Section 1.2), which is a script including two geographical events triggered in sequence. Several sound effects trigger at various locations, with the intention of referring to two separate geographical locations. First, it refers to the location of a house from which a gunshot is heard from afar, and then from the same house but at a closer distance when some burglars' conversation is heard. Second, we also referred to the location of friendly field agents in the vicinity of a field. The intention was to provide clues in a sequence, to lead the player to take appropriate actions regarding the orders to the field agents. The script was triggered during all the test sessions, however it played out at diverse geographical locations.

The interviews reveal that the players in four out of five cars connected the gunshot heard during the first event with the dead body found during the next event. However, none of these players referred to the action as relating to a specific house. It is possible that the intended building was not visible during some of the game sessions, or that the device failed to support their investigation.

The players in the fifth car never mentioned any relation between the two events, but rather talked about them as separate occurrences. They instead interpreted the gunshot as if they themselves were the target. Furthermore, these players linked the second event to a house that they had seen outside the window of the car. A close look at the video recordings of the game-play (Table 13.3) reveals that variations in the motion of the cars might have influenced those variations in the interpretations of game events.

In the transcript in Table 13.3, the fifth car is driving past a sports ground and stops at a red light. The first event is triggered and a walkie-talkie call from a field agent is heard (07:49). The players immediately look in the direction the agent is referring to. The gunshot is heard (07:55) while the car is still halted at the red light.

Thus, the car is actually standing still when the event is executed. In the other trials, the car was moving when the script was triggered. We suggest that the variations in speed might have influenced their interpretation of the game narrative. The players in the fifth car interpreted the gunshot as being directed towards them. It is not so surprising that the players did not link the gunshot to the dead body found moments later. A possible interpretation is that a player that is standing still might feel more exposed and vulnerable than if the car is moving at high speed. In this way, motion might contribute to a feeling of confidence.

Table 13.3 Excerpt from the dead-body script in the fifth car

Time	System output	Road context	Visual focus
07:49	Agent:"We're on the other side of sports ground"	Car is standing still at red light	Look towards sports ground
07:55	Gunshot	Standing still	Look towards screen
08:01	Choices	Standing still	Looks at the screen

13.3 Discussion

Backseat Playground is an ambitious implementation which on a technical level shows how we can build location-based games for passengers. Conceptually, it is a design pattern which makes possible narrative-driven applications which are geographically dependent, but not specifically made for each place where they provide interesting content. The evaluation with the children was promising but also raised some questions. The constraints for interaction with roadside objects, that is, the limited time in each encounter, and the enclosed position of the passengers, seem to plays some tricks on the gamers.

It is, of course, difficult to interact with small objects. But what was more troublesome was that our particular audio design did not make small objects more salient. What was interesting to see, however, was that our system occasionally made the passengers believe that they had seen objects which had not been sighted. We argue that this effect emerged due to the motion of the car, which gives them little time to get a good view of individual geographical objects. They then confused the soundscape with the actual view of the road setting.

The design of passenger applications can benefit from the balance between transparency and transformation when adding new experiences to the road. But that balance needs to also be considered in design. First, it seems like the cursory experience of the landscape makes it difficult to visually identify objects, but easy to trick the passenger. It might be difficult to change that balance to improve identification while at the same time preserving the potential to trick the player. Second, new techniques might increase the precision of mapping digital content onto the geography. But then the passenger has to put even more effort into identification work, which leaves less time for the experience of individual objects.

A critical challenge, given the players' motion, is to fit a temporally unfolding game, with its associated location-dependent narratives, to an unpredictable travel path. Here, the results are promising since the players made sense of the different episodes as being part of an overall narrative. However, the players occasionally had difficulty associating fictive content to several sequentially appearing locations, such as hearing a gunshot at one location and then associating that event to a sound appearing somewhat later.

Immersion is a central concept within game theory. It can occur when difficult sensory-motorical and mental tasks are combined (Björk and Holopainen 2004). In all, the players struggle to keep up with things, leading them to invent new interaction strategies to cope with the situation, although missing out on many details. This could in some cases be interpreted as a failure. But from a game design perspective it is not necessarily negative, since these types of applications should provide interesting challenges, rather than solve problems as effectively as possible. Furthermore, almost all the players responded that they felt as if the game was going on outside the window. Several players also struggled to distinguish between what they actually had seen and what they believed they had seen. We argue that all this, taken together, shows that the game provided a very immersive experience.

At the same time, the motion influenced the passengers' emotional experiences in ways which were difficult to understand. We think that a lower speed created a sense of vulnerability, which had consequences for game play. When the vehicle was standing still during an intense moment in the game, the players' interpretation of the event differed from that of moving players. It appeared as if a lack of speed made the player feel more vulnerable than if the car was rolling. High speed might contribute to a feeling of confidence where the player feels more like an observer, while standing still would suddenly turn the player into a victim.

References

Appleyard D, Lynch K, Myer JR (1964) The view from the road. MIT Press, Cambridge

Björk S, Holopainen J (2004) Patterns in game design. Charles River Media, MA

Brunnberg L, Gustavsson A, Juhlin O (2009) Games for passengers—accounting for motion in location-based applications. In: Proceedings of the international conference on the foundations of digital games (ICFDG), 26–30 April 2009. Disney Wonder Cruiseship, FL, pp 26–33

Charles F, Cavazza M, Mead S et al (2004) Compelling experiences in mixed reality interactive storytelling. In: Proceedings of ACM SIGCHI international conference on advances in computer entertainment technology, June 3–5, Singapore

Crawford C (2005) Chris Crawford on interactive storytelling. New Riders, Berkeley

Crow D, Pan P, Kam L et al (2003) M-views: a system for location based storytelling. In: Proceedings of UbiComp 2003, Seattle, WA

Gustafsso A., Bichard J, Brunnberg L, Juhlin O, Combetto M (2006) Believable environments: generating interactive storytelling in vast location-based pervasive games. In: Proceedings of the 2006 ACM SIGCHI international conference on advances in computer entertainment technology. Hollywood, CA

Jakl A (2004) The workflow of C++ game-development on a series 60 platform device. Bakkalaureatsarbeit 238-003-045-2, Fachhochschul-Bakkalaureatsstudiengang. Multimedia Technology and Design, Hagen

Laaksolahti J (2003) Towards socio-emotionally rich interactive narratives, Lic. thesis, Department of Computer and Systems Sciences, Stockholm University

Leshed G, Velden T, Rieger O et al (2008) In-car gps navigation: engagement with and disengagement from the environment. In: Proceedings of CHI 2008, pp 1675–1684

Lynch K, Southworth M (1974) Designing and managing the strip. In: Banerjee T, Southworth M (eds) City sense and city design—writings and projects of Kevin Lynch. MIT Press, Cambridge

Malaka R, Schneider K, Kretschmer U (2004) Stage-based augmented edutainment. In: Proceedings of smart graphics: fourth international symposium, Banff, Canada

Mateas M, Stern A (2003) Façade: an experiment in building a fully-realized interactive drama. In: Proceedings of game developers conference

Szilas N (2003) IDtension: a narrative engine for interactive drama. In: Proceedings of technologies for interactive digital storytelling and entertainment (TIDSE) conference, Darmstadt, Germany, pp 187–203

Venturi R, Scott Brown D, Izenour S (1972) Learning from Las Vegas: the forgotten symbolism of architectural forms. MIT Press, Cambridge

Chapter 14
Multiplayer Gaming in Traffic Encounters

Finally[1] we turn to traffic encounters in an attempt to provide an inspirational pattern of game play for children in the back seat. The experiential qualities of such encounters were discussed in Chapter 8 and 9. Our hypothesis is that a game could be particularly engaging if it included the vivid and dynamic mobile context, such as when the geographical surroundings are included. Contingent traffic encounters such as rapid frontal meetings, protracted overtaking, or gatherings, e.g., traffic jams or queues at red lights, constitute an essential part of the experience of traveling along a road. We suggest that these meetings can also be used to create fun and compelling game experiences.

We have previously discussed how the speed of the vehicle influences the game experience for better and for worse. The brevity of the encounters with geographical objects makes it difficult to handle game play, but also supports immersion in the game. A central challenge in this chapter is to discuss how having even less time, as can be expected during encounters in opposite lanes, for example, should be handled, and how it will be experienced. Here our study shows that minimalism is critical.

A number of academic research projects make use of proximity between players as a resource in mobile computer gaming (Barkhuus et al. 2005; Björk et al. 2001; Sanneblad and Holmquist 2003). These games are played via the interface of a mobile device using traditional graphical user interfaces, with buttons and stylus as interaction mechanisms. Thus, the players have to choose between looking at their surroundings and engaging in the game. The problem of providing a proper balance of digital interaction and physical interaction has been raised by Trevisan et al. (2004). They argue that the multiple sources of information available, and the two worlds of interaction, demand that the users make "choices about what to attend to and when." They suggest that we move beyond the first design agenda of creating a seamless, invisible fit where things are blended together, to see mixed reality as consisting of discrete elements between which users alternate. The issue is to design the boundaries to allow alternation but preclude improper combinations. This is not

---

[1] This chapter draws upon research presented as Brunnberg and Juhlin (2006). Reprinted from the publication with permission from Springer Verlag.

O. Juhlin, *Social Media on the Road*, Computer Supported Cooperative Work 50,
DOI 10.1007/978-1-84996-332-9_14, © Springer-Verlag London Limited 2010

least important in this case where the temporal boundaries are extremely limited (Koleva et al. 1999).

We have therefore turned to the area of tangible user interfaces, which were originally developed to close a "gap" between parallel but related activities in a real and a virtual world. Tangible user interfaces allow more embodied interaction with the computer. For example, Ping Pong Plus was designed by Hiroshi Ishii and his colleagues already in 1999 as a form of "digitally-augmented cooperative play" (1999). Table tennis has been augmented with an interactive surface, which incorporates sensing, sound, and projection technologies. The players can focus either on real objects, such as the ball, or look at the augmented effects when it hits the table. There are a number of projects exploring the field of tangible interfaces and games (Magerkurth et al. 2004; Mandryk et al. 2002; Mueller et al. 2003), although in stationary settings depending on pre-set infrastructures such as projectors or tabletops.

14.1 The Road Rager

We have designed a game prototype, called the "Road Rager." It enables game play by wireless ad hoc Mobile ad hoc networking technology between car passengers as they convene within a limited range in a similar way to the applications Sound Pryer, Hocman, and Road Talk. In this case, we wanted to design a user interface that can be handled and experienced while watching for cars in the vicinity during the limited time span of an encounter in traffic. Screen-centric interaction risks causing the player to focus on the computer, rather than look out the windows, and thus spoils the specific benefits of the game. Consequently, a key challenge concerns the possibility to enable the player to balance her attention between the computer and traffic, when the time available for identification and interaction with the opponent is very restricted.

The game is developed for a PDA equipped with WLAN capability. The game device is aware of the player's aiming direction by means of a digital compass, and the geographical position through a GPS-receiver (Fig. 14.1).

The devices automatically initiate a game-event when two players are in close proximity, i.e., within approximately 100–200 m of each other. The player takes on the role of a character with magic powers. Her goal is to acquire power in preparation for the yearly witchcraft convention. Power is measured in stars and frogs, which are gained or lost when dueling with other players. A duel is automatically launched when two players are within wireless range. The event ends when one player becomes enchanted, or if they move out of range. If a player charms her opponent, the objects she possesses are traded for more powerful ones; e.g., frogs are exchanged for stars. If the connection is broken they receive stars or frogs depending on their results up to that point.

To account for traffic safety we have minimized the player's urge to request assistance of the driver. More specifically, there is no support in the game for predicting traffic encounters or making them happen more frequently by changing travel routes or driving styles. Further, it is essential that the player should feel comfortable with

Fig. 14.1 Clutcher, PDA, and Bluetooth GPS

Fig. 14.2 LEDs on top of Clutcher

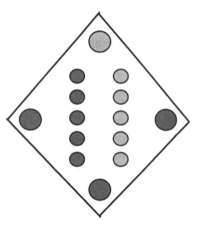

the embodied interaction provided by the game, even though they are buckled-up and remain so.

The tangible interface, called the Clutcher (Fig. 14.1), is equipped with fourteen LEDs and a button. Four of the LEDs, hereafter referred to as "locator LEDs," are placed in each corner (Fig. 14.2) to inform the player of the direction of the opponent. Ten smaller LEDs are placed in two rows. They are sequentially turned on and off to indicate the amount of magic power the player possesses.

14.2 Balancing Focus of Attention through Design

According to Trevisan et al. (2004) designers can influence what users look at and interact with by controlling attention through the design of the synchronization and integration of the user interface. Synchronization refers to the ways in which an event controlled by the system is temporally unfolded. The system can present media, demand input, or request a task either simultaneously or in a sequence. Integration refers to choices of what types of interaction will occur, e.g., how the user will receive feedback and how the media are distributed to output devices. Furthermore, integration refers to where the media is presented vis-à-vis the user's attention, i.e., in the central or peripheral context of the focus of attention.

The users' attention can also be influenced through the design of game characteristics such as how the game is *explored* or how it should be *manipulated* (Eskelinen 2001). Exploration refers to the players' experience of moving and traveling within the game. In this case, the players' view from the windscreen becomes integrated with that experience, and especially the ways in which they look at surrounding vehicles to *identify* adversaries. Manipulation refers to tasks provided in the game, where players actively change the state of "temporal, spatial, causal and functional relations and properties" (Eskelinen 2001). As argued previously, a game can work without interesting narratives or other forms of exploration, but it must always have manipulative challenges to be a game. Finally, a specific focus of attention can be afforded by the reward structure in a game.

Three tools (the *Magic Wand*, the *Sludge Thrower*, and the *Electro Squeezer*) were designed, which in various ways combine user interfaces, tasks, and rewards, in order to investigate the possibilities of enabling and experiencing combined attention.

The *Magic Wand* (Fig. 14.3) requires that the player combine her attention to be successful. The player has one chance to cast a spell, while very close to the opponent, to get a high score. Therefore the player needs to know exactly who she is contending with. The identification is made possible by the "locator LEDs" on the Clutcher (Fig. 14.1), which give clues as to the direction of the opponent. When the adversary is located, i.e., when the player has decided who in that direction she is contending with, she visually focuses on that car and makes the gesture when they are very close. It is the most rewarding of the tools if the player identifies the opponent and waits until they are close (approximately twenty meters) to cast the spell, to further favor visual identification. If the spell is cast directly after peer connection the gain is only minimal.

Fig. 14.3 Casting spells

The tool affords a sequential order of tasks that must be performed to be successful. The player must first identify the opponent and then wait until the other car is really close before engaging in manipulation. The user interface is designed to allow a visual focus on the traffic both during identification and manipulation. The player can simultaneously look at traffic and the LEDs on the Clutcher as a form of sight, when trying to identify the opponent. The player can continue to look at traffic while making gestures in a circular pattern to cast a spell when engaging in game manipulation. Furthermore, sounds are played while the Clutcher is moved, and when the spell is properly cast.

The *Electro Squeezer* is designed with minimal demands on the player to combine her attention and identify the adversary in order to be successful (Fig. 14.4). It only requires that she recognize that an opponent is within wireless range, which is conveyed by a specific sound, before starting to manipulate. There are no limits as to how many times the player can score but the rewards are small. The tool sends out fictive electric shocks and plays a specific sound if the Clutcher is squeezed. Thus, there are no demands for either simultaneous or sequential ordering of tasks.

Fig. 14.4 Triggering electric shocks

The *Sludge Thrower* (Fig. 14.5) is designed to require a degree of interaction with traffic somewhere in between those of the previous tools. It enables the player to throw virtual sludge at the opponent and score points if it hits. Similarly to the Magic Wand, the process requires that identification and manipulation be carried out sequentially. The design to support identification is also the same. However, the tools have different manipulative tasks. The Sludge Thrower only requires that the Clutcher be aimed towards the opponent to be successful. Furthermore, the integration of modes of interaction is similar to that of the Magic Wand. The player can

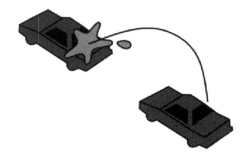

Fig. 14.5 Throwing sludge

throw magic sludge in the same way as she would throw a smaller real object to score points. The gesture recognition registers when the player moves the Clutcher forward and downward. The player will hear a sound indicating that something is flying through the air for approximately two seconds and then a sound indicating a hit or a miss. This interaction can be done at the same time as looking out of the windows. There are no limits as to how many times the player can score.

14.3 User Feedback

Road Rager is intended for game play between unacquainted contenders in chance encounters on the road. These meetings may take place anywhere along the road network. In order to ensure encounters with other players, as well as to be able to observe the game play, we set up a field trial which was restricted to a preset circular route where the subjects used the prototype during a limited period of time, in three different cars. Fourteen children, between 8 and 10 years old, tested the game. As a word of caution, it has be to be acknowledged that the test situation was unrealistic in certain ways. The children encountered the same cars several times and soon learnt what they were searching for, which would be unlikely in a real game situation.

The way the players directed their attention varied between the three tools. For each tool we have structured the material accordingly. First, we discuss whether the players (i.e. the child holding the device and the partners) understood how the tool was supposed to be used. Second, we analyze the players' focus of attention during game play. Finally, we present the players' experience of using the tool.

Casting magic spells. The Magic Wand is designed to require a high degree of visual focus on traffic, in conjunction with a focus on the computer interface. It was difficult for the players to meet both these demands as discussed with reference to the following two excerpts.

Table 14.1   Handling the magic wand

Time	Sound	Hand movement	Visual focus	Comments
10:22	Magic Wand		F looks out P looks at device	
10:26	Connect		F looks out P looks at device	P: aaa
10:27		P lifts the device	P looks out F looks at device	F: aaa
10:28		P moves the Clutcher in a circle	P and F look out through the windscreen	
10:29	Spell			
10:30		F points at a passing car they meet in opposite lane	P looks down at the screen. F looks out through the left window. P quickly glances at F's hand then back to screen	F: there!
10:31			P and F look at screen	P: where?

P, player; *F*, partner; *R*, Researcher

In the excerpt above, the player already has the Magic Wand activated when the game-event begins (10:26). Both the player and the partner quickly look down at the screen when they hear the sound icon which indicates that the ad hoc network is connected. They both look out through the windscreen and the player immediately makes the gesture to cast a spell (10:28). Then he directly focuses on the screen. Not even his partner's pointing towards the opponent drags his attention away from the computer (10:30). He seems confused, which is further supported by his comment "where?" while he is looking at the display, and by his refusal to look where his partner is pointing. Thus, the player casts the spell almost immediately after the connection sound is heard with very limited attempts to identify the opponent. He does not perform the tasks of identification and manipulation in a sequence as intended in the design, but rather almost juxtaposes them. However, during manipulation the player simultaneously maintains visual focus out through the windscreen while interacting with the computer, i.e., listening to the audio feedback and interacting with gestures. Thus, here the player combines his focus of attention.

Table 14.2 Device-centric interaction

Time	Sound	Hand movement	Visual focus	Comments
05:51	Connect		P looks at PDA screen	
05:52	Spell+Hit	P moves the Clutcher in a circle	P looks at the PDA screen	P: help!
05:55			Fl looks down at the PDA screen	F2: was it someone who hit us?
05:58	Electro Squeezer Hit		P and Fl look at the PDA screen	F1: try and take this one

The excerpt in Table 14.2 presents another type of game play in which the Magic Wand is used. The player has the tool activated before coming into wireless range of the opponent, as in the previous example. When the sound icon, indicating network connection, is heard (05:51) the player looks at the screen on the PDA and immediately makes the gesture to cast a spell (05:52). As in the previous case, the player goes straight into manipulation, casting the spell immediately after the connection sound is heard. She does not really attempt to identify the opponent and does not wait for the cars to come close enough to get a high score. Then both the player and a partner look at the PDA screen (05:55). One of the partners asks whether they got hit (05:55) and they then get into a discussion about what tool to use next (05:58). However, in contrast to the other case, the player pays no visual attention to the traffic when engaged in manipulation, and solely focuses on the computer screen. Thus the player displays what we term "device-centric attention." This type of gaming did not fit with our intention to require a visual focus on the traffic.

There could be several explanations of the juxtaposition of identification and manipulation as well the device-centric attention. It seems like the players understood the concept of the wand in general and how it depended on identifying the adversary and delaying the casting of the spell until they were really close. This general understanding of the concept is visible in other parts of the field test. On one occasion a partner says, "I think we see them... be prepared... I think we should take the Sludge Thrower, it has better range than the Magic Wand." Thus, we need to look at other possible explanations. The demand for interaction could be set too high given the brief duration of game play. Or the players could just have become too excited to wait until the opponent was identified and was close enough. However, the concept of a Magic Wand cannot be ruled out altogether since its proper use is difficult to evaluate during such a short field test.

It is not surprising that the players commented in the interviews that they did not like the Magic Wand. Some of the children had thought that the Magic Wand was going to be the most fun and useful tool before the test. Erik said they had thought the wand would be the best tool "because you died right away." However, they soon changed their minds because, as Bill said, "it didn't turn out that way. You earned more by choosing a less effective tool."

Throwing sludge. The Sludge Thrower provides information on the direction to the opponent and requires that a gesture be made in that direction to be successful. Thus, it provides valuable information on where to look for the adversary, but does not require that they know exactly where in that direction the car is in order to score.

The majority of the children quickly got the idea of how to handle the Sludge Thrower. Most of them practiced throwing sludge when there were no opponents around. There were two ways of using the tool requiring that the players balance their focus of attention in different ways. First we will look at game play where the player successfully engages in interaction with combined attention.

During the game-event the player changes tool to the Sludge Thrower (23:27). He holds up the Clutcher towards the windscreen. He looks at the LEDs and then out in the direction indicated (23:31). After another quick glance at the LEDs he throws sludge in the same direction (23:34). He looks out in that direction as the device plays a sound indicating that the sludge is flying through the air. Thus, identification and manipulation are smoothly performed in sequence two times. Furthermore, the player holds the Clutcher in his line of sight. The player shifts visual focus between it and the traffic. Here we are close to what we were aiming for. The player focuses both on traffic and on the digital device.

The excerpt in Table 14.3 also displays a collaborative approach to attending both to traffic and the device. The partner is actively searching for the opponent (23:27). He identifies a suspected car and points it out to the player (23:36). The player then throws sludge in that direction (23:37). Thus, the partner makes the identification for the player.

There was also a type of use of the Sludge Thrower, in which visual attention was solely on screen, like that previously discussed. We will, in the following, discuss such a case, even though detailed transcriptions have been excluded for brevity. In this case, both the player and the partner look down at the screen on the PDA when the sound indicating peer connection is heard.

The player holds the Clutcher in her lap. She soon changes her visual focus to the LEDs and throws sludge in the direction indicated by the green light. They meet the

Table 14.3 Combining identification and manipulation

Time	Sound	Hand movement	Visual focus	Comments
23:17	Connect		P and F look at the screen	F: now
23:22		P casts an unsuccessful magic spell	P looks at the screen. F looks out through the windows and searches actively for opponent	F: I think they are behind us
23:25		P casts a magic spell	P first looks at the LEDs and then glances out through the windows for a second	
23:27	Sludge Thrower	P changes tool to Sludge Thrower, F points towards the left side-window	P looks at the screen, F looks out through the windows and searches actively for the opponent	F: wait! here …
23:31		P holds up the Clutcher aims towards the left side-window	P first looks at the LEDs and then out through the windows for the opponent	
23:34	Sludge + Miss	P throws Sludge	P looks at the LEDs and then out again	
23:36		F points towards a blue car parked in the opposite lane		F: there was Troll-pelle!
23:37	Sludge	P throws Sludge in direction F is pointing	P and F look in the direction toward the opponent	
23:39	Sludge Hit		P and F look down at the screen	P: yes! R: did you get him? P: yes, I got him!

opponent driving in the opposite direction and the locator LEDs switch in response and indicate that the adversary is now located behind them. They observe the locator LEDs and turn the Clutcher backwards so that the green LED lights up. Once more she makes a gesture to throw sludge with her eyes steadily on the Clutcher. Neither the player, nor the partner, even once look out through the windows during this game-event, but identify the direction to the opponent simply by looking at the locator LEDs. Still, as in the previous case, their interaction follows a sequence of identification and then manipulation.

To sum up, the Sludge Thrower was used both in a way where the players divide their attention between the traffic and the digital interaction, and in a way with device-centric attention. This was similar to the way the Magic Wand was used. However, the Sludge Thrower provided a more interesting gaming experience than the Magic Wand, since the game play was often successful and was conducted sequentially from identification to manipulation as intended in the design of this tool. The Sludge Thrower also provided a better experience according to the interviews. Several of the players thought that the Sludge Thrower was the most fun tool to use, even though it was considered somewhat difficult. A player said, "I think the Sludge Thrower is easiest to shoot with…but it is harder to hit with it." Another player preferred the gesture per se.

We suggest that the differences in the success-rate and playing-experience of the Sludge Thrower and the Magic Wand can be understood with reference to the classical semiotic notion of indexical and symbolic signs. The gesture of the Sludge Thrower, that is, the required movement of the Clutcher forward and downward, can be interpreted as an indexical sign (Fiske 1982), in the sense that it gets its meaning from the local context. Throwing implies that something in the context gets something thrown at it. In this case, the availability of an adversary in the direction of the gesture supports an interpretation of the gesture as a throw. The spell, on the other hand, is a symbolic sign, which means that it gets its meaning from a social convention. In brief interaction, such as in a traffic encounter, the indexical throw gesture is more intuitive and easier to understand than the more abstract gesture of a circle referring to a spell. When time is short, and players are excited, it is possible that this minimal difference is of importance.

Triggering electric shocks. The Electro Squeezer requires no visual attention on the traffic for successful scoring. The player only has to pay attention to the sound indicating that an opponent is within wireless range. Then he can directly start to score points by pressing the Clutcher. Consequently, all the children quickly understood the concept.

Again, we identified two types of focus of attention during game play. We will start by discussing the type of gaming where the players combine their focus of attention. For brevity, we do not provide the transcriptions.

Just before the event the player and partner discuss what tool to use. The connect sound is heard. They look at the screen and the player selects the Electro Squeezer. The partner says "Push! Squeeze! You don't have to aim." He looks out of the windows in search of an adversary, while holding up the Clutcher in the line of sight. The player squeezes the Clutcher while looking out. He suddenly says "there!" and then glances down on the PDA screen. He lifts his gaze and smiles, as he continues to squeeze the tool. Both the player and the partner looked at a car, in the opposite lane. The player keeps on squeezing while holding up the Clutcher, aiming it towards the passing car. The partner waves towards the car (Fig. 14.6). In this event, the player engages in what we have referred to as combined attention even though it is not required to score; i.e., he looks out through the windows while simultaneously interacting with the computer.

We also observed a type of gaming where the players' attention was centered on the devices. In the following event, the player and partner immediately look down at the screen as the connect sound is heard (Fig. 14.7). The player holds the Clutcher in her lap and they both look at the LEDs, while she persistently squeezes the tool. After a while the player exclaims, "aaa! there is only one left." The player observes

Fig. 14.6 Combined attention

Fig. 14.7 Device-centric attention

the power LEDs, which present the scores in the current exchange, taking no notice of the surrounding traffic.

Thus, the players used the Electro Squeezer in the same two ways as when interacting with the previous tools. The difference is that in this case, the visual focus on traffic, as displayed by the boys above, was not required to score points. We suggest that it occurred since the players found the visual presence of the opponents interesting and fun. In the interviews, the boys discuss the experience of encountering someone physically in a multiplayer game. The best part of the game, according to them, was:

> Bill: ...the feeling...
> Erik: when you encountered someone...
> Bill: ...you become sort of ... it gets exciting somehow.

Some children preferred this tool because they didn't have to aim. The interviews reveal that they considered this to be especially good when something blocked their view of the opponent. Still, for other children this tool was not considered as fun as the Sludge Thrower, because it was only about squeezing.

14.4 Discussion

This study provides initial feedback on how to design for interaction when the boundaries in a mixed reality world are very short-lived and when people move quickly around. The study is a starting point for understanding the possibilities of designing for traffic encounters.

The interviews and the observations of the players during game play made it clear that these temporary encounters created a thrilling gaming experience, even for the partners in the cars. Several children mentioned that the feeling when someone was in the vicinity, and they were searching for the opponent, was fun and thrilling.

We have gained insights into how the users balanced their focus of attention between the traffic and the gaming device. We identified a type of gaming, which was observable in the use of all three tools, where the visual focus of attention was directed solely towards the screen or the tangible interface, and never out towards traffic. This was a successful form of interaction, in terms of scoring, for the Sludge Thrower and the Electro Squeezer, but a failure when using the Magic Wand. Thus, for those tools where identification was not necessary, the players occasionally did not engage with the traffic, and even when it was required they still did not do so. In that sense, it also failed to live up to the design intention of requiring players to identify the opponent and thus engage in looking at the traffic in those situations. On the other hand, both the Sludge Thrower and the Electro Squeezer were also used in a way where the players combined their visual focus of attention on traffic with engagement with the computer.

The Magic Wand provided for a sequential unfolding of the tasks of identification and manipulation, which was not applied by the players. Instead they went straight into manipulation as soon as the connection sound was heard. Perhaps the pressing situation in those brief encounters pushed the player to go directly to action. We cannot conclude that demands for sequential unfolding of tasks should be completely ruled out in future designs. In game design, the easiest solution is not always the best. However, it is clear that this type of sequence of tasks, which requires a delay for more exact positioning, should not be a general design principle. Further, the Magic Wand, which was designed to require identification, and thus visual focus on traffic, generated the least amount of attention out of the windows. Possibly, this tool is too complex and demanding for the limited time available for game play in such brief encounters.

The Sludge Thrower provides a both fun and illusory experience, and we observed frequent occurrences of combined attention. Here, the sequential unfolding of tasks was smoother. Even though it is only slightly different than the Magic Wand, the difference seems to be crucial. First, the Sludge Thrower requires less strict positioning and gives the players many chances to score. Second, the Sludge Thrower recognized an indexical gesture while the Magic Wand recognized a symbolic gesture with a more abstract meaning. Thus, the Sludge Thrower provided a tighter blend in the manipulation, but was more forgiving in terms of identification.

When using the Electro Squeezer the focus of attention was very much on the surrounding traffic, although it was not required to score points. Still the players enjoyed it. We suggest that the experience of being able to see the opponent makes a very simple game play more exciting. Thus, the success of the Electro Squeezer supports the general design concept of drawing on meetings to make a game which is both comprehensive and challenging in an interesting way.

In general, it is difficult to enable game play when the lifetime of the game-event is so short. There is just too little time to engage in extensive identification before getting into manipulation. However, our study also showed that the weak approach to identification was appealing to the children. On several occasions, the players successfully combined their visual orientation towards the traffic with a focus on the computer interface. And they enjoyed identifying whom they were playing against, even though it was not necessary for scoring. Weak identification, in this sense, adds to the exploration of the game landscape.

Furthermore, indexical gestures, such as throwing, make interaction more intuitive. Other examples for future design could be scooping, patting, or hugging. These gestures are less complex than obscure symbolic gestures of various kinds.

To sum up, we have in this paper been concerned with how to combine and balance a player's focus of attention between traffic and a computer, while at the same time providing a game which is comprehensive, interesting, and challenging. All in all, it seems possible to exploit contingent traffic encounters to create a both compelling and fun game experience. But minimalism is critical for success. The features and tasks of the game have to be cut down to the minimum. Even such a simple task as was supported by the Magic Wand was too complicated. Of course, games should not be designed to be easy, but to provide interesting challenges. However, in this case, the challenges of the use context themselves are so difficult that the designer as a first priority should focus on making the concepts achievable. Then, social situations such as traffic encounters, could become new use contexts for mobile multiplayer games.

References

Barkhuus L, Chalmers M et al (2005) Picking pockets on the lawn: the development of tactics and strategies in a mobile game. In: Proceedings of Ubicomp'05—the seventh international conference on ubiquitous computing, Tokyo, pp 358–374

Björk S, Falk J et al (2001) Pirates!—using the physical world as a game board. In: Proceedings of Interact'2001, conference on human–computer interaction, Tokyo, Japan, pp 423–430

Brunnberg L, Juhlin O (2006) Keep your eyes on the road and your finger on the trigger—designing for mixed focus of attention in a mobile game for brief encounters. In: Proceedings of the fourth international conference on pervasive computing. Springer, Heidelberg, pp 169–186

Eskelinen M (2001) The gaming situation. Game Stud Int J Comput Game Res 1 (1), http://www.gamestudies.org/0101/eskelinen/. Accessed 15 July 2010

Fiske J (1982) Kommunikationsteorier—En introduktion. Wahlström & Widstrand, Stockholm,

Ishii H, Wisneski C et al (1999) PingPongPlus: design of an athletic-tangible interface for computer-supported cooperative play. In: Proceedings of CHI'99, conference on human factors in computing systems, Pittsburgh, PA, pp 394–401

Koleva B, Benford S, Greenhalgh C (1999) The properties of mixed reality boundaries. In: Proceedings of the sixth European conference on computer-supported cooperative work, Copenhagen, Denmark, pp 119–137

Magerkurth C, Memisoglu M, Engelke T (2004) Towards the next generation of tabletop gaming experiences. In: Proceedings of GI'04, conference on graphics interface, London, ON, Canada, pp 73–80

Mandryk RL, Maranan DS, Inkpen KM (2002) False prophets: exploring hybrid board/video games. In: Extended abstracts of CHI'02, conference on human factors in computing systems, Minneapolis, MN, pp 640–641

Mueller F, Agamanolis S, Picard R (2003) Exertion interfaces: sports over a distance for social bonding and fun. In: Proceedings of CHI'03, conference on human factors in computing systems Ft. Lauderdale, FL, USA, pp 561–568

Sanneblad J, Holmquist LE (2003) Designing collaborative games on handheld computers. In: Proceedings of SIGGRAPH'03 sketches & applications, international conference on computer graphics and interactive techniques, San Diego, USA

Trevisan DG, Gemo M et al (2004) Focus-based design of mixed reality systems. In: Proceedings of the third annual conference on task models and diagrams, Prague, Czech Republic, pp 59–66

Chapter 15
Post Script: A New Balancing Act for Research on Traffic and Mobile Technology

Our analysis of road use and social interaction started off as a reaction against taking people's descriptions of life in traffic as a private activity as a strict guideline (Bull 2004; Redshaw 2008). It is often claimed that we enjoy commuting in cars because it gives us private time to relax and escape from the social pressures of family life and work. Obviously, this view does not lead us to account for the social coordination and negotiation which are required in order to drive safely. Perhaps we should instead see such accounts of driving as indications of how smoothly the social interaction between unacquainted strangers runs. The experience of loneliness in traffic should then be understood as a social situation with strangers, where the driver very seldom gets to account for his actions, and where social negotiations in most cases run very smoothly, which in a sense makes the social invisible. This is, of course, a description that does not fit everything that happens in traffic. There are many accidents and other situations where the driver finds himself in an awkward social situation. People get angry and try to tell him off by various means, or he becomes involved in an accident and finds himself surrounded by people demanding that he account for his actions. The point here is that we, in both those situations, should refrain from de-socializing the activities based on accounts of road use as a private activity. There is, as we have discussed, much to learn about vitality, fit, and control of traffic, from detailed investigations of social interaction in traffic.

We argue that social interaction has consequences for major topics in transportation science such as efficiency, safety, and control. Traffic coordination should be seen as a "situated practice," where both formal and informal rules are used and negotiated in specific situations. The ways in which drivers come to agree on how to share a particular section of road depend on local and contingent interpretations of the codes. Thus, the success of road use, in the sense that only few encounters lead to accidents, depends to some extent on our social skills and mechanisms for settling such issues on the fly. We have also seen how people manage to perform other tasks than driving, such as speaking on a mobile phone, through interactional adaptation to other road users and the people they are talking to. Since both driving and talking on the phone involve being with people, they are both adapted to each other. There is nothing odd about one or the other. The driver can adjust his coordination with the other road users to his conversation, just as he can adjust his conversation

O. Juhlin, *Social Media on the Road*, Computer Supported Cooperative Work 50,
DOI 10.1007/978-1-84996-332-9_15, © Springer-Verlag London Limited 2010

to the demands of traffic. Finally, we have also seen how social interaction in traffic is a temporally extended and ongoing practice, despite taking place during brief moments. The interaction consists of what conversation analysts would call a single turn, such as when a person makes a proposition which is then affirmed by someone else. But we also discussed examples which were somewhat more extended, such as when a pedestrian showed that she wanted to cross a road. The driver just continued at a constant slow speed, which made the pedestrian pull back. We also discussed even more prolonged ongoing social practices such as the road inspectors having to return several times to specific locations, and make continuous inquiries in order to decide how to handle a specific road object.

How we coordinate ourselves with others influences the efficiency, or the fit, of street use. How well a section of the infrastructure meets the demand depends on how well a particular social practice—for example coordinated maneuvering along a shared road—maps onto the technical resources for doing so. These technical resources do not only include tarmac and concrete. In several of the case studies, the drivers were also using modern technology, such as mobile phones and hand-held computers. The lorry drivers used them to make calls, and the road inspectors to organize their work tasks. Again, successful usability of a particular computer device depends on how it fits into social interaction. The lorry driver coordinates his use of the mobile phone with people around him. The usability of the new computer device is also coordinated with people around the road inspectors' truck.

How much mobile technology, such as mobile phones, diverts drivers' attention away from traffic must be understood in a context that accounts for their engagement in interactional adaptation. The path from "distractions" to unsafe driving is not as straight as experimental research and psychological research assume. Thus, traffic research really needs to improve its understanding of social interaction in traffic to get a grip on how, e.g., mobile technologies influence safety.

Safety is an important aspect of life on the roads and is a goal of government institutions and researchers, as well as the road users themselves. Therefore, social interaction might not always be a problem needing to be done away with, such as by replacing human drivers with artificial ones. Instead increased interaction might be exploited to increase safety, such as discussed in the chapter presenting the application called Road Talk. It is intended to enhance the means for drivers to share information and knowledge about the state of the roads while they are driving. It is a resource for community-based traffic information to increase vitality and access. The Place Memo application is also intended to improve the fit between the current technologies and their use in traffic, as well as expand the possibilities for collaboration in road inspection. Safety and efficiency have been the main targets in the design phase. It is also important to account for traffic safety in such cases where it is not the main focus of the application, such as when designing journey games. The intention was to prevent the game play from interfering with the driving in any sense. This decision made us focus on passengers in the back seat, and we avoided any dependence on driver assistance for the gameplay. The interfaces were also designed to allow the player to remain buckled up yet still feel comfortable with the embodied interaction provided by the game.

The control of road use, as, for example, pursued through official traffic codes and policing activities, is also socially negotiated. Driving schools teach how to apply traffic codes in situations where there are other people around who adhere to other rules. They also teach students about situations where it is better to apply informal rules. We discussed how mobile technologies and SMS services support social interaction to defeat control technology related to speed limits, i.e., automated speed traps. All these examples show the importance of social interaction in a setting where we often disregard those aspects in everyday life.

We have argued that the role of social interaction in road use goes beyond traditional topics within transportation research, such as safety and efficiency, and perhaps also beyond our common understanding of traffic. Let us return to a driver who depicts her car use as a period of solitude on the way home from a hectic work day. It is not rare that people think about this situation as being alone for a while (Bull 2004; Redshaw 2008). Perhaps it is fair to understand this as an experiential statement or conception, rather than a description of the social maneuvering task at hand. Still, we argue that her experience is of a social kind, albeit of a type termed "accompanied solitude." The driver is anonymous, among other drivers, and she can rest her eyes on them in a way that resembles the wanderings of the flâneur. She can glance at them and fantasize as did the Baudelarian figure who strolled around city streets looking at people. Although that activity is ubiquitous in traffic, there are also other types of road users who engage in social interaction in traffic even more. Motor bikers' brief encounters combine the pleasures of riding with social interaction. Again, new technology already plays a role in this form of experiential social interaction. The motorcyclists turn to the web and chat forums to get more out of their meetings on the roads. These examples point to the importance of understanding driving as a socially sensual activity, which includes delight and play. The need to broaden the scope to understand the experiences of social life in traffic is also evident in the interaction between roadside inhabitants and passing drivers. We coined the concept of "intermediate interaction" to account for how roadside inhabitants communicate with anonymous and transient visitors. Road signs are used to advertise commercial activities along the road, to establish identities, or just play around. Lynch's concept of legibility, that is, the degree to which road users can communicate via symbolic physical features, is well suited to account for this form of social interaction (Lynch, theory of Good City Form).

We have invented several applications than focus on sense, enjoyment, and play. Motorcyclists could bring internet servers and browsers into traffic. This would provide them with the benefits of the Internet while they are engaged in their cherished traffic encounters. Hocman allows them to meet physically and digitally at the same time, which would enrich the aesthetics and their community life. Car drivers could use Sound Pryer, a shared car stereo, to allow them to listen to music from other car stereos in the vicinity. This allows them to break down the sense of isolation or enjoy peering into the audioscape of nearby cars.

These applications provide means for drivers and other road users to present themselves and show their identity, thereby increasing the legibility of road use. They offer resources for a playful relation to identity and social life. We do not attempt to provide technologies that bring about some clear or unambiguous representation of individuals and communities in the sense that Kevin Lynch imagined. Hocman and Sound Pryer should be seen as lighthearted resources, which allow people to show who they are and to play around with their identities in meeting with strangers.

The focus on playful representations of street life becomes even more obvious in the games we have designed and developed for children in the back seat. These are intended to transform and make transparent the meaning of swiftly passing geographic objects. The Backseat Game and the Backseat Playground link gameplay to the spatial surrounding of the car. This relation should include local meanings of geographical objects, i.e., make visible to passing road users what is going on alongside the road and the meanings residents give to activities and objects. But the games also gain by altering their meaning, in a sense that would probably be awkward to local inhabitants. Both these approaches add to the gaming experience of the passenger and we might even say that the use of local geographical objects in games is a highly promising feature. The players often became immersed in the game, as well as interested in local geographical objects. In particular, the possibility to explore the road setting in a new way pleased the children. At the same time, we find ourselves on a boundary for game design. Fitting game manipulation into brief encounters between a player and a geographical object or a passing vehicle proved to be a challenge. Therefore, we strongly argue for minimalism in design. For example, gesture-based interaction needs to be indexical, that is, draw its meaning from the encounter, in order to be conceivable during the limited time span of an encounter. Again, references to objects as part of a narrative exploration seem to fit better within this context than providing challenging tasks to perform.

We have not said very much about road use as a means to access geographical locations, although this is obviously a key concern for most road users. Already from the start we stated that the amount of transportation work, that is, where and when people go to places, will not be a topic of this book. Instead we invited the reader to think about how the time on the roads is actually spent. We allowed ourselves to establish a temporary conceptual boundary, or in other words, to create a design space. Of course, there is no absolute boundary between topics such as access and sense, which is evident when it comes to the applications we have designed. If the road users adopt them in the ways we intended, their road use will be more efficient, safe, and enjoyable. This might make road use more appealing which would attract even more people to road use. An increase of the amount of transportation is a possible outcome. Still, our temporary limitation allowed us to discuss social life on the roads. It can be seen as a conceptual demarcation allowing us to study roads as open public spaces, of benefit for various reasons for many people.

We have investigated the various ways people engage in traffic and live their lives on the road. The key point is that the streets and highways are a shared resource and we need to negotiate and establish agreements about how it should be used on a micro scale. Two drivers cannot use the same spot of tarmac at the same time. Instead they need to achieve agreement about who comes first. This book also wants to influence such a negotiation on a more aggregated level, and particularly where the activities concern the design of new technologies to support road use. It is important that we account for variations of road use also at this level. In the end, the way we decide to use this shared resource becomes a balancing act, as Lynch (1981) stated in his *Theory of Good City Form*. When the studies and technical opportunities of that time were put together it was obvious that efficiency, safety, sense, and control were intermeshed and had to be negotiated. Our focus on the time spent in traffic added to the list of things needing to be reconciled in the design of mobile IT applications. Most important, we need to acknowledge the social interaction in traffic as a resource to achieve traditional goals in policy making such as increased efficiency and safety. But we suggest that the balance between these demands and other social demands is also of importance. The sense quality in road use is seldom taken into account in traditional transportation research. Therefore, applications such as Sound Pryer and Hocman are important inspirational patterns because they make social and experiential aspects visible parts of the balancing act. We know that people balance safety concerns with other needs and demands. Obviously, you need to negotiate efficiency and safety just to go somewhere, since you would, of course, be most safe if you were never to leave your house. Applications which are intended to increase sense demands make this list a bit longer.

This book is also an attempt to reconcile several disparate research traditions around the design of new information technology for road use. Sociology, with its specialization on methods and theories to increase our understanding of social interaction, is an obvious starting point. The intention here is to combine this approach with both transportation research and such domains of computer science as focus on social interaction and user experiences, to provide some form of socio-technical amalgamation. Transportation research has a long tradition of focusing on information technology and computing. But this research very seldom touches base with areas such as computer-supported collaborative work (CSCW) and human–computer interaction (HCI). And when it does, it concerns traditional usability studies of IT use in traffic. The latter fields have a historic interest in desktop technologies and practices. Although there has been a recent turn towards studying mobile practices and technologies, this rarely extends to road use. It is desktop computing which is the vantage point from which the journey to other use-contexts starts, and that makes road use seem a bit too far off. The distance is evident for example in Bellotti and Bly's paper (1996) called "Walking away from the desk top computer," as well as in Mark Weiser's canonical paper on "ubiquitous computing" (Weiser 1991). In terms of physical mobility, the research has come to focus on pedestrian practices (Östergren 2006). It is as if the research community has taken the title of Bellotti and Bly's paper literally. When they let go of the desktop use context, they just take a couple of steps. We argue that the theoretical and technical perspectives within human–computer interaction have much more to offer. Perhaps this book will inspire these research fields to extend their interest to the design of interactive roads, that is, to develop new concepts that account for the social interaction in traffic as well as the experiential qualities in road use.

Let us finally make explicit an area where studies of traffic encounters have implications for the design of other types of mobile services, and where the focus on mobile pedestrian practices might inhibit the design of innovative applications. An increasing number of mobile applications are being developed within research which draws upon mobile social encounters (Juhlin and Östergren 2006). They envision a form of urban life where face-to-face meeting-support systems contribute to people's encounters. Pedestrian style technology provides, for example, music sharing in cafés and on pavements, as well as gaming between passengers on public buses. Most of the applications are developed for public interaction between unacquainted people. But if we compare the technology designed for people who are walking around or sitting down, with the technology developed for road users, we discover something of a duration paradox.

The physical speed of the users affects the duration of the meeting. A meeting between café guests is generally much longer than a meeting between two drivers. A longer meeting may seem more appropriate for the technologies we have discussed, since it would provide more time for interaction. But a longer meeting also increases the exposure of a participant more, which make her vulnerable. A café visitor can be harassed by another visitor, or be persuaded to reveal so much personal information that her future anonymity is compromised. A short meeting, such as a traffic encounter, provides for fewer turns of interchange and scant information. But there is less risk of being cross-examined on the information communicated, and less risk of being lured into revealing too much. We argue that face-to-face meeting support systems are unlikely to be used by pedestrians since their attention is so occupied with staying away from each other. Short meetings provide opportunities where people could possible interact in new ways if their non-recognition was preserved (Goffman 1963). But they are often awkward, since the participants have to attend to other activities as well. Here, mobile face-to-face meeting support systems, such as Hocman and Sound Pryer, could spur interaction between strangers. But then the interaction would be different from more prolonged and rich meetings between people. It will not look like social relationships between friends. If that challenge is addressed, there will be opportunities for designing support that could help public interaction find new and interesting forms.

Finally, social interaction in traffic is important, even though the communication is highly restricted and has to occur during a limited time period, in most cases through "body movements" of vehicles. People mostly succeed in achieving agreements on how to share the road space through interaction, although they are anonymous and have minimal hierarchical social relations to each other. In some sense, we already travel along interactive roads. Still, there are a number of interesting possibilities to extend it in various ways if we just critically consider the time spent in traffic.

References

Bellotti V, Bly S (1996) Walking away from the desktop computer: distributed collaboration and mobility in a product design team. In: Proceedings of the ACM conference on computer supported cooperative, Boston, MA

Bull M (2004) Automobility and the power of sound. Theory Cult Soc 21(4–5):243–259

Goffman E (1963) Behaviour in public places—notes on social organization of gatherings. Free Press, New York

Juhlin O, Östergren M (2006) Time to meet face-to-face and device-to-device. In: Proceedings of the eighth international conference on human computer interaction with mobile devices and services—mobile HCI 2006, pp 77–80

Lynch K (1981) A theory of good city form. MIT Press, Cambridge

Östergren M (2006) Traffic encounters—drivers meeting face-to-face and peer-to-peer, Doctoral dissertation, IT University of Göteborg, Studies in Applied Information Technology

Redshaw S (2008) In the company of cars—driving as social and cultural practice. Ashgate, Aldershot

Weiser M (1991) The computer for the twenty-first century. Sci Am 265(3):94–104

Index

O. Juhlin, *Social Media on the Road*, Computer Supported Cooperative Work 50,
DOI 10.1007/978-1-84996-332-9, © Springer-Verlag London Limited 2010